British politics today:
the essentials

MANCHESTER
1824
Manchester University Press

Politics Today

Series editor: Bill Jones

British politics today:
the essentials

Bill Jones

Manchester University Press

Manchester and New York

distributed in the United States exclusively
by Palgrave Macmillan

Published by Manchester University Press
Oxford Road, Manchester M13 9NR, UK
and Room 400, 175 Fifth Avenue, New York, NY 10010, USA
www.manchesteruniversitypress.co.uk

Distributed in the United States exclusively by
Palgrave Macmillan, 175 Fifth Avenue, New York,
NY 10010, USA

Distributed in Canada exclusively by
UBC Press, University of British Columbia, 2029 West Mall,
Vancouver, BC, Canada V6T 1Z2

British Library Cataloguing-in-Publication Data
A catalogue record for this book is available from the British Library

Library of Congress Cataloging-in-Publication Data applied for

ISBN 978 0 7190 7938 2   *hardback*

ISBN 978 0 7190 7939 9   *paperback*

First published 2009

18 17 16 15 14 13 12 11 10 09   10 9 8 7 6 5 4 3 2 1

Typeset by R. J. Footring Limited, Derby
Printed in Great Britain
by CPI Antony Rowe Ltd, Chippenham, Wiltshire

Dedicated to the students on the lecture course at
Liverpool Hope University, 2007–8:
Angela, Luke, Phillip, Oliver and Dale

Contents

Figures, tables and boxes

Figures

Tables

Boxes

Preface

Way back in 1979, Dennis Kavanagh (then here at Manchester) and I wrote a book entitled *British Politics Today*, for Manchester University Press. It was a short book comprising a series of essays on British politics, which were little more than our fleshed out and tidied up notes. Our stated aim was not to provide the last word on any aspect of British politics, but to introduce each topic and hope students would be encouraged to avail themselves of the recommended reading at the end of each chapter. It ran through seven editions and sold about 120,000 copies. It also became the foundation volume of the 'Politics Today' series, which now has over two dozen books to its name. Over the years, with each successive edition, it became a little bigger as material was added but not subtracted. Eventually, it was not so much shorter than some of the bigger attempts at comprehensive textbooks on the market. Perhaps because of this, it became obvious that the shelf life of the book was approaching its end. It was too short to be a properly comprehensive text, yet it had progressed too far to fulfil its original function.

This new volume aims to return to the original concept: a pared down, relatively easy read for students at A level, first-year undergraduates and any other student or general reader seeking a concise introduction to the British political system. The book is based on the lecture course I wrote for my students at Liverpool Hope University, 2007–8, and it is to this charming – if tiny – group of young people that the book is dedicated: Angela, Luke, Phillip, Oliver and Dale. As well as thanking them, I would also like to acknowledge the assistance given to me by Dennis Kavanagh – when we wrote the original book over two decades – and in the latter stages of preparing this book, by copy-editor Ralph Footring. He interprets his role in a much wider and creative fashion than is usual but the results are very much appreciated by this author. David Hesp also helped with valuable advice.

Note on reading recommendations

Each chapter is concluded with some recommended reading. This comprises the relevant chapters from the big textbooks as well as more specialised works and the occasional website.

Major textbooks

Bill Jones, Dennis Kavanagh, Michael Moran and Philip Norton (2007) *Politics UK* (6th edition), Pearson.
Dennis Kavanagh, David Richards, Andrew Geddes and Martin Smith (2006) *British Politics* (5th edition), Oxford University Press.
John Kingdom (2003) *Government and Politics in Britain: An Introduction* (3rd edition), Polity.
Robert Leach, Bill Coxall and Lynton Robins (2006) *British Politics*, Palgrave.
Michael Moran (2005) *Politics and Governance in the UK*, Palgrave.

Epol

This is the exceptionally useful online journal of the Political Education Forum. It contains short articles on the whole gamut of British politics by leading academic authorities as well as classroom teachers. It can be accessed via:

http://politicaleducationforum.com/site/content_home.php

Acknowledgement of copyright material

Every effort has been made to obtain permission to reproduce copyright material in this book. If any proper acknowledgement has not been made, copyright-holders are invited to contact the publisher.

The regions of the UK

1

Defining politics, government and democracy

Defining politics

Before embarking on a politics course, it is as well to clarify what we mean by the world of 'politics'. It's a vague enough kind of word, 'politics', tainted by much negative association, so what precisely do we mean by it? To illustrate, let's consider whether any of the following headline-type statements can be said to be 'political':

1 Prime Minister's press secretary briefed against Chancellor.
2 Sons contest mother's will leaving fortune to daughter.
3 Leader of Opposition suggests United Kingdom renegotiates membership of European Union.
4 Potato shortage hits poorest families.
5 Strikes close down benefit offices.
6 John pips Colin for chess team captaincy.

Virtually all of them can be said to have some political content: 1 and 3 are clearly political but even 2 and 6 contain something of politics with a small 'p'. So what unites the big and small 'p' senses of the word?

The answer is the element of *conflict* and the need to *resolve* such conflict. So we talk of 'family politics', 'work politics', 'boardroom politics', even 'chess club politics', all with a small 'p', while 'Politics' with a big 'P' is concerned with how we – individuals and groups – relate to the state. In relation to the latter, a range of issues leap to mind. For example:

- How much can the state's government tell us what to do?
- How much obligation do we owe to the state?
- How should the state be governed and what part should we play in such activities?

There are many definitions of political activity but the following one puts conflict at its centre:

> Politics is essentially a process that seeks to manage or resolve conflicts between people, usually in a peaceful fashion. In its general sense it can describe the interactions of any group of people, but in its specific sense it refers to the many and complex relationships which exist between state institutions and the rest of society. (Jones *et al.*, 2007, p. 9)

Conflict

What is such conflict about? This is not easy to answer but it often boils down to scarce resources: 'who gets what, when, how' in Harold Lasswell's famous definition (Lasswell, 1936). But conflict can arise not just over material resources like money and property but also over things like status and authority. This, after all, is why Tony Blair and Gordon Brown fought throughout Blair's ten years in power, each seeking to exercise dominance over the other. Voltaire wrote tellingly about the source of political conflict: 'There has never been a perfect government, because men have passions; and if they did not have passions there would be no need for government'.

Conflict resolution

How are the conflicts resolved? It all depends on the political system involved. Autocratic governments seek to repress dissent and impose settlements, irrespective of the desires and interests of those involved. President Mugabe, of Zimbabwe, leader of a one-party dictatorship, for example tried in 2007 to stem runaway inflation by banning firms from making price increases, accusing them of collaborating with opposition elements to bring down his government. During 2008 he also used state-organised violence to determine the results of presidential and parliamentary elections. Democracies like Britain, however, use representative institutions to negotiate between competing interests through the medium of political parties contesting elections.

The 'good government is like good parenting' analogy

I tend to think that good government is a bit like good parenting, as suggested by liberal writers like L. T. Hobhouse in the nineteenth century, who argued that the state had a responsibility to nurture 'good citizens'. Both parenting and government aim to encourage good behaviour and to achieve prosperity and happiness for their respective objects. More precisely:

- Children have inbuilt rebellious tendencies, as do voters. It follows that, like good parenting, government should avoid being overbearing if possible:

persuasion is of the essence. An arrogant government alienates voters in no time at all.

- As with rules for children, government always works best when citizens have been properly prepared. The ban on smoking in indoor public places from 2007 is a good example of effective preparation, as it seems to have been accepted more or less without serious complaint. The introduction in 1989 of the poll tax (or community charge), on the other hand, generated riots in central London, which helped bring down the Thatcher government, which came up with the idea.
- It follows that rules should be reasonable and sensible. The two above examples also illustrate that when they are not, consent is not achieved. By the same token, any attempt to insist children go to bed at, say, 5.30 p.m. is likely to be met with furious refusals.
- Of course, rules must be applied consistently, without exception, favour or discrimination. Any deviation from this rule creates chaos in both families and political systems.

The parenting analogy, however, implies excessive intrusion. Perhaps the criterion here should be the prevention of harm to others: for example, children should be prevented from bullying their fellows just as adults

---

Box 1.1 What does government do?

In his book *The Third Way*, Anthony Giddens describes what he thinks the purposes of government are:

- to provide means for the representation of diverse interests;
- to offer a forum for reconciling the competing claims of those interests;
- to create and protect an open public sphere in which unconstrained debate about policy issues can be carried on;
- to provide a diversity of public goods, including forms of collective security and welfare;
- to regulate markets in the public interest and foster market competition where monopoly threatens;
- to foster social peace through the provision of policing;
- to promote the development of human capital through the education system;
- to sustain an effective system of law;
- to have a directly economic role, as a prime employer, in macro and micro intervention, and in the provision of infrastructure;
- more controversially, to have a civilising aim – government reflects the widely held norms and values, but can also help shape them, in the educational system and elsewhere;
- to foster regional and transnational alliances and pursue global goals.

Source: Giddens (1998), pp. 47–8.

should be. It is when harm to oneself is involved that problems arise. Parents naturally step in to prevent their children harming themselves – playing with sharp objects for example – but libertarians argue that adults – mature individuals – *should* be allowed to inflict harm on themselves should they so decide: through drugs, dangerous sports and the like. This is also when cost to taxpayers becomes a factor. Both drinking and smoking – self-destructive pleasures – cost us billions in medical care, so should they be discouraged? Gambling can also break up families and causes untold misery to growing children, so should it also be discouraged? To conclude, possibly the major reason for being wary of pushing my comparison is that it might encourage politicians to vie for the 'parenting' role. No one wants to see a version of George Orwell's 'Big Brother' installed in Number 10.

Representative democracy and its requirements

Britain is, arguably, the oldest democracy in the world – though it took many centuries for it to evolve into its current 'representative' form. The conditions necessary for such a system of government need to be identified:

Box 1.2 The nature of democracy

Journalist Gary Younge gave the following clear-sighted analysis of the essence of democracy (*Guardian*, 18 February 2008):

> In December, the president of Uzbekistan, Islam Karimov, stood for re-election. Karimov, a one-time ally in the 'war on terror' who in 2002 had one opposition leader boiled alive, has long faced criticism from human rights groups and the United Nations. Having already served two terms, he was not even eligible to stand. A minor detail for a man like Karimov. His three opponents all endorsed him and did not ask Uzbeks to vote for them. Those who would not endorse him were disqualified and imprisoned. Karimov won the day with 88.1% of the vote.
>
> There is a profound difference between holding an election and having a democracy. Elections are the best means that we have come up with so far for giving people a voice in the running of their affairs. Democracy is the system which ensures that voices are heard by empowering them with the ability to change those who run our affairs.
>
> Elections, in and of themselves, are a purely technical matter. The authorities name the day, tell the voters, provide the booths and the equipment. The voters make their choice. The authorities then tally the results. But, as we know from countless incidences, from Kenya to Florida, the technical elides effortlessly into the political. Which day? Which voters? Where are the booths? How does the equipment work? Who's counting? Whose votes count? All this has a bearing on the result. That's why democracy, if it is working, gives us the right to kick out the authorities.

- full adult franchise – everyone must have the vote;
- secret ballot – to ensure voters are not coerced or influenced, as used to be commonplace in Britain in earlier times;
- a choice of candidates – so that voters can choose to vote for the candidate or party they prefer;
- regular elections – to ensure no government becomes entrenched and so that voters are able to eject a government they have come to dislike and to elect another in its place;
- elections that are fought on equal terms (e.g. in relation to finance) for all parties and candidates;
- access to the media for all parties and candidates – to allow free expression of their views.

References

Giddens, A. (1998) *The Third Way: The Renewal of Social Democracy*, Polity.
Jones, B., *et al.* (2007) *Politics UK* (6th edition), Pearson.
Lasswell, H. (1936) *Politics: Who Gets What, When, How?*, McGraw-Hill.

Further reading

All the major textbooks provide some discussion of politics and democracy in their opening chapters:

Jones, B., *et al.* (2007) *Politics UK* (6th edition), Pearson.
Kavanagh, D., *et al.* (2006) *British Politics* (5th edition), Oxford University Press.
Kingdom, J. (2003) *Government and Politics in Britain: An Introduction* (3rd edition), Polity.
Leach, R., *et al.* (2006) *British Politics*, Palgrave.
Moran, M. (2005) *Politics and Governance in the UK*, Palgrave.

Other texts

Axford, B., *et al.* (1997) *Politics: An Introduction*, Routledge.
Crick, B. (2000) *In Defence of Politics* (5th revised edition), Continuum.
Duverger, M. (1966) *The Idea of Politics*, Methuen.
Heywood, A. (1997) *Politics*, Macmillan.
Paxman, J. (2002) *The Political Animal*, Michael Joseph.
Riddell, P. (1993) *Honest Opportunism*, Hamish Hamilton.

Websites

International Political Science Association, www.ipsa-aisp.org.
Political science resources, www.socsciresearch.com/r12.html.
Political Studies Association, www.psa.ac.uk.

2

An overview of the British political system

Questions and answers: the political system

Most readers will be familiar with the political system, though they are not likely to have thought about it analytically, unless they have studied it more systematically at some time. This short chapter aims, at the risk of being too simplistic, to reach out to include those who have never studied the subject and also those who have found it unappealing. The aim is to establish some very basic building blocks of understanding and to stimulate further study. I use a question and answer approach to get inside the topic, and Figure 2.1 draws together all the elements of government.

What is the fundamental idea underpinning the British system of government?

Democracy.

Is this idea qualified to any degree, or is it meant to be applied in a pure form?

It is not applied in a pure form but in one utilising 'representatives'. There is a spectrum of democracy running from 'pure' or 'direct' to degrees of 'representative':

Direct ━━━━━━━━━━━━━━━━━━▶ Representative

The British system and most others are well to the right of this spectrum; that is, they involve 'indirect democracy' via *representatives*. But this system throws up the problem of how representatives are prevented from assuming too much power and ruling in their own interests.

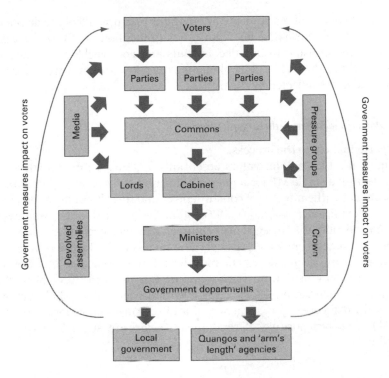

Figure 2.1 *British government institutions: how they relate. The arrows indicate directions of influence/implementation*

How is the answer to this problem approached?

Via a system of 'responsibility' or 'accountability'. Our representatives, who are elected to govern us, are answerable, at least in theory, to someone, or some group of people, at every stage of their decision-making.

And these stages are?

Decision-making is subject to accountability at three key stages.

First, voters elect Members of Parliament (MPs) to the House of Commons; they can eject them in any future election should they wish.

Second, the largest party in the Commons provides the Prime Minister, in the form of its leader, who then appoints a team of ministers: effectively the government. MPs in the Commons of all parties can defeat the government on any issue. The discipline of the governing party makes this unlikely but any slackening in loyalty can put the government under intense pressure.

Third, civil servants in the departments of state do the day-to-day work of government and owe their allegiance to the ministers placed in charge of them. In theory, civil servants are anonymous instruments of the democratic system and 'responsibility' for failure, not to mention credit for success, is taken by the minister. In practice, officials are more visible these days and, if they still mostly avoid public blame for mistakes, their future careers are usually adversely affected by them.

How does the general public apply control?

Via 'participation' in the process.

There are 44.5 million voters potentially, organised into constituencies, each electing a single MP for a maximum period of five years. There are 646 constituencies (the number of constituencies and their boundaries do change over the years), each of about 60,000 voters. Every British or Commonwealth citizen resident in the UK aged over eighteen can vote, except for some people in mental homes, convicted prisoners and members the House of Lords. The simple-majority electoral system may be reformed one day but the 1998 report of the Jenkins Commission, set up by Tony Blair in December 1997 to examine possible voting reform, was eventually left on the shelf. Labour is hugely divided between reformers and anti-reformers and most agree there would have to be a positive referendum vote before any such change could be introduced.

How do voters exercise control over governments?

They can elect them out of office at election times.

They can seek to influence them via pressure groups (see Chapter 8).

They can join a political party (Box 2.1) and influence them through the party machinery.

They can stand as a candidate and seek to exercise *real* power and influence from the inside.

How are governments formed?

The largest party in the Commons after a general election is invited, according to tradition, by the Queen to form a government. If there is no overall majority, the Queen has the right to ask anyone who seems able to form a minority or a coalition government. Minority governments are sometimes formed but are usually short-lived, as, lacking a majority, they cannot guarantee any period when measures can be voted through.

The second largest party becomes the official opposition.

The Prime Minister nominates a Cabinet of twenty or more members to fill the main offices of state plus a clutch of junior ministers, all of whom have to belong to one of the two Houses of Parliament (Commons or Lords). The ministers are 'our' representatives in the centre of government, representing

Box 2.1 The main political parties

Only 3% of voters join parties but the parties:
• select candidates;
• provide personnel for Parliament and local councils;
• provide ministers and prime ministers.
Their ideologies are changeable but their aim is always to win power.

The Conservative Party
The Conservative Party was the party of government for two-thirds of the last century. It represents the interests of business and property and has traditionally had a flexible, pragmatic approach to ideology, although Margaret Thatcher, as will be seen, changed all that. Its membership has been declining and ageing over recent years.

The Labour Party
Labour used to be the workers' party but failed to attract their support in the 1980s; once, it favoured 'high tax, high spend' social policies and the nationalisation of major industries, but eighteen years of opposition convinced the party that such policies were no longer worth offering. Neil Kinnock moved the party towards the political centre after its massive defeat in the 1983 general election. John Smith continued in this direction until, following his death in 1994, a further leap towards the centre took place under the combined leadership of Tony Blair and Gordon Brown, advised by Peter Mandelson. Membership revived up to 400,000 but then fell off badly in the later years of Blair, to little more than 200,0000.

The Liberal Democrats
This party was born out of the merging in 1988 of the Liberals and rump of the Social Democratic Party (formed in 1981). Its centrist message was usurped by Blair, who was not naturally sympathetic to traditional Labour ideas. The Lib-Dems were initially constrained from active opposition to the Labour government elected in 1997 by the promise of a share in government – plus hope of a new voting system (not fulfilled to date).

The nationalist parties
Clearly, this strand of political thinking is very important in Wales (a governing coalition in the Welsh Assembly was formed between the Welsh nationalist party, Plaid Cymru, and the Labour Party in summer 2007) and Scotland (which had a minority Scottish National Party government after May 2007).

the party elected and implementing the manifesto policies so endorsed. The extent of their control and their success define the degree of democracy we have – just how *much* control we have is a subject of great debate.

What has the House of Lords got to do with our political system?

The Lords ceased to be part of the effective heart of government after the 1911 Parliament Act, when its powers were reduced to delaying measures for up to two years, and this was further reduced in 1949 to one year. So, in practice now, the Lords have very little impact on the big issues but can be important at the margin, especially as a source of amendments, revising of clauses in legislation and providing provocative/useful debate. Ministers can be drawn from the Lords and sit in the Cabinet should the Prime Minister wish. Furthermore, by endowing peerages on supporters, the Prime Minister can enable people to join the government without having to win a seat in the Commons; this provides a useful 'backdoor' into ministerial ranks.

Is the Prime Minister as powerful as the US President?

Yes, in the sense that, with party backing – which there is by definition, as the premier is its leader – the Prime Minister can railroad through any legislation, even if it is bad or unpopular, or both, as in the case of the 1989 poll tax.

No, in that Prime Ministers are only as powerful as the majority which supports them; in the United States, Presidents are in power until the next election, subject to impeachment proceedings, resignation or death.

It has to be made clear that the two systems are very different and there is a completely different relationship between the legislature (discussing and creating laws) and the executive (implementing laws).

How important is the civil service?

Very, inasmuch as it advises ministers and carries out the day- to-day running of government. Interpreting government decisions gives a degree of power to senior civil servants and advising ministers in theory gives them hidden power to run the country – Sir Humphrey Appleby in *Yes Minister* reveals how this can happen in a comedic fashion but its popularity with politicians (especially Margaret Thatcher) at home and abroad attests to the fundamental truth that senior advisers can be more devious and instrumental in decision-making than the nominal head of the department or even the government as a whole. The British civil service is non-partisan and permanent; it still tends to be led in the most senior positions by graduates from Oxbridge universities.

Margaret Thatcher was keen to reduce the size of the civil service and to introduce devolved departments, called 'agencies', to undertake the routine work while ministers concentrated on the bigger issues.

Is local government important?

Most definitely, but the gradual stripping of power from local authorities since the middle of the last century and the strangling of their financial freedom of action has made local government less attractive to able people and less interesting to voters, who rarely turn out in force for local elections.

How important is Europe to British politics?

Crucial. The European Union touches British politics in all kinds of ways: legally, European law is superior to domestic law; economically, it provides the framework in which the British economy thrives or dies; politically, it is the focus of most domestic as well as foreign policy, most areas of policy have important European dimensions and ministers and civil servants often work as much in Brussels as they do in London.

Can pressure groups exercise effective power?

Not really, as they concentrate on issues and causes and leave overall power to the parties. There are thousands of them, trying to influence all levels of government and in a variety of ways, from petitions to national demonstrations in Trafalgar Square. There are two basic types:

- 'sectional' groups, representing 'constituencies' like workers or business people;
- 'cause' groups, representing ideas or ideals like abortion law reform or environmental protection.

Some groups, like the unions, can exert occasional power via strikes or influence in the Labour Party, but mostly such groups depend on their 'insider' status: their proximity to the inner decision-making centres. 'Outsider' groups often are the ones which make the most noise but they tend to achieve the least in terms of outcome.

What is the role of the media?

The media perform a crucial role, as they are the mediating agent, interpreting messages between the government and people and influencing both the context in which decisions are taken and those decisions themselves. Good relations with and effective use of the media are central to the successful conduct of politics. A major criticism of New Labour under Blair was that it focused too much on media presentation but any government these days is driven by the 24–7 media coverage, the need to 'feed the beast' and the desire to win points over the 'enemy' parties.

Recommended reading

Jones, B. (2004) *The Dictionary of British Politics*, Manchester University Press.
Wright, A. (2003) *British Politics: A Very Short Introduction*, Oxford University Press.

Aside from the above two sources that give concise treatments of the British political system, the major textbooks will provide more than full elaborations. However, at this stage the early student is probably better off consulting the websites below.

Websites

British Government and Politics on the Internet, from the School of Politics, International Relations and Philosophy, Keele University, www.keele.ac.uk/depts/por/ukbase.htm (an excellent resource).
European Consortium for Political Research, www.essex.ac.uk/ecpr.
Political Education Forum, www.politicaleducationforum.com/site/content_home.php (useful for students intending to study politics at university).
UKPOL, www.ukpol.co.uk.

3

The historical development of British government

The story of British democracy's evolution is one of the most remarkable in the history of government, as it tells the tale of how an original absolute monarchy, in charge of making, implementing and interpreting the laws of the land, slowly morphed – through the monarch's reliance on advisory councils – into a system which represented all parts of the country, which, to be effective, required the acquiescence of such representative bodies and finally acquired the crucial characteristic of being elected by each citizen in the country. 'From absolute monarchy to representative democracy in 1000 years' would not be a bad approximate description of the process. Below, the main stages in the process are described.

Concise chronology to the eighteenth century

Early days

The story of 'Britain' begins effectively with England's emergence as a unified kingdom – Knut (Canute) became king of a unified England in 1016, which went on to expand to the outer limits of the shores of the British Isles. England under the Saxon monarchs featured a council of nobles called the 'Witenagemot'; this comprised those who attended the king at any one time – at home in his palace or when travelling. The importance of the body arose because it was held that Saxon kings *should* listen to advice and, consequently, most did. Those who did not, such as Ethelred II ('the Unready'), were not respected partly in consequence.

King John

It was established therefore that monarchs listened to advice, which they needed anyway to gather support for their regime and to raise finance for their activities: maintaining law and order, building palaces, waging wars and so forth. When Norman kings took over in 1066 – thus adding large tracts of France, and later Ireland, to England, creating the so-called 'Angevin empire' – this aspect of the political culture was absorbed but this did not mean that kings became especially enlightened. King John (reigned 1199–1216), for example, was forced to do a deal with his nobles at Runnymede in 1215, subsequently named the Magna Carta, which established certain basic rights regarding taxation and fair trials for citizens.

Curia Regis

The Curia Regis was the court of the Norman/Angevin kings and effectively exercised the functions of government, promulgating new laws during its meetings, held three times a year. Its three key officials – dispenser, steward and chamberlain – exercised considerable power until the court declined in importance during the twelfth and thirteenth centuries. Subsequently, the wider Curia developed into the embryonic parliament and the king developed his own council of ministers during the medieval period.

Simon de Montfort

This immigrant from France led the so-called 'reform movement' aimed at limiting royal power; the movement found expression in the Provisions of Oxford, of 1258. Following a period of civil war, de Montfort summoned a 'Parliament of Knights and worthy citizens' in 1265, an event which in retrospect has been viewed as the embryo of the House of Commons.

Model Parliament, 1295

While it did not in reality provide any template for the future, this gathering, summoned by Edward I to finance his wars, was notable for its degree of representation: seven earls, forty-one barons, seventy abbots, two knights from each shire and two representatives from each city and borough.

House of Lords

This originated in the meetings monarchs held with advisers before and after the Norman Conquest. Initially, nobles mingled with knights and wealthy landowners in parliamentary gatherings, but special sessions of the Curia were held with nobles only and slowly these meetings and the rest began to assume separate characters. The Lords was not described as such until 1544, but by then contained the most powerful men in the country plus representatives of the Church: abbots and bishops. The number of lay lords varied: forty-nine in 1295; seventy-three in 1453; but down to thirty-six by the reign of Henry VII as a result of the high noble death rate during the Wars of the Roses (1455–87) (see below for more on the Lords).

House of Commons

This lower House of Parliament, comprising the non-baronial representatives of communities across the country, was summoned in 1213, 1254 and 1258; and in 1265 these representatives assembled at de Montfort's Parliament (see above). These men were usually rich landowners and the monarch was concerned to extract revenue from them. By the end of the fourteenth century, taxation was raised 'by the Commons with the advice and consent of the Lords'; the Commons had established some control over finance – a crucial lever in the process whereby power was gathered from the monarch. But the Commons was very much the junior partner to the Lords in the Middle Ages and had no separate meeting place until 1547, when St Stephen's Chapel in Westminster was adopted for this purpose. From then on, however, it acquired more and more power and influence.

1536, Wales

Wales was not annexed to England until 1536, despite the fact that it had been conquered long before, during the thirteenth century.

Civil War, 1642–49

This resulted from the tension between monarch and Parliament which had been in evidence since the beginnings of the royal propensity for advice and need for financial assistance. Charles I had sought to rule without Parliament – in 1620 he established the Long Parliament, compliant with his wishes, which lasted until 1640 – but in the end it rose up against him, led by the remarkable soldier and statesman Oliver Cromwell – himself from relatively humble beginnings and a member of the Commons. Cromwell's forces prevailed and the king was executed on 30 January 1649.

On 19 May 1649, England became the 'Commonwealth of England'. Cromwell proclaimed himself Lord Protector in 1653, after suppressing a revolt in Ireland and dismissing the residual forms of Parliament to establish the Protectorate. He died in 1658 and thereafter – in a country exhausted by two decades of turmoil – moves were made to restore the monarchy: the restoration occurred in April 1660, when Charles II acceded to the throne.

Glorious Revolution, 1688–89

The restored monarchy discovered it was very much *not* business as usual. The monarchy had been bested by a body with some claim to represent the country and from now on monarchs ignored public sentiment at their peril. Consequently, the attempts of James II to introduce Catholicism to what was now, largely, a Protestant nation repelled the political class in his own country. William of Orange was approached by seven leading politicians – Whig and Tory – and invited to overthrow his father-in-law. This was an astonishing act of treason according to one point of view, but it is always the victors who write the history and, in 1689, William proceeded to become such a person, and with the minimum of bloodshed. On 11 April 1689, William and his wife Mary were crowned king and queen, but they had accepted the Declaration of Right, subsequently embodied in the Bill of Rights, which effectively gave Parliament the final say in making the law of the land. The historic importance of this 'Glorious' revolution is that it opened the door to genuine democratic government through a representative parliamentary assembly.

Constitutional change in the eighteenth century

1707, Scotland

Already sharing the same monarch since 1603, in 1707 the Scottish and English Parliaments merged to create the Kingdom of Great Britain.

The Georgian dynasty

As Queen Anne had no heir, a great-grandson of William I was invited – a second imported monarch – to rule (in addition to his native Hanover). While he preferred his homeland to these damp shores and never really learnt the language, his dynasty dominated the century, with his son and grandson becoming George II and George III. George I was happy to leave governing to his ministers, all of whom were Members of Parliament.

The first Prime Minister

George I communicated with his committee of ministers, or Cabinet, as it had come to be called, via the most senior finance minister. For a long time this was the First Lord of the Treasury, Robert Walpole: effectively the first 'Prime Minister'. He was followed by a number of exceptional talents, especially Pitt the Elder and his son, Pitt the Younger, who became Prime Minister at the remarkably early age of twenty-four, in 1783.

Political parties

Inevitably, if a large number of people in an assembly hold substantial power, they will seek to group together the better to win votes. In the eighteenth century, the two main groupings were:

The Whigs

This group was formed in the late seventeenth century, when it resisted the Catholicism of James II, but became associated thereupon with Nonconformity, the industrial interest and reform. They dominated during the century via the so-called Whig 'junto', which lasted until the Tories took the lead under Pitt the Younger. The Whigs went on to form the basis of the Liberal Party in the nineteenth century.

The Tories

This group supported James II after 1680. Although they accepted the Glorious Revolution, they then supported the 'Jacobite' 'Pretenders' to the throne; as a result, they stayed out of power until the reign of George III.

Patronage

This was a crucial means of controlling power in the eighteenth century; it was used by the aristocracy and the monarch to control personnel in the Commons and to reward supporters from all walks of life. The monarch owned over 100 offices, as well as many sinecures, pensions and contracts – monarchs could therefore deploy their largesse in such a way as to advance their own policies. The large landowners used their power of appointment to help determine who sat in the Commons via the 'rotten boroughs' and 'pocket boroughs' that were in their gift.

The Enlightenment

The twentieth-century philosopher and historian Bertrand Russell argued that Descartes set the ball rolling in the seventeenth century with his individualistic assertion that 'I think, therefore I am': a tacit rebuttal of the religious and feudal ideas of his age. The ferment of ideas called the Enlightenment which swept through Europe in the eighteenth century arguably began in the late seventeenth century in Britain with the advance of science: Isaac Newton and thinkers like Thomas Hobbes. Essentially, Enlightenment thinkers applied the tests of reason and humanity to existing social, economic and political conditions and came up with answers fundamentally challenging traditional assumptions about religion, the role of the individual and relationships between state and citizen.

In France, Voltaire flayed the *ancien régime* with his wit and rational critiques; his works and those of similar writers affected the intellectual atmosphere in which all political activity took place. Freedom of speech and movement, tolerance of differing views and beliefs, the sanctity of the individual and the reality of people's basic rights plus the obligations of the state to the citizen were all ideas picked up and applied in Britain by the likes of John Locke, Adam Smith, David Hume and Tom Paine. Baron Montesquieu, the French Enlightenment thinker, contributed the idea of the 'separation of powers': the idea that the three functions of government – legislative, judicial and executive (making laws, interpreting laws and implementing them, respectively) – should be embodied in separate institutions, thus balancing each other's power and preventing tyranny by any single centre. Meanwhile, across the Atlantic the framers of the US constitution produced their classic Enlightenment document – the American constitution – built around the same notion of the separation of powers. All this ferment of ideas and activity created a sense in which the British form of government, already praised for its emphasis on liberty, was ripe for further reform.

The influence of the French Revolution, 1789

Events in France had a huge impact on encouraging reform and a movement for democracy throughout Europe.

> Bliss it was ... to be alive,
> But to be young was very Heaven.

So wrote the young poet William Wordsworth (*The Prelude*, 1805) of the French Revolution, which began in 1789. While the course of the revolution took much of the passion out of the reform movement, 'liberty, equality and fraternity' were ideas which, thanks to the likes of Tom Paine, crossed the Channel. Such thinkers helped to advance the idea that individual citizens had the right to help determine how they were governed, rather than by a hereditary monarchy or by religious ideas, which many now regarded with scepticism.

Developments in the nineteenth century

1801, Ireland

England had conquered Ireland by the end of the thirteenth century and English nobles proceeded to rule as 'absentee landlords' for the most part. English settlers were deliberately 'planted' in Ireland, with more marked success in the north. Protestantism, however, was not accepted by the Catholic country. Catholics were discriminated against and denied civil rights, as well as robbed of much of their lands via a form of what would be called 'ethnic cleansing' in modern-day parlance. After the 1798 rebellion, Ireland was merged with Britain in the Act of Union, and its Parliament dissolved.

Great Reform Act, 1832

The government of Lord Liverpool (1812–27) was widely seen as reactionary, seeking to douse possible flames of revolution in Britain. There were

> ### Box 3.1 Two signposts on the way to democracy
>
> **Putney debates, 1647**
> These occurred in October–November 1647 between advocates of a post-Civil War settlement retaining the monarchy and the Lords, and those of the radical 'Leveller' proposal that there be 'one man, one vote' and authority vested in the Commons. The debates lasted nearly two weeks but Cromwell grew anxious at their radical tone and when the king escaped on 11 November the discussion was effectively terminated.
>
> **Peterloo massacre**
> This famous event occurred on 13 August 1819, when 60,000 people were assembled to support the idea that the new industrial towns should be granted representation by MPs. As Martin Wainwright wrote in the *Guardian* on the 188th anniversary of the event (13 August 2007):
>
>> Less than 2% of the population had the vote at the time, and resentment was sharpened by 'rotten boroughs' such as the moribund Wiltshire village Old Sarum which had 11 voters and two MPs. Manchester, Leeds and Liverpool had none.
>>
>> Plans to elect a 'shadow parliament' put the wind up the Tory government which was also frightened that the power of Henry 'Orator' Hunt, the main speaker at Peterloo, might turn the Manchester crowd into a mob. The local volunteer yeomanry, described as 'younger members of the Tory party in arms', was ordered to disperse the meeting, with fatal results.
>
> The eleven deaths, however, were not in vain, as the indignation generated by the massacre led directly to the formation of the Chartists and fed into the movement for the Great Reform Act.

widespread signs of unrest – in Spa Fields and the Peterloo massacre, for example – and repressive legislation like the so-called 'Six Acts'. George Canning, who became Prime Minister in 1827, was a more liberal Tory but was followed by the Duke of Wellington, who considered the British constitution to be 'perfect'. It was finally Lord Grey's Whig government that passed the Great Reform Act in 1832. Amid threats to create new peers to overcome passionate resistance in the Lords and much popular agitation, the bill was passed, inaugurating the age of democratic government in Britain.

The Act did not expand the electorate to much more than half a million out of a population of 14 million – but that was double what it was before – and it did abolish anomalies like 'rotten boroughs' and constituencies, like Old Sarum, which had virtually no voters but still returned an MP.

The system was placed on a new basis and a beginning was made on the road to democracy. The Great Reform Act was followed by further Acts of 1867, 1884 and 1885, which expanded the electorate to some 5 million voters and achieved a rough correspondence between population and representation throughout the country.

Now it was elections that determined the colour of government and not the will of the monarch or the aristocracy. Queen Victoria was not without influence, but the role of the monarch had been reduced effectively to one of ceremonials and symbolism.

Political parties

Now that voters really mattered, political parties began to organise in the country – hence the many old buildings – Conservative and Liberal Clubs – which are still to be seen, which acted as headquarters for them. This section tells the story of the British parties up to the end of the twentieth century.

Conservative Party

This emerged from the Tory Party, a name which is still interchangeable with its modern nomenclature. In the wake of the 1832 Act, Robert Peel was active in establishing the basis of the modern party, registering members and drawing up a programme – the Tamworth Manifesto. Conservative associations formed at that time are still to be found all over the country. The party represented and advanced the interests of the landed gentry but increasingly came to represent those of industry, commerce and property in general.

In the twentieth century, the Tories seemed to be the 'natural party of government', in that they were in office two-thirds of the time, to Labour's one-third. Churchill more or less accepted Labour's changes in the 1950s but when the economy began to decline in the 1960s the Conservatives urged a return to a more 'free market' economy. Edward Heath, Prime Minister 1970–74, did not really deliver such an outcome but he did succeed in negotiating the UK's entry into the European Community, a historic and still controversial decision. By the end of the decade Margaret Thatcher had become leader and after 1979 she pursued a robust policy of making the British economy competitive again. This entailed allowing traditional and inefficient industries to go bankrupt, confronting and subduing the trade unions and imposing her formidable personality upon her party. By 1990, it had had enough and John Major took over, until his political capital was exhausted as the 1997 election approached.

Liberal Party

This emerged in the 1860s from an amalgam of: Whigs, the Manchester Radicals and disenchanted Conservatives – often followers of Robert Peel. Its outposts in the country can still be seen in the form of the many 'Reform' and

Liberal clubs in towns, cities and countryside. The party tended to speak for the 'newly' rich entrepreneurs, advocating 'classical' free market economics and opposing aggressive foreign policies in favour of encouraging world trade.

Labour Party

At the end of the nineteenth century, trade unions realised that they could better advance the cause of their members by organising to get representatives directly elected to Parliament. In 1900, an embryonic body was established which won seats in the 1906 election and later played a role in government during World War I. By 1924, the party had tasted government via the short minority premiership of Ramsay MacDonald, the illegitimate son of a Scottish crofter. It experienced a second period of government in 1929–31, but then suffered a long period of opposition until its leaders shared power with Winston Churchill in his coalition government during World War II. In 1945, it won a surprise landslide under its leader Clement Attlee, who led the historic postwar government that introduced nationalisation of the key utilities, as well as the welfare state. Labour also ruled in 1964–70 and 1974–79 (under Harold Wilson and James Callaghan), but suffered a long period in opposition until 1997, when Tony Blair won a landslide victory.

'Golden age' of Parliament?

In the middle of the nineteenth century, when there were no clear party whips, it was possible for debates actually to determine the outcome of policy discussions. Bills were often redrafted on the floor of the House and ministers sometimes had to back down or even resign. This did not last long, as parties in Parliament soon realised they had to produce a programme/manifesto to win elections and then organise their MPs to vote in a disciplined fashion in order to drive it through.

Developments in the twentieth century

Lords–Commons conflict resolved

With the Commons controlling financial decisions and coming to dominate the major debates of the day, it became increasingly difficult for a Prime Minister to sit in the Lords. The Conservatives, moreover, controlled the majority in that chamber by virtue of the hereditary peers. The conflict was brought to a climax by the Liberal government of 1906, when Lloyd George's challenge to 'Mr Balfour's Poodle' lit the blue touch paper to a massive constitutional battle, which the Lords eventually lost in 1911, when its powers were reduced to that of delay of a bill by twenty-four months. From now on no

Prime Minister could sit in the Lords and the number of ministers who could do the same effectively became limited as well.

Parliamentary terms

In 1715 the Septennial Act was passed, extending the maximum term a Parliament could run from three to seven years and, indeed, most of them did run for approximately that period in the eighteenth century. During the nineteenth century, however, the average was four years and the 1911 Parliament Act reduced the maximum to five years. Wartime terms of Parliament were extended temporarily but in modern times governments look to renew their mandates usually after four years, and leaving it any later can box the Prime Minister into a corner, with too little time to solve problems.

Votes for women

Mary Wollstonecraft wrote a pamphlet in support of women's rights as early as 1792 and John Stuart Mill urged votes for women around the middle of the nineteenth century. But the cause did not progress and it took the militant grouping the 'suffragettes' under the Pankhursts to add momentum to the campaign. During World War I, women worked in the war effort and the movement won votes for women aged over thirty in 1918. In 1928, full voting rights were accorded to women.

1920, Government of Ireland Act

After much political and then military conflict, the Government of Ireland Act partitioned the north from the rest of the country, sowing the seeds of 'the Troubles' from the late 1960s onwards.

Further constitutional changes in the twentieth century

1948   The Lords' powers of delay reduced to 12 months.
1969   Votes given to those aged 18 and over.
1998   Scottish Parliament and Welsh Assembly set up by Blair government. Northern Ireland Executive established (but subsequently repeatedly suspended until 2007).
1999   The Assembly set up for Northern Ireland.
       Most hereditary peers abolished from the Lords but the final stage of reform – a wholly or at least partially elected Lords – is still awaited.
2007   Hard-line Protestant Ian Paisley became First Minister in the Northern Ireland Executive and former IRA leader Martin McGuinness his Deputy.

Epilogue

From being an absolute monarchy at the close of the Dark Ages, British government saw the evolution of an advisory council into a bicameral legislature that assumed much of the monarch's power but paradoxically chose to vest it in the leader of the biggest party elected to the lower house of the legislature. Instead of an 'absolute' monarch, we now arguably have a secular 'president' – certainly when the office was in the hands of Thatcher and Blair. Something which has transformed the way politics is conducted since the inception of democracy are the media, which now permeate and ventilate – for good and ill – every aspect of the system, from elections to appointed quangos.

Recommended reading

The major textbooks deal with this as follows:

Jones, B., *et al.* (2007) *Politics UK* (6th edition), Pearson: chapter 2.
Kingdom, J. (2003) *Government and Politics in Britain: An Introduction* (3rd edition), Polity: variously in the first four chapters.
Leach, R., *et al.* (2006) *British Politics*, Palgrave: chapter 3.

Other texts

Black, J. (2000) *Modern British History since 1900*, Macmillan.
Jones, B. (2004) *The Dictionary of British Politics*, Manchester University Press.
Schama, S. (2002) *A History of Britain, Vol. III*, BBC Publications.

Websites

British Government and Politics on the Internet, from the School of Politics, International Relations and Philosophy, Keele University, www.keele.ac.uk/depts/por/ukbase.htm.
European Consortium for Political Research, www.essex.ac.uk/ecpr.
Political Education Forum, www.politicaleducationforum.com/site/content_home.php (useful for students intending to study politics at university).
UKPOL, www.ukpol.co.uk.

4

The social and economic context of British government

This chapter examines how economic changes have affected Britain over the centuries, and presents some thoughts on the absence of a modern British revolution.

Political structures like elections and legislative institutions provide the shell within which political activity is conducted. What goes on within depends upon the kind of society and economy a nation has and, ultimately, how its political system evolves and copes with challenges. For example, if a country's economy is primitive, its political processes will be very different from those in a country that is highly industrialised, with an educated workforce. Britain clearly falls squarely in the latter category. An agricultural society, moreover, is unlikely to produce the same pattern of wealth inequality as an industrial one.

Britain's economic history

Britain's economy during Anglo-Saxon times (from the fifth to the tenth century AD) comprised mostly agriculture and the export of tin, a commodity much sought by the Romans. After the Norman invasion, agriculture remained dominant, with peasants and small farmers, bound by oaths of allegiance to the squires and nobles who owned their land, often providing the workforce. The Black Death in the fourteenth century wiped out half the workforce and helped to push up the wages of those who worked the land. Wool became the dominant commodity in medieval times; it was produced in the heartlands of England and exported to the textile cities of Europe. So important was wool that the seat of the Speaker of the House of Lords in the fourteenth century was symbolically stuffed with English wool. By the seventeenth century, Britain had moved into textile as well as wool production.

Imperial beginnings

About this time, England began to explore the world with a purpose more fiercely acquisitive than most of the other European powers. Its maritime location and navigational expertise gave it a number of advantages in exploring, trading and then colonising the newly discovered worlds of the Americas, Africa, Asia and the Far East. Especially lucrative was the slave trade – taking slaves from Africa to America and the Caribbean – which proceeded apace from the sixteenth century. Also profitable was the spice trade with India and China, which involved conflict with rival country Holland in those years.

Industrial Revolution and the emergence of Marxism

In the eighteenth and nineteenth centuries, technological breakthroughs, especially in the manufacture of cotton, coincided with the availability of both abundant coal resources and plentiful indigenous plus immigrant labour from Ireland, to produce a transformation in the economic structure of the country. This was a transformation – for good or ill – destined to engulf the whole world. The social and geographical impact of these changes included:

- the influx into the towns of thousands of agricultural labourers who now took work in the mills and factories;
- the emergence of great metropolises in the north and midlands, born of the new industries;
- the formation of municipal governments, which sought to solve the acute sanitation and health problems of urbanisation;
- a huge surge in exports to the expanding Empire and elsewhere, creating immense individual and national wealth;
- the creation of a small group of exceptionally rich 'capitalist' industrialists, often a new breed of entrepreneur but also frequently linked to the traditional aristocracy.

Thus, these changes led to the emergence of a small, rich 'upper class' of property owners and a huge, often impoverished urban working class. This inevitably had a transforming effect on British politics. The emergent middle-class industrialists were determined to resist the attempts of the aristocracy to hang on to the political control they had enjoyed for centuries. Meanwhile, the working class multiplied as the country's population surged. Once equipped with the vote, the working class became wooed by both major parties but it took the recently formed trade unions – organisations set up to protect industrial workers – to initiate the formation of a new party to advance the interests of the working class and the disadvantaged generally.

Karl Marx, a highly intellectual observer, of German origin but living in London during the nineteenth century, believed he had discerned the motive forces of history: conflict between differing 'classes' in society. Marx argued that at every stage in human history there had been a dominant and a subservient class, with the former being the one which controlled the means of wealth production, be it agriculture, wool, cotton or whatever. The subservient class would be convinced by the blandishments of the dominant class that these social arrangements were quite right and proper – no more than 'common sense' – but this state of affairs was due to end: as capitalists maximised profits, workers would come to realise the extent of their exploitation and would begin to develop a 'revolutionary consciousness'.

This polarisation of society into a small *bourgeoisie* and the *proletarian* masses would eventually express itself, he predicted, in a sweeping away of the former dominant class, an interregnum period and then the formation of a 'classless society'. However, even though Marx's analysis of the forces creating and changing society was remarkably accurate, in the view of many historians, history did not quite work out according to his 'scientific' rules. This is included in the following section, on class.

Class developments

If class – as is usually the case – is defined primarily in terms of occupation, things have evolved in a completely different way from Marx's predictions. Notably, there has been neither a polarisation of society nor the subsequent development of a classless society. In 1911, the working class comprised 74.6% of the labour force, while professionals (including managers and administrators) comprised only 7.5%. Following the Edwardian period, the economy expanded to include 'traditional industries' like mining, ship building and steel, but after World War II competition from other parts of the world reduced such industries to basket cases by the 1980s, along with the newer activities of vehicle production and electronics. By 1991, the equivalent figures were:

Box 4.1 Classifying class

Many sociologists have produced ways of classifying social strata but the most widely used is the ABC scale, which is as follows (with current percentages of the overall population in parentheses):

A   Upper middle: professional, higher managerial (3% of all households)
B   Middle: middle managers (16%)
C1   Lower middle: junior managers, routine white collar (26%)
C2   Skilled: plumbers, carpenters, mechanics (26%)
D   Semi-skilled and unskilled: manual workers (17%)
E   Residual: dependent on long-term benefit (12%)

37.7% working class and 34.0% professional. As Moran notes, '"The workers" as traditionally understood, are now in a minority' (Moran, 2005, p. 43). Nonetheless, that there are still class differences based on income and wealth can be in no doubt (see Figure 4.2, p. 30).

Why no revolution?

It goes without saying that there has been no modern revolution, despite astonishing levels of inequality in the nineteenth century and now in the twenty-first century. Why should this be?

- Some commentators argue that the British are not ideological and reject extremist measures.
- Marxists tend to explain it in terms of 'false consciousness' – the fact that the 'capitalist hegemony' of the institutions of the state – government, business, education, the media, for example – enable it to 'brainwash' society into thinking capitalism is the only possible way of organising the economy and that inequality is a natural, unavoidable and necessary concomitant of such a system.
- Others argue – perhaps more convincingly – that workers are extremely wary of risking what little they have for the speculative gains that might

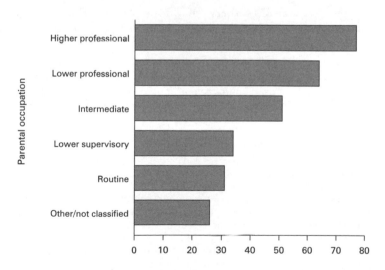

Percentage of children attaining five or more GSCE grades A* to C

Figure 4.1 *Attainment of five or more GSCE grades A* to C, by parental occupation, 2002, England and Wales*
Source: Office for National Statistics.

be won via the turbulence of revolution. It is perhaps not surprising that it is often middle-class people who advocate revolution – the working class cannot afford that luxury.

Social mobility and education

The most effective means of moving 'up' in social class is through education, especially higher education. However, it is also true that education reflects social class: children from 'lower' social categories tend to do less well than those from higher strata, as Figure 4.1 illustrates.

Private education

Some 7% of children are educated privately in schools which are expensively equipped and staffed and so are able to offer generally good GCSE and A level results (see Box 4.1, p. 26). Schools like Rugby, Shrewsbury, Marlborough and the most prestigious of the lot, Eton and Harrow, attract the children of the wealthiest. Places in the elite universities of Oxford and Cambridge go

---

Box 4.2 Private education and success in Britain

Writing in the *Guardian* (23 February 2008), historian David Kynaston ruefully noted the conclusions of a report published the previous autumn by the Sutton Trust:

> This ranked the success of schools, over a five-year period, at getting their pupils into Oxbridge. Top was Westminster school with a staggering 49.9% hit rate. In other words, if you pay your annual boarding fees of £25,956, you have a virtually evens chance of your child making it to Oxbridge – the pathway to the glittering prizes that will almost certainly lie ahead. Altogether, there were 27 private schools in the top 30; 43 in the top 50 and 78 in the top 100. Put another way, the 70th brightest sixth-former at Westminster or Eton is as likely to get a place at Oxbridge as the very brightest sixth-formers at a large comprehensive. I found it hard not to be angered as a citizen – and ashamed as an Oxford graduate – to see these figures.
>
> Importantly, this grotesque skewing is not confined to Oxbridge admissions. The Independent Schools Council, which represents the private schools, claimed in November that pupils at its schools were now five times more likely than the national average to be offered a place at one of the Russell Group universities, the top 20 out of more than 100 universities. 'These results show once again,' justifiably boasted the ISC's chief executive, 'the superb job done by ISC schools in preparing pupils for entry to leading universities'.

A report in the next day's *Guardian* revealed that, of the 30,000 candidates achieving three A grades in their A levels, only 176, or 0.5%, were drawn from those – the poorest – receiving free school meals.

disproportionately to the privately educated (or 'public school' educated, as we oddly refer to it) – about a half, even though they represent such a small proportion of children. These favoured recipients then go on to dominate the top jobs and professions: directors of big companies, judges, top posts in the armed forces and the civil service, and so on (see Box 4.2).

Expansion of higher education

In the early 1960s, only 5% of children went on to university; by the end of the century, the figure was over 40%. Studies show that the biggest beneficiaries of this expansion were middle-class children – working-class ones experienced only a small increase in the proportions entering higher education.

White-collar occupations

Following World War II, there was a massive increase in 'white collar' or 'middle class' jobs as the public sector grew and old occupations declined. Recent research has shown that the children of those born during the twentieth century generally enjoyed 'upward social mobility', in that their occupations were 'higher' than those of their parents. However, more recent studies suggest social mobility has stalled: white-collar occupations have ceased to expand so rapidly.

Inequality

Capitalism always produced 'winners' (e.g. people who established successful businesses) and 'losers' (e.g. those whose businesses failed, who worked for someone else at a low wage, or who lost their job or otherwise fell on hard times). The juxtaposition in city areas of great houses not far away from slums, not to mention beggars on the streets, was (and is) ample illustration of extremes of wealth and poverty. During the twentieth century, such inequalities diminished a little but towards the end of the century differences began to increase as directors of British companies began to receive salaries on a par with those in the United States. At the same time, the Conservative government of Margaret Thatcher brought down top tax rates to only 40% and pursued economic policies that – necessary or not – caused widespread unemployment. Since then, the gap has become wider, though with some amelioration at the very bottom through the efforts of Labour's Gordon Brown, who devised redistributive budgets in his decade as Chancellor of the Exchequer; Figure 4.2 illustrates (see also Figure 4.3).

The Joseph Rowntree Foundation published a report in July 2007 which revealed that the gap between rich and poor was wider than at any time over the previous forty years. Richard Lapthorne of Cable and Wireless was given

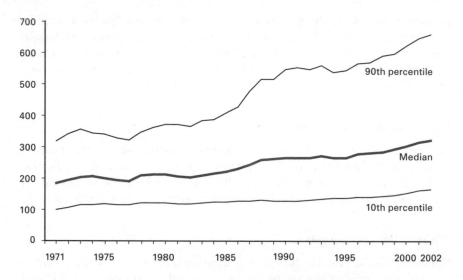

Figure 4.2 *Distribution of real household disposable income, 1971–2002*
Source: Office for National Statistics.

remuneration of £11 million over three years; Stuart Rose, chief executive
officer of Marks and Spencer, was given £7.8 million for turning the company
around; and the boss of mining group Xstrata received a salary 544 times
that of the average mineworker employed by his company. The ratio of his
earnings to the income of those on benefits must be even more astronomical.
Bosses of private equity firms – which take over public companies to make
them private and then often sell off assets and sack staff – can make sums of
money running well into the billions for individual takeovers. The economic
recession of 2008–9 did, though, reduce the scale of such rewards.

The Gini coefficient

This is an index produced by relating the wealth and income of the rich to
those of the poor; a high rating means high inequality, while a low one means
less inequality. According to this index, Sweden, Denmark and Holland are at
the top while Britain is low down the table, along with the United States. High
indexes correlate highly with social dissatisfaction and crime, suggesting it
could be a cause of social instability. In his book *Who Runs Britain?* Robert
Peston (2008) reflects on how the index soared during the Thatcher years of
the 1980s, eased down a little under Major before climbing again under Blair
and Brown until Brown's redistributive policies after 2001 produced reductions. This was only temporary, however, as the inequality gap took off yet
again after 2005 (see Figure 4.3 and Table 4.1).

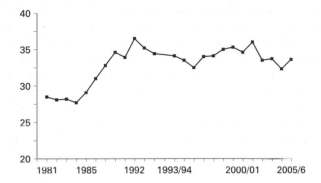

Figure 4.3 *Income inequality: rise in inequality. Gini coefficient (expressed as a percentage) for equivalised disposable income, 1981–2005/6*
Source: Office for National Statistics.

Table 4.1 *Number and percentage of children living in households with income less than 60% of median, 1979–2004*

	Before housing costs		After housing costs	
	Number (million)	Percentage	Number (million)	Percentage
1979	1.7	12	1.9	14
1981	2.4	18	2.7	20
1987	2.6	21	3.1	25
1988–89	2.9	23	3.3	26
1990–91	3.2	26	3.9	31
1991–92	3.4	27	4.1	32
1992–93	3.5	27	4.3	33
1993–94	3.3	25	4.2	32
1994–95	2.9	23	4.0	31
1995–96	2.8	22	4.0	31
1996–97	3.2	25	4.2	33
1997–98	3.1	25	4.1	32
1998–99	3.1	24	4.1	33
1999–2000	3.0	23	4.1	32
2000–1	2.7	21	3.8	30
2001–2	2.6	21	3.7	30
2002–3	2.6	21	3.6	28
2003–4	2.6	21	3.5	28

Note: Figures before 1994 relate to the whole of the UK and those after to Britain only.
Source: Family Resources Survey.

Income inequality in 2005/6 increased compared with the previous year. This increase was due to greater inequality of earnings and self-employed income, rather than the tax and benefit system. This followed a fall in inequality of disposable income between 2001/2 and 2004/5. In this period, there was faster growth in earnings at the bottom end of the income distribution, which, to some extent at least, was due to increases in the minimum wage. Tax credits also increased the income of households with children in the lower part of the income distribution.

Income equality still remains high by historical standards – the large increase which took place in the second half of the 1980s has not been reversed.

The super-rich

Peston's book identifies the extent of the burgeoning inequality in Britain since the late 1980s. In 1989, the average pay for senior directors running the top 10% of companies was £222,000 per annum, when the median pay (that's the middle point in the scale of richest to poorest) for employees was £11,648. This produced a ratio of 19–1. Since then, employee pay has about doubled, while bosses' pay has increased nine-fold. In the United States, whose trends we tend to follow a few years later, the ratio is a staggering 300–1.

Some big earners pull in more than they can possibly spend; Sir Philip Green, for example, earned £1.2 billion in 2005. He was also able to borrow £10 billion in his attempt to buy out Marks and Spencer 'with minimal negotiation and no strings attached' (Peston, 2008, p. 12). According to one analysis, the top 0.1% of British earners scoop up 2% of all personal income. In the United States, the equivalent percentage take 6% of total income, with the top 1% absorbing an astonishing 21.2% of economic output.

Should we worry? Well, the super-rich seem to have been chosen by party leaders as their cash cows; Labour has chosen them in preference to trade unions, its traditional source of wealth. Labour has also done everything possible to persuade the super-rich to take advantage of lenient British tax laws and live here while their wealth in offshore tax accounts is left unmolested by Her Majesty's Revenue and Customs. Most opinion polls show a large majority resent these huge rewards, and even deem them immoral, yet when very moderate tax proposals were aimed at the super-rich in the autumn of 2007, a barrage of objections were levelled at the Chancellor, who eventually backed down. Maybe allowing people to become so very, very rich is morally bad for any society with even the slightest aspiration towards equality. On the other hand, maybe having them live in the country, distasteful inequality notwithstanding, creates advantages for the whole of society, as the super-rich spend their money and create new businesses within it. Wilkinson and Pickett's book *The Spirit Level* (2009) suggests high economic inequality creates severe social dysfunction.

Underclass

The US sociologist Charles Murray discerned a near permanent group of people at the 'bottom' of US society who were, in effect, not subscribing to the values of society; for instance, they did not live in stable families but often in single-parent ones where children were allowed to run free and lacked good male role models of steady workers and caring fathers. Murray suggested such a group also thought little of living off welfare and indulging in crime or drugs. It followed that their children tended to grow up with an inadequate moral compass and very vulnerable to anti-social influences. He called this group – maybe 5% of society – an underclass. In the 1990s he journeyed over to Britain, where he diagnosed, in articles for the *Sunday Times*, a similar phenomenon. In 1994 he wrote an article entitled 'The new Victorians and the new rabble', in which he predicted rich middle-class people were likely to retreat to 'gated' communities, where they would live protected and isolated lives while the rest of society lived at the mercy of a 'rabble' expressing many of the underclass values. Most commentators dismissed this as highly unlikely

---

Box 4.3 Oxbridge and social mobility

In the *Observer*, 16 March 2008, Carole Cadwalladr examined the stranglehold Oxbridge seems to exert over the British establishment:

> [The Sutton Trust] calculates that 81 per cent of the judiciary went to Oxford or Cambridge, 82 per cent of all barristers, 45 per cent of 'leading' journalists, and 34 per cent of front-bench ministers and shadow ministers.

Somewhat appalled, she emailed the television presenter and author Jeremy Paxman for a comment and received the following peremptory reply:

> God, this is a boring subject, isn't it? Surely the reason is perfectly obvious. Oxford and Cambridge are the finest universities in Europe and two of the best universities in the world. They are also intensely beautiful, operate on a small college basis and employ some of the cleverest men and women in the world as teachers. They therefore attract some brilliant students. Only someone whose chip was so big that it completely obscured their eyes could be surprised – or consider it undesirable – that these two universities contribute lots of people to some of the more prominent areas of British life.

Yes, but isn't it the case that even though only 7% of schoolchildren are educated privately, about half of all entrants into this key entry point into the ruling elite are from this tiny, rich and privileged segment of our society? Meanwhile, Cadwalladr reveals that only 20% of entrants originate from comprehensives.

Paxman (educated at Malvern College and Charterhouse) seems to ignore the inequity of the Oxbridge intake, and the case made by David Kynaston (also privately educated) in Box 4.2 (p. 28) that, effectively, parents buy places for their children in elite occupations and contribute to the stifling of social mobility.

but in July 2007 Professor Danny Dorling of the University of Sheffield published a report which suggested that, indeed, an increasing segregation in urban centres could be discerned where middle-class people lived lives wholly separate from working-class people, and vice versa.

Regional differences

The biggest divide between the regions is a north–south one, with the north being less developed than the south, especially the south-east. With high levels of unemployment following the decline of traditional industries in the north, there has been a constant attraction of the south and a drift there as a result. As the economy has become more oriented towards service industries, London has become the centre for financial and business services. Attempts to encourage businesses to devolve into the regions have been only partially successful and the south-east still has far and away the most dynamic part of the economy; it is arguably part of a robust European triangle of economic activity that includes northern France, Belgium and the Netherlands.

Gender

Women have been treated as second-class citizens by men in the past; in the nineteenth century a man was allowed to beat his wife and to own her property, while she had no legal redress and could not divorce an abusive spouse. Since then, legal inequity has been removed in many areas but social attitudes and treatment in the workplace have not always kept pace with the legal changes. Women still tend to receive lower wages than men and tend to be employed in lower-status, lower-paying jobs: clerical positions, shop assistants, secretaries, nurses and so forth. They are also often employed only part time, while others suffer discrimination if they wish to have children and still keep their jobs. On 24 July 2007, the Equal Opportunities Commission published a report into gender equality. It found that:

- only 20% of MPs are female;
- a 'pensions' gap leaves retired women with 40% less income than male contemporaries;
- women receive 38% less per hour than men when working part time and 17% if full time.

Ethnicity

Britain used to be a relatively homogenous country, the major division within society being that of social class. It would be fair to say that class as a divider has been blurred and that ethnicity has become a new and potent dividing line in the early twenty-first century. Successive influxes of refugees – such as Huguenots (French Calvinists) in the fifteenth and sixteenth centuries, and Jews fleeing from pogroms in Russia throughout the nineteenth century – had been absorbed without too much difficulty but the influx of the impoverished Irish during the Industrial Revolution was more difficult and the Irish were often the victims of various forms of discrimination.

Immigration after 1945 was different, in that immigrants from the Caribbean were black and therefore more obvious. The same went for immigrants from the 'New Commonwealth' – India, Pakistan and then Uganda – and this was exacerbated when they tended to live in certain parts of big cities, such as West Indians in Willesden and Asians in Southall.

More recent immigration has been in the form of asylum seekers from the world's trouble spots, like Afghanistan, Somalia and Iraq, and economic migrants from eastern Europe as these countries entered the European Union after 2004. Immigration was an issue in the inner cities even before Enoch Powell's infamous 'rivers of blood' speech in 1968, but the racist far right found little electoral purchase, despite widespread grumbling. During the general elections of 2001 and 2005, immigration became an issue as party leaders argued over how many illegal immigrants were living in Britain – some said a quarter of a million but the real figure was later estimated to be closer to a half million.

The 2001 census revealed, according to the Office for National Statistics, that there were 4.6 million people of minority ethnicity in the UK: 7.9% of the total, increased from 6% in 1991. Half of these minorities were Asian, with mixed-race people accounting for 15%. Half of all minorities live in the London area. Leicester's proportion of white residents fell from 70.1% in 1991 to 59.5% in 2008; by 2026, calculates Sheffield University, it will be 44.5% (see Hinsliff, 2008). In 2007, some 591,000 immigrants arrived – the largest groups were from Pakistan, Bangladesh and Sri Lanka – but 400,000 long-term migrants left.

Conclusion

The socio-political context is crucial. The biggest shaper and moulder of society is the economy and historically Britain has inherited a free enterprise system under which some have prospered while many not done so well. Inequality tends to generate political demands – based on arguments of equity and need – for some kind of redistribution. Gender inequality has created demands for equal rights and immigration has created demands for action to limit its volume and effects.

References

Cadwalladr, C. (2008) 'It's the clever way to power', *Observer*, 16 March.

Dorling, D. (2007) *Poverty, Wealth and Place in Britain 1968 to 2005*, Policy Press (see also www.guardian.co.uk/society/2007/jul/18/guardiansocietysupplement. economicpolicy and http://image.guardian.co.uk/sys-files/Society/documents/2007/07/17/JRFfullreport.pdf).

Hinsliff, G. (2008) 'Ethnic middle classes join the "white flight"', *Observer*, 20 April (see www.guardian.co.uk/world/2008/apr/20/race.communities).

Kynaston, D. (2008) 'The road to meritocracy is blocked by private schools', *Guardian*, 22 February.

Moran, M. (2005) *Politics and Governance in the UK*, Palgrave.

Murray, C. (1994) 'The new Victorians and the new rabble', *Sunday Times*, 29 May. Published in book form as *Underclass: The Crisis Deepens*, Health and Welfare Unit of the Institute of Economic Affairs in association with the *Sunday Times* (September 1994) (see www.civitas.org.uk/pdf/cw33.pdf).

Peston, R. (2008) *Who Runs Britain… And Who's To Blame For the Economic Mess We're In?*, Hodder & Stoughton.

Wilkinson, R. and Pickett, K. (2009) *The Spirit Level: Why More Equal Societies Almost Always Do Better*, Allen Lane.

Recommended reading

Kavanagh, D., *et al.* (2006) *British Politics* (5th edition), Oxford University Press: chapter 5.

Leach, R., *et al.* (2006) *British Politics*, Palgrave: chapter 3.

Moran, M. (2005) *Politics and Governance in the UK*, Palgrave: chapter 3.

Other texts

Halsey, A. and Webb, J. (eds) (2000) *Twentieth Century Social Trends*, Macmillan.

Kynaston, D. (2007) *Austerity Britain, 1945–51*, Bloomsbury.

Peston, R. (2008) *Who Runs Britain… And Who's To Blame For the Economic Mess We're In?*, Hodder & Stoughton.

Website

National Statistics, income inequality, www.statistics.gov.uk/cci/nugget.asp?id=332.

5

Political culture in Britain

Definition of the term

'Political culture' is a rather nebulous concept, although Iain McLean's *Dictionary of Politics* manages a reasonably crisp definition: 'The attitudes, beliefs, and values which underpin the operation of a particular political system.' These will include, he writes, 'knowledge and skills'; 'positive and negative emotional feelings' towards the system of government; and 'evaluative judgments' about it (McLean, 1996, p. 379). Factors contributing towards these feelings, emotions, values and attitudes include historical experience, the economic system and the constitution. Below I identify a number of factors and suggest how they might influence the political culture.

The importance of political culture

Perhaps because it is somewhat vague, this concept is often overlooked in political analyses but, in truth, it is of central importance. Searching for metaphors, one considers ideas like the 'soil' from which political systems spring or the 'blood' circulating around that system. People often wonder why characteristics persist or systems do not export successfully – the reasons are often connected with political culture. For example, Russian history shows a marked authoritarian tendency; the tzars were succeeded by a man sometimes described as the 'Red Tzar', Joseph Stalin. Following the implosion of the Soviet Union, many hoped democracy would take the place of communism but Vladimir Putin's regime showed strong authoritarian tendencies. Similar problems with former communist regimes can be discerned in eastern Europe and central Asia. Finally, the United States and Britain hoped democracy would take root in Iraq after their joint invasion in 2003 but the combination of Muslim extremism, residual Baathist attitudes and hostility to western ways have scarcely succeeded – at least so far – to nourish the distinctly slender sapling of democracy in this region.

Historical experience

Two historical features can be identified that have been especially important in the development of Britain's political culture:

- *Sequential solving of major problems.* Unlike many other European countries, Britain met the challenges of the day in sequence and not all at once: in the sixteenth century, a settlement was reached between church and state; in the seventeenth century, conflict between king and Parliament was settled in the form of a limited monarchy; while the nineteenth century saw the gradual expansion of the franchise, to include all classes of voters by the early twentieth century.
- *Empire.* This, arguably unjustifiable, centuries-long adventure proved hugely popular for a nation with a strong maritime tradition. Thousands flocked to live in the new colonies and enjoy a standard of life much higher than back home. Moreover, the British tended to exult in their status as the centre of a worldwide empire; the song *Rule Britannia* reflects some of this 'jingoistic' sentiment. The downside of this nationalistic hubris was the racist attitudes which empire tended to encourage in those people who lived in the colonies and how they influenced attitudes towards those indigenous to the 'colonies' who later emigrated to the 'mother country'. Service in the armed forces also tended to encourage disdainful attitudes towards 'native' peoples.

The economy

The means by which wealth is created and distributed is of key importance in determining political culture. Britain's experience as the first industrial power meant it suffered a major division between the rich and poor. As Karl Marx well noted, these helped make the conditions conducive to social disturbance or revolution, but this did not happen in Britain, largely because the working classes decided to hang on to what they had, rather than risk it all in a potentially bloody revolution. Nevertheless, ideologically committed young people tried (in vain) to enthuse workers at the factory gates with ideas of insurrection and a revolution to achieve social justice. In addition, the ruling elite were wise enough, when crises occurred, to bend before the forces of change in order to cling onto their riches, power and privileges.

Consequently, Britain was able to evolve from an agricultural to a highly industrialised country with only minimal dislocation. The British have accepted the bases of the free enterprise system without too much dissent.

Using capital to set up a business, to hire and fire people as the business requires, is more or less accepted, together with the right of entrepreneurs, with the energy, expertise and luck to succeed, to make and keep their profits. They may not share the 'American dream' of fabulous wealth and they may grumble bitterly at the differences between rich and poor, but rising up violently in order to even things out has never recommended itself as a course of action to most British working people. Most people would accept that free enterprise economics is the best and the only way to create wealth; this acceptance has now reached the status of 'common sense' for most British people.

Most would also like to earn more money and enjoy an ever-improving standard of living. As disposable income has increased, British people, in common with most of the developed world, have indulged in acquiring more and more material goods, as well as extensive air travel. Marx would have condemned this happy materialism, had he been alive today, as the persistence of the 'false consciousness' which the ruling class had inculcated into the working masses, assisted by the institutions of the state and the capitalist owned media; the argument would be that such diversions prevented workers from realising they were being exploited by the capitalist owners of factories, enterprises and the like. Antonio Gramsci, a twentieth-century writer who shared Marx's basic analysis, elaborated such a perspective for present times, especially in respect of the media.

The constitution

As Britain does not have a written constitution – it has tended to change gradually over the centuries – it is not easy to hold definite views upon it. However, like any country, Britain has its own unique system of government, parts of which are warmly supported and others of which are not. Free speech might not seem to be something most of us feel passionately about, but imagine the uproar if the Home Secretary suddenly banned all news media from criticising the government, as is the case in many autocratic regimes. This would certainly ignite some fairly passionate demonstrations.

Maybe we have become a little spoiled with our liberal democratic government and fail to appreciate its virtues – no one would wish it, but having them snatched away for a while would probably remind us that our political rights are priceless. Other rights we would miss if they were removed would include the rights of everyone to set up their own organisations representing common interests, like political parties or trade unions, and to vote in choosing the government in regular elections.

Some aspects of the constitution are more controversial. Some of these are ancient and regarded as possibly past their utility:

- The House of Lords has been mostly stripped of its hereditary peers but still (in 2009) awaits comprehensive reform.
- The role of the monarchy is disputed by some who feel an elected head of state might be preferable. Since the lives of the royal family have become something of a soap opera, respect for the monarchy has declined and it has arguably lost status, but the millions who filed past the Queen Mother's coffin in 2002 showed that the institution retains enormous support and affection.
- The Church of England is the official established church of the country and the Queen is its head. However, the authority of the church has declined over the last two centuries and arguably now, with its diminished congregations, it has ceased to have any real relevance.

Other aspects are more modern and have not yet been fully accepted by the nation:

- *Membership of the European Union (EU)*. This took place in 1972 and since then the organisation has developed massively into a more integrated and powerful institution embodying most of eastern as well as western Europe. Some people, mostly to the right of the political spectrum, would like to see Britain withdraw from the EU or for its powers to be drastically reduced. British opinion has become increasingly Eurosceptical over the last decade.
- *Devolution*. The devolved assemblies, created in 1998, have experienced three elections but still some people resist them. A reducing number would like to dismantle them and restore the old 'Union', while an increasing number would like to abolish them in favour of independence.

Extremism

Most historians agree that British political culture does not display any disposition to extremism. A variety of aspects of the country's political culture help explain this:

- *Ideological*. The British political fringe has included all the usual exoticisms of anarchists, Trotskyists, communists, Maoists, fascists and the like, but there has been no occasion when beliefs substantially adrift from the centre have ever taken root. In the 1930s, both communism and fascism were represented by political parties but neither prospered; rather, they won the support only of zealous minorities, to some extent in thrall to their overseas models.
- *Political methodology*. The same can be said under this heading. Extreme ideologies tend to embrace extreme methodologies, such as violent revolution and the cult of the personality in the case of both communism and fascism. But the British instinctively recoiled from the idea of revolution during the

general strike of 1926, when it was at its most feasible, and have tended to prefer the historically established indigenous machinery of incremental change and representative democracy via the House of Commons. This does not mean that violent displays do not occasionally occur, as in the city riots in the early 1980s or the 'poll tax' riots in London in 1990, but these were episodic events and not part of a wholesale rejection of the political system.

Deference

'Political deference' has been held to mean respect for the government, the law and the absence of a militant tradition. 'Social deference' has been seen as the acceptance that some people are innately superior, by virtue of their social rank. So a 'gentleman' was seen as one who spoke in a 'received pronunciation' fashion, dressed well, was polite and had 'leadership' qualities. For this reason, the armed forces tended to recruit the privately educated into their officer ranks during the nineteenth century. It was the wastage rate of such people in World War I that led to more recruitment into the officer classes from the middle classes. In similar fashion, the traditional professions – the law, the civil service and banking, not to mention the new profession of broadcasting – looked first to recruit from the same privately educated middle classes; the Conservative Party drew most of its MPs from the same sources. Labour, too, drew some of its leading lights from the ranks of the 'gentleman's schools'. However, the lower ranks seldom took kindly to such subservience and deference was often accorded only through gritted teeth. The 1950s was probably the last decade when British society could be said to be deferential in this sense.

During the 1960s, a form of 'cultural revolution' took place when such attitudes were re-examined and found wanting. Perhaps this is explained by:

- new British writers like Kingsley Amis, whose books poked fun at the established order;
- the imported music from the United States – jazz and rock and roll – which expressed individual expression and rebellion (and British musicians soon began to equal the popularity of their US models);
- the emergence of an elite, educated at grammar schools, many of whom went on to study at the elite universities and who resented the hegemony of a class which had scarcely distinguished itself in many respects;
- the increasing prosperity of the middle classes, which encouraged them to be more assertive;
- the apparent failure of the existing ruling elite to sustain the postwar boom and spread prosperity throughout society (the replacement of the Edwardian Harold Macmillan as Prime Minister by the aristocratic Alec Douglas-Home, in 1963 seemed to symbolise this stasis);
- the identification of a new group in society – teenagers – whose natural mode is one of questioning and straining rules to their limits;

- the decline of religion as a social glue which legitimised social differences and respect for 'superiors'.

The upshot of these changes was a decade when a bonfire was made of the rules of deference regarding respect for social hierarchies, sexual restraint and conventional expectations of how life should be led. This was symbolised by: the emergence of 'hippy' culture in the late 1960s, which offered alternative lifestyles; a reform of the law which outlawed homosexual acts between consenting adults; and an increasing tendency to regard politicians as objects of derision. This last was encouraged by the BBC television programme *That Was The Week That Was*, which saw the advent onto our screens of David Frost and others who made their names by poking fun at the established order. It was no coincidence that the Conservatives, fearful of appearing old-fashioned, elected two grammar-school products as leaders, in the persons of Edward Heath in 1965 and Margaret Thatcher ten years later.

Satire. This has established itself as central to our perception of politicians since the 1960s – witness the popularity of television programmes like *Spitting Image, Yes Minister, Bremner, Bird and Fortune* and *The Thick Of It*. Some argue that such fun making has served to reduce respect for our political leaders;

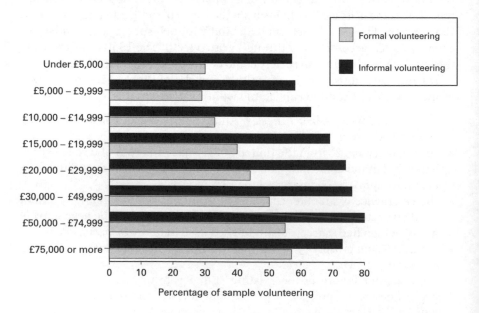

Figure 5.1 *Volunteering, by annual gross household income, 2001, England and Wales*

Source: Home Office Citizenship Survey 2001, Office for National Statistics.

this may be true to a degree, as it certainly worried leaders like Heath, but those more nimble in adapting their image, like Tony Blair, have been able to deflect a fair amount of criticism by deploying self-deprecating wit.

Civil society

This is the complex web of relationships which exist between citizens – social, economic and via voluntary groups. While not specifically political, such contacts enable people to 'learn' the rudiments of democratic decision-making and the requirements of fitting in, adjusting and compromising. Britain has long had a history of encouraging a mass of voluntary bodies – for instance scout groups, charity organisations, support groups for those who need them – and, as such, has long been held to provide a healthy 'soil' in which democracy can grow. Figure 5.1 shows how volunteering is heavily influenced by the income group (and hence social group) people belong to. Figure 5.2 illustrates 'community spirit' in Britain as perceived by people in recent decades; significantly, it shows how the number of people discerned as 'going their own way' increased sharply from 1988 to 1992, suggesting a decline in this form of 'social capital'.

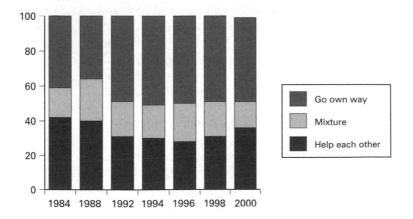

Figure 5.2 *Community spirit in neighbourhoods, 1984–2000, England and Wales*
Note: Respondents were asked, 'In general, what kind of neighbourhood would you say you live in? Would you say it is a neighbourhood in which people do things together and try and help each other or one in which people mostly go their own way?'
Source: Home Office British Crime Survey 2001, Office for National Statistics.

Crime

The decline of deference has also had an impact on crime. When people more or less accepted their position in society, they were not too unhappy that the upper social strata received more financial rewards and more power. However, once everyone began to feel an equal entitlement to success, those lower down in the hierarchy were not willing to accept inferiority and turned to illegality as a means of advancing their socio-economic status. This is one of the reasons, perhaps, why there was a huge crime wave between the advent of Thatcher in 1979 and the demise of John Major's government in 1997. It followed that a reduction in crime rates has become a major political demand over recent decades.

Welfare state

After the introduction of pensions in the early twentieth century, welfare measures were added incrementally until the major extension of them after 1945, when Labour won its historic landslide. Free education and free health care were the major additions and very quickly became part of the nation's life. Further measures like sick and unemployment pay added to a raft of support measures from the state, which almost amounted to 'cradle to grave' provision. It is fair now to say that the British have become used to such assistance and are closely attached to the National Health Service, so much so that any party seeking to dismantle it would lose support – even the suggestion that the Conservatives might do so became an electoral liability in 1997 and in 2001. It would be fair to say that the British have become habituated to welfare services, expect to receive them and will punish at the ballot any party which begins either to remove or to weaken them.

Vulnerability to attack?

A report in the *Guardian* (15 February 2008) by the armed forces think-tank the Royal United Services Institute suggested that 'multiculturalism' as a long-term policy carried a number of risks that our political culture is vulnerable to attack from without and within:

> The United Kingdom presents itself as a target, as a fragmenting, post-Christian society, increasingly divided about interpretations of its history, about its national aims, its values and in its political identity.... The problem is worsened by the lack of leadership from the majority which in misplaced deference to 'multiculturalism' failed to lay down the line to immigrant communities, thus undercutting those within trying to fight extremism. The country's lack of

self-confidence is in stark contrast to the implacability of its Islamist terrorist enemy, within and without. 'Fractured institutional integrity' means that when the unexpected occurs, the response is likely to be incoherent and ad hoc, short-termist and uncertain. Uncertainty incubates the embryonic threats these risks represent. We look like a soft touch. We are indeed a soft touch.

Less accepted, more 'negotiable' values

It would be a mistake to believe that political culture was in any way set in time: it is constantly changing, reflecting different living conditions and events. As we have seen, while some aspects of our political culture seem well established, others are in flux. The Lords is no longer accepted as legitimate in its unelected state, the ailing Church of England has lost its congregations and much of its former authority, while British people have yet fully to embrace either the EU or the notion of devolution.

MPs' expenses and an erosion of trust

At the time of writing, British political culture is undergoing something of an upheaval, though how fundamental it is and how lasting it will prove is impossible to gauge. The banking crisis of 2008–9 led to a deep economic recession, with associated unemployment and bankruptcies. Widespread anger was felt against the leading bankers, whose incompetence, coupled with greed for obscenely large bonuses, it was believed, had caused the crisis in the first place.

Just when the public began to realise they could not, for example, prevent the much loathed Sir Fred Goodwin, former head of the Royal Bank of Scotland, receiving his £700,000 annual pension (though he did later agree a reduction of £200,000), along came the MPs' expenses scandal. This revealed that many MPs were making unreasonable claims for their parliamentary expenses: for upkeep on second homes when some lived within commuting distance; for substantial amounts of food; for gardening costs; and for absurd items like lavatory seats (John Prescott) and porn films (Jacqui Smith's husband). While bankers were not accountable, MPs were and they were subjected to a furious backlash from constituents and other ordinary voters.

The outcome of this fusion of discontents was a shift in political culture so that not only a root-and-branch reform of MPs' expenses was thought necessary but also a raft of constitutional reforms, like fixed parliamentary terms, more power for select committees and, even, radical reform of the voting system. At the time of writing it is too soon to judge how much change, if any, will result from this eruption of anger: it could be temporary and fade away or, equally, provide the trigger for some genuine change to reduce the collapse of trust in politicians and the political system.

Conclusion

Writing in the 1960s, Almond and Verba produced *The Civic Culture*, a major study in political culture. They saw Britain as having the 'ideal civic culture', that is, one that 'combined or balanced the values of citizen participation and self-confidence with a trust in the elites and a responsiveness to their laws' (quoted in Jones and Kavanagh, 1994, p. 25). In Britain, judged the authors: 'Citizens are sufficiently active in politics to express their preferences to rulers, but not so involved as to refuse to accept decisions with which they disagree. Thus the civic culture resolves the tension between popular control and effective governance' (quoted in Watts, 2003, p. 18).

Clearly, such an analysis requires an update. Participation rates have plummeted along with trust in elites, especially after the expenses debacle, and perhaps stability is no longer so assured. The erosion of deference has made the country easier to live in for many people but at some cost to authority and trust. A more enthusiastic embrace of market forces has added dynamism to the economy but also instability as wealth and income gaps have grown apace. British civil society is still robust but has suffered a decline since the days of Almond and Verba's book. It is by no means certain that, if written today, such a study would produce such an optimistic set of conclusions.

References

Almond, G. A. and Verba, S. (1963) *The Civic Culture: Political Attitudes and Democracy in Five Nations*, Princeton University Press.
Jones, B. and Kavanagh, D. (1994) *British Politics Today*, Manchester University Press.
McLean, I. (1996) *Oxford Concise Dictionary of Politics*, Oxford University Press.
Watts, D. (2003) *Understanding US/UK Government and Politics*, Manchester University Press.

Recommended reading

Kavanagh, D., *et al.* (2006) *British Politics* (5th edition), Oxford University Press: chapters 4 and 5.
Kingdom, J. (2003) *Government and Politics in Britain: An Introduction* (3rd edition), Polity: chapter 7.
Leach, R., *et al.* (2006) *British Politics*, Palgrave: chapters 3 and 4.
Moran, M. (2005) *Politics and Governance in the UK*, Palgrave: chapter 5.

Other texts

Beer, S. (1982) *Modern British Politics*, Faber.
Beer, S. (1982) *Britain Against Itself: Political Contradictions of Collectivism*, Faber.
Kavanagh, D. (1972) *Political Culture*, Oxford University Press.
Mackenzie, R. and Silver, A. (1968) *Angels in Marble*, Heinemann.
Rose, R. (ed.) (1974) *Studies in British Politics*, Macmillan.

6

The changing constitution

Unwritten

Constitutions provide the 'rules of the game' for states, determining how their political systems are allowed to operate – how often there will be elections and what kind of voting system is to be used, what constitutes a majority in the legislature, what powers the head of the executive has, and so forth. If they know nothing else about the constitution, most British people know that their country has no written document upon which it is inscribed. But, like many other well known 'truths', this is not quite correct. Much of the constitution is actually written down, in the form of Acts of Parliament relating to, for example, who can vote. What Britain lacks is a *complete codified document* like the US constitution. Autocratic regimes also produce constitutions from time to time, but autocrats tend to ignore the rules or change them if they prove inconvenient, so, unsurprisingly, they are more commonly associated with democracies.

Historical emergence of constitutions

From the earliest days there were no written constitutions – monarchs ruled more or less as they pleased and that was that. Most countries up to the eighteenth century did not question the idea of monarchical rule and it would have been difficult in any case to suddenly stop off and formulate a new system. The situation of the embryonic United States was therefore unusual: the successful rebellion of the original thirteen states against British rule provided a tabula rasa, a clean slate. Their constitution was drawn up by a committee of very ingenious and able men in 1787 and became possibly the most important constitution ever drafted. From thereon, more and more nations produced similar documents; for example, France has introduced a number, the most recent being the 1958 version for the Fifth Republic. The Soviet Union also had a famously liberal constitution dating from 1936, though in practice Joseph Stalin totally ignored its major provisions.

Usually constitutions are created by consensus. Significantly, such innovations as devolved assemblies in the UK have been put out to referendums before being implemented. However, Britain's system of government, originating long before rules were formally written down, was created more out of conflict than agreement: for example, *constitutional* monarchical rule was born out of the Civil War, the execution of one king and the fleeing of a second. However, once all the seventeenth-century constitutional matters were sorted out, together with the laying of the democratic foundations for the nineteenth century, they hardly arose at all during the eighteenth century. Constitutional matters did, though, feature much in the nineteenth century and the early twentieth but then lay quiescent until the 1990s, when they topped the political agenda once again.

'Dignified' and 'efficient'

Walter Bagehot, the most famous authority on the British constitution, made a distinction in the nineteenth century between those aspects which were 'dignified' – those that had a mostly ceremonial function, like the monarchy, Privy Council and, to a degree, the House of Lords – and the 'efficient' or 'working' aspects – like the Commons, departments of state and the law courts. (Moran, 2005, p. 71, points out that 'dignified' is not precisely the correct word to describe some of the behaviour of the Royal Family in recent decades.)

Parliamentary sovereignty

Basic to the whole system of British government is the notion that it is only the Queen in Parliament who can make the law, or indeed unmake it. Unlike in the United States, the courts cannot strike down a law as being contrary to the constitution. No other body can set aside its statutes. After the Glorious Revolution of 1688, the King agreed to be bound by the laws of Parliament, and the courts of law too. Parliament is at the peak of the constitution and, as the Commons is (now) the dominant element of it, elections to that body determine which party leader forms the government.

Sources of the constitution

Moran (2006) notes the eclectic nature of the British constitution:

- *'Normal' statutes.* These are laws passed affecting the power of the state. For example, habeas corpus, codified by an Act of 1679, limits the right of the state to detain anyone without trial. Since then, the Prevention of Terrorism Act 1974 was passed to increase state powers in relation to those suspected of terrorist offences; as it was a 'temporary' measure, it has been renewed every year since and was further strengthened by the Anti-terrorism, Crime and Security Act in 2001.

- *'Super' statutes.* These are those that Parliament cannot easily over-rule, as they originate in treaties in connection with the European Union (EU), the establishment of devolved assemblies in Scotland, Wales and Northern Ireland, or, another identified by Moran, the abolition of most hereditary peerages in the Lords, which is not something that Parliament could be likely to reverse in the foreseeable future. Hence, these are statutes of a heavier timber than the normal ones applying to electoral law and so forth. This is especially true of EU law, which is superior to domestic law and over-rules it. In 1972, on joining the European Community, the UK agreed to be bound by the 1957 Treaty of Rome and then by the Single European Act of 1986 and the European Communities (Amendment) Act in 1993, which implemented the Maastricht Treaty.
- *Case law.* This comprises the interpretations of various laws in court cases. Often, application changes with circumstance, so accumulated judicial opinion can acquire the status of law in itself.
- *Common law.* This kind of law dates back to Norman times and has been distilled from 'custom and precedent', often relating to traditional rights and freedoms upheld by courts over centuries, freedom of speech and assembly being among them. Common law, however, is over-ruled by statute law.
- *Royal prerogative.* These powers are in effect the residual powers of the monarch regarding summoning and dissolving Parliament, appointing judges, creating peers, signing treaties, declaring war and the like. Because they are in the hands of the crown, Parliament's approval is not

---

Box 6.1 Prime Minister's powers of appointment over the Church of England

In its constitutional Green Paper of 4 July 2007, the government declared the Prime Minister should no longer use the royal prerogative 'to exercise choice in recommending appointments of senior ecclesiastical posts, including diocesan bishops, to the Queen'. The Prime Minister should not have 'an active role' in the selection of the candidates. Currently, the Church of England chooses two names for diocesan posts, including that of Archbishop of Canterbury, and presents them to the Prime Minister in order of preference. The Prime Minister has the power to choose the second name or to ask for more names. It was proposed that, instead, the Church's Crown Nominations Commission should put just one name to the Prime Minister, who would then convey this recommendation to the Queen.

deemed necessary. Over time, however, the Prime Minister and Cabinet have come to exercise these powers, causing reformers like Tony Benn to criticise the Prime Minister as a 'medieval monarch in Downing Street'. Upon acceding to power in 2007, Gordon Brown declared he would pass over these prerogative powers to Parliament. At the time of writing, some such transfers of power are embodied in the Constitutional Renewal Bill.

- *Conventions.* These are perhaps quintessentially British phenomena, in that they lack the force of law but have been followed for so long that they have come to be seen as automatically applicable. Examples include the practice whereby the Prime Minister, since early twentieth century, will sit in the Commons and not the Lords, that the Queen will dissolve Parliament when the Prime Minister requests it and that the Prime Minister will resign if defeated on a motion of confidence.
- *Institutional rules.* Moran points out that the internal rules of our major institutions virtually have constitutional significance; for example, Erskine May's nineteenth-century work *Parliamentary Practice* (often known just as *Erskine May*) has become the bible of parliamentary procedure in the Commons.
- *Works of authority.* There are a number of hugely respected works on the constitution – for example Edward Coke's *Institutes of the Law of England* (1628–44) and A. V. Dicey's *An Introduction to the Study of the Law of the Constitution* (1885) – which have considerable persuasive power where clarity is sought.

Amendment of the constitution

In the United States there are several hurdles to be cleared before any aspect of the constitution can be amended; Britain is unusual in having no special 'entrenchment' of its constitution. However:

- Bills with constitutional content usually have their committee stage on the floor of the Commons rather than in a standing committee;
- it has now become accepted that major constitutional proposals should first be subject to a referendum, as in the case of devolution;
- devolution itself has, arguably, removed some constitutional items away from the orbit of Westminster, but power is still only delegated – it can be limited or abolished altogether should Parliament so decide.

Separation of powers

During the eighteenth century, the French political thinker Baron de Montesquieu believed England had a 'separation of powers', which produced a balance whereby the legislature, executive and judiciary checked each other. The framers of the US constitution were influenced by his analysis and embodied it in their creation. However, he was mistaken, as the executive is actually formed out of the largest group in the legislature and the 'independence of the legislature' is mostly a fiction. In the United States this mistake has perhaps had good consequences, as the legislature is elected separately from the executive and the senior judiciary is appointed by the President. Separate elections give separate legitimacy and power not found in British government, meaning that a British Prime Minister has more power in some respects than a US President, who has to contend with the elected Congress; the Prime Minister, on the other hand, can be deposed if he or she loses party backing, while the President is guaranteed office until it officially expires after four years.

Moran's 'core' and 'contested' elements of the constitution

In the United States, the constitution occupies a revered place in national life, in which its authority is unquestioned. In Britain, there is nothing to equal such respect, although Moran – recognising that such considerations delve into 'political culture' – makes a useful distinction between those aspects of the constitution which are accepted without cavil (the core elements) and those which attract controversy (the contested elements).

Core elements

Moran identifies a number of items:

- *Rule of law.* The government is not allowed to exceed the limits of its own laws or it is judged to be 'ultra vires', and procedures exist for citizens and groups to challenge government if it does transgress. The addition of EU law has led government to be cautious to ensure that new laws are compatible with it.
- *Procedural democracy.* These are the rules whereby a government is elected, serves its time in office and then is subjected to another judgement by voters. Moran is right to say that these rules are so ingrained 'that it occurs to virtually nobody to change them', but some minor changes are made from time to time and, it might be observed, these rules cannot be so widely absorbed if only 60% of the electorate can be bothered to vote in a general election, as in 2001.
- *Accountability.* That governments should explain themselves and be subject to challenge and dismissal is never questioned.
- *Liberal freedoms.* By the same token, virtually no one challenges the right of someone to freedom of speech or assembly. However, especially in the wake of restrictions resulting from terrorist acts, recent changes in the law have shown that even these core elements are not infrequently altered and diminished to a degree.

Contested elements

- *Territorial unity.* The emergence of passionate nationalist movements in Wales, Scotland and Northern Ireland shows that this has become an element of the constitution that is looking increasingly tenuous.
- *Parliamentary supremacy.* Membership of the EU has seen a challenge to parliamentary sovereignty, which many Euro-sceptics have opposed. And from 'below', devolution has ushered in challenges based on a new legitimacy delegated to assemblies within UK territory.
- *Crown legitimacy.* In the nineteenth century, the Queen and her family were above criticism and occupied a near sacred position, albeit mostly ceremonial, at the heart of the constitution. During the twentieth century, the Royal Family still commanded huge public support, especially during World War II, when they symbolised the national struggle. But after the late 1960s, when the royals made the mistake of allowing the light of publicity to steal away their magic, their position began to be criticised. The demise of deference and the growth of intrusive tabloid reporting meant that the marriage of Prince Charles to Diana Spencer was pored over like no other, and it is hardly surprising it failed to survive.

Current constitutional issues

A written constitution?

Since the 1980s, pressure has grown for the official writing down or 'codification' of the uncertain aspects of the constitution. Constitutional reformers, for example members of the pressure group Charter 88, have long argued for such a document, on the following grounds:

- The executive has grown over-mighty and needs to have limits clearly applied to it.
- The erosion of civil rights requires the clearest possible statement of what rights every citizen is entitled to.
- The specific powers and responsibilities of each part of the state need to be delineated, to prevent power being misused.
- People would be able to refer to a document to learn about their rights.

More conservative elements argue in opposition:

- The checks and balances work well enough at present, and the real problem of British government is not the centralisation but a fragmentation of power, to new assemblies and groups.
- A written constitution would put enormous power in the hands of unelected judges, whose interpretation of disputes would create new aspects of constitutional law.

- It would introduce an inhibition to change, which is inimical to British government, whose unwritten constitution has allowed government to adapt and develop organically.

In February 2008, it seemed the Justice Secretary and Lord Chancellor, Jack Straw, had opted in favour of a written document. Speaking at George Washington University, Washington, DC, he revealed plans to draw up a written constitution within two decades. Reformers tended to regard this statement with a 'we'll believe it when we see it' scepticism.

A British Bill of Rights?

In the same speech, Straw also expressed his wish that a British Bill of Rights be drawn up:

> In the United Kingdom many duties and responsibilities exist in statute, common practice or are woven into our social and moral fabric. But elevating them to a new status in a constitutional document would reflect their importance in the healthy functioning of our democracy. (See *Guardian*, 14 February 2008)

After criticising the idea of a specifically British Bill of Rights as confusing to the voter, Marcel Berlins, legal editor of the *Guardian*, was equally dismissive of Straw's vision:

> Written constitutions have been needed to control the governance of countries that have emerged from some kind of upheaval – by revolution, independence from a colonial master, geo-political re-arrangement (such as the break-up of Yugoslavia or the Soviet Union), the overthrow or accession of a dictator, or some other drastic change, as in post-apartheid South Africa. Britain has encountered none of these. Its constitution – untidy, only partly written, bits and pieces to be found here and there – continues, on the whole, to serve the country well. It is in no danger of collapse or breakdown. Let the government forget its dreams of a perfect constitutional document. We don't need one. (*Guardian*, 18 February 2008)

Reference

Moran, M. (2005) *Politics and Governance in the UK*, Palgrave: chapter 5.

Recommended reading

Jones, B., *et al.* (2007) *Politics UK* (6th edition), Pearson: chapter 15.
Kavanagh, D., *et al.* (2006) *British Politics* (5th edition), Oxford University Press: chapter 10.

Kingdom, J. (2003) *Government and Politics in Britain: An Introduction* (3rd edition), Polity: chapter 3.
Leach, R., *et al.* (2006) *British Politics*, Palgrave: chapter 10.
Moran, M. (2005) *Politics and Governance in the UK*, Palgrave: chapter 5.

Other texts

Bogdanor, V. (ed.) (2003) *The British Constitution in the Twentieth Century*, Oxford University Press.
Brazier, R. (1994) *Constitutional Practice*, Oxford University Press.
House of Commons Library (2008) *The Royal Prerogative*, SN/PC/0361, 3 November.
Institute for Public Policy Research (IPPR) (1992) *A New Constitution for the United Kingdom*, Mansell.
Norton, P. (1993) 'The constitution: approaches to reform', *Politics Review*, vol. 3, no. 1.
Oliver, D. (2003) *Constitutional Reform in the UK*, Oxford University Press.

Website

University College London's Constitution Unit, www.ucl.ac.uk/constitution-unit.

7

Political ideas

What are the major current ideologies in British politics?

Socialism and *Conservatism* were once the commonplace rival ideologies in Britain but both have been so diluted since the latter part of the twentieth century that they cannot really be said to survive in any recognisable original form. It would be more accurate perhaps nowadays to use the term 'bodies of belief'. There are four main broad bodies of belief in current British politics, all based on blends of existing (though fading) ideologies:

- *New Labourism* (or *Blairism*), based on socialism, social democracy and Thatcherism;
- *Conservatism*, based on traditional Conservatism, Thatcherism and Blairism;
- *Liberal Democracy*, based on liberalism and social democracy;
- *Green thinking*, based on various blends of environmentalism.

To unravel these bodies of belief in their modern incarnations, it will be necessary to examine: the central elements of socialism and Conservatism; the post-war consensus; revisionist Labourism, Thatcherism and Blairism, followed by Cameron's reworking of Blairism; then Liberal Democracy will be looked at plus Green thinking and aspects of the political fringe.

What is meant by socialism and social democracy?

Critique of capitalism

Socialism developed during the nineteenth century, based on a critique which, among other things, claimed that capitalism: created huge differences in wealth and income; concentrated economic production on luxury goods for the rich; denied workers any proportionate and fair return for their labour;

encouraged a competitive and inhuman attitude towards fellow humans; and destroyed craftsmanship and pride of workmanship.

Utopian socialism

Early socialists believed it was possible to create a society which was just and fair, less money obsessed and more committed to allowing people to develop their talents and interests according to their wishes. William Morris's *News from Nowhere* (1890) provides a charming vision of what a socialist society might be like; for example, there would be no money and items from shops could simply be acquired upon request. The basic assumption on which this approach was based was that human nature was essentially benign and cooperative: people were merely awaiting the arrival of the circumstances whereby their desire to share and assist communal endeavour could be made possible. However, this was a romantically vague, utopian aspiration rather than a realistic programme of action with specific policies for governing. It is fair to say that support for utopian socialism was strictly limited to the ranks of the shining-eyed faithful. Recognisably socialist policy programmes arrived after the Labour Party formally adopted socialism as its ideology in its 1918 constitution and after it had tasted the somewhat salutary experience of governing as a minority party in 1924 and 1929–31.

Attlee's version of socialism

As a coalition partner of Churchill's Conservative Party during World War II, Labour gained valuable hands-on experience of government and was prepared to answer the challenge of its surprise landslide 'socialist' victory in the 1945 election under Clement Attlee. In practice, his version of socialism meant that: one-fifth of the economy was nationalised, run by boards answerable to ministers; a welfare state was created, which entailed free health and education plus a range of benefits for the less well-off; and more planning was introduced for both the economy and the environment. But 'Attlee socialism', if it can be so-called, was only partial; it fell way short of abolishing the private sector, which still flourished under postwar Labour.

What is meant by traditional Conservatism?

This is not an easy question to answer, in that Conservatism has never been a clear ideology – it is 'more a state of mind', remarked Tory Lord Chancellor Lord Hailsham – possibly because, as the body of ideas supporting the governing class, it has tended to adapt and incorporate elements as necessary. It might almost be said that Conservatism is a constant 'work in progress'. But sifting through its positions over the 150 or so years of the party's existence, certain constants can be identified. These ideas should not be seen as exclusively the property of one tradition, nor as the invariable badge of those who have belonged to it, but as components of what has been perceived as the party's traditional ideology.

- Human nature is basically selfish and uncooperative.
- Society is held together by social institutions like the family, school, monarchy, Parliament and so forth. Change that might weaken such bonds, according to this approach, should be resisted.
- Freedom is the most important purpose of politics: freedom for individuals to pursue their destiny; and freedom for energetic people to set up businesses and better themselves.
- Government should be limited to minimum tasks, like keeping order and a sound currency – other things are not the proper task of government. To prevent too much accumulation of power, checks and balances within government are desirable and necessary.
- Property ownership is educational, in that it illustrates the connectedness of the defence of property with social and political stability.
- Political change is generally to be avoided unless absolutely necessary and only then in a gradual and judicious fashion. To Conservatives, the body politic is a delicate and sensitive entity that might wither and die if interfered with in the wrong way.
- Political ideas which demand sweeping change – for example socialism – are faulty, as they are removed from everyday realities and will cause only harm.
- Elites are suited to government by virtue of birth, education and inclination and are superior to those not enjoying such advantages.

Michael Oakeshott, a much admired philosopher of the right, sums up Conservatism memorably thus:

> A propensity to use and enjoy what is available rather than to wish or look for something else; to delight in what is present rather than what may be.... To be conservative, then, is to prefer the familiar to the unknown, to prefer the tried to the untried, fact to mystery, the actual to the possible, the sufficient to the superabundant, the convenient to the perfect, present laughter to utopian bliss. (Oakeshott, 1962)

What was the 'postwar consensus'?

This arose from a synthesis of views after World War II. The war had a profound effect on British political culture, in that it imposed six years of shared danger and national unity. People from all classes mixed freely in the forces and to a lesser degree on the home front too. Rationing meant that food shortages were to a large extent shared and people must have noticed that some of the poorest people had been able as a result to eat better than ever before in their lives. At the end of the war, many expected Churchill's astonishing leadership to be rewarded by a landslide victory, but such had been the social metamorphosis within the nation as a result of the war that it was Attlee's socialist party which received the huge victory. This was the backcloth on which Attlee was able to introduce his far-reaching changes to ownership and the welfare state. Once the Conservatives were back in power in 1951, they respected most of the changes Labour had made, recognising perhaps how profoundly the nation had been changed by its wartime experience. Apart from a few repeals of certain minor measures, the Conservatives presided over Labour's 'postwar settlement' as it is sometimes alternatively called.

The elements of this consensus are usually held to be agreement upon:

- Keynesian economic policies, which overturned the orthodox view that saving is the correct economic response to recession by arguing that judicious government spending can revive the economy in such circumstances and reduce unemployment;
- the mixed economy, comprising a substantial public sector with an even bigger surviving private one;
- the welfare state, comprising pensions and other benefits plus free schools and the National Health Service, available for all citizens irrespective of status;
- a collaborative role for the unions in the political system (during the war their wholehearted cooperation – involving especially Ernest Bevin, who later became Labour's Foreign Secretary – had changed the way they were regarded by the Conservatives, who were now happy to consult them on major changes);
- acceptance of compromise and consultation as the best way of governing (such processes had been established during the war as the most cost-effective way of solving political problems);
- regarding the alliance with the United States as the best form of security against the threat of the Soviet Union.

What is meant by the 'mixed economy'?

This term has been used as a distinction from the 'wholly privately owned economy', though such a term was never used in practice. Its provenance is found to a degree in the socialist idea, embraced by Karl Marx and summed up by Pierre-Joseph Proudhon, that 'property is theft', that the value which a worker imparts to a product is denied him or her by capitalism, in that the owner of the means of production – be it a factory or a workshop – reaps the lion's share of the profits earned. In 1918, the famous clause four of the Labour Party's constitution dedicated the party:

To secure for the producers by hand or by brain the full fruits of their industry, and the most equitable distribution thereof that may be possible, upon the basis of the common ownership of the means of production and the best obtainable system of popular administration and control of each industry and service.

This clause was for decades emblazoned on party membership cards. Initially, no one was really sure what this meant in practice, merely that private ownership of the economy was bad and should be ended. The notion of 'nationalisation' soon took hold thereafter but lacked a practical form until Herbert Morrison, as Minister of Transport in 1930, set up London Transport, run by a public corporation under the loose control of a minister and account-able ultimately to Parliament. For a Labour Party casting around for workable policies, this was a perfect, cautiously moderate, compromise between abol-ishing private property and maintaining liberal parliamentary democracy. When Labour won its landslide in 1945, this was the template used in taking control of 20% of the economy, in the form of the public utilities – gas, elec-tricity and water – plus the coal industry. Those on the left wished to extend control into something rather like that in the Soviet Union and other commu-nist countries, but Attlee and his moderate colleagues favoured the retention of a substantial private sector. The economy was therefore to be 'mixed'.

What happened to the postwar consensus?

- *Economic decline.* The consensus survived far into the postwar period – until the mid-1960s – but was gradually undermined by Britain's declining economic performance. British exports managed to revive quite vigorously immediately after the war, as the transfer to peacetime production was achieved relatively smoothly. However, by the mid-1950s British goods were being outsold by those from other countries, most gallingly includ-ing Germany and Japan, the defeated wartime foes. During the 1960s, the decline became more evident as even British consumers ignored home-produced goods, seeing them as overpriced, of poor quality and poorly designed. As businesses began to fail, trade unions, used to being con-sulted, began to object that members were being laid off. Acute industrial relations problems added to Britain's dire economic reputation.
- *Ideological polarisation begins.* Unions and the more socialist wing of the Labour Party began to agree that more radical economic change was re-quired to revive the economy. The model they tended to invoke, however, was the command economies of the communist bloc, which, at the time, in-fluenced by the Soviet Union's technological achievements in the nuclear and space race, seemed to be emerging as possibly superior to western capitalism. Meanwhile, on the right, politicians like Enoch Powell and his disciples were arguing that the consensus approach was not allowing market forces to operate freely and therefore successfully. The election of Margaret Thatcher

as Conservative leader in 1975 ensured that Powell's ideas plus those of 'monetarist' economists like Milton Friedman were installed as the official policies of British government when she came to power in 1979.

• *Polarisation is entrenched.* By the end of the 1970s, the rival ideologies were in face-to-face confrontation. From Thatcher on the right to Tony Benn on the left, there has probably never been such a wide political spectrum in British politics. The debacle of the 'Winter of Discontent' (1978–79) engineered a sea change in British attitudes, in which trade union power was held to be excessive. Thatcher was elected to deal with the problem and revive the economy, two tasks which, according to her values, were achieved by the time she left the stage in 1990. For its part, Labour had swung far to the left but the rebuff it received in the form of the party's drubbing in the 1983 election prompted Michael Foot's successor as leader in that year, Neil Kinnock, to begin the slow, hard process of dragging Labour back onto the centre ground, where elections are won rather than lost.

Evolution of ideologies

Labour revisionism, or social democracy

When the Labour Party came to power in 1964, Attlean 'socialism' had been somewhat attenuated by 'revisionism', which argued that the major changes needed to emasculate capitalism had already occurred and that the task of Labour was now to fill in the details of removing inequality and class divisions to achieve the ideal of a fair and just society which Labour members envisioned. This brand of socialism or, rather, *social democracy* as it was called in various parts of Europe, accepted the efficacy of capitalism as the means whereby wealth is created, but retained socialist values in how resultant wealth should be distributed. Critics on the left, of which there were (and are still) many, claimed the values underpinning socialism had been compromised into vacuities, while defenders claimed they were merely adapting such values to modern conditions.

What is meant by Thatcherism?

Clearly, this body of ideas is attached to the person of Margaret Thatcher, Conservative Prime Minister 1979–90. She emerged as a candidate for leader of the party in 1975 in the wake of Edward Heath's second election failure in 1974. Labour under Harold Wilson had governed from February in that year from a minority position but scraped a thin majority in the October election. Substantial elements in the Conservative Party believed Heath's U-turn from his more robust right-wing 'Selsdon' manifesto of 1970 was unforgivable and wanted a leadership election. Many wished to wound the imperious and not much loved Prime Minister, but only one person was prepared to strike: Margaret Thatcher. The thrust of her message was an increased intensity of opposition to what she saw as a failing Labour government.

The 'ism' associated with her name can be distilled into the following elements:

1 Monetarism is the key to managing the economy. She argued that if government control can the supply of money circulating in the economy, inflation will also be controlled. This means interest rates will be of key importance to encourage growth or to rein in inflationary tendencies.
2 Economic freedom – regarding employment, making a profit, buying and selling property – is the foundation of all freedom.
3 Market forces should be left alone by governments to 'work their magic'.
4 Governments should intervene in the economy and society only when absolutely necessary. It follows that publicly owned services should be 'privatised' if this would make them more efficient.
5 Trade unions should not be allowed to accumulate so much power that they can hold the nation to ransom. If they attempt to do so, they should be confronted and their powers reduced by law.
6 The welfare state tends to create a 'dependency culture' which destroys the will of individuals to determine their own destiny. An 'enterprise culture' needs to be put in its place.
7 National interests should be defended at all costs.
8 Citizens have a duty to be well behaved and to be aware of their obligations to other people.

Most who lived through her era would probably agree that all these precepts were probably less relevant to Thatcherism than the amazing strength of personality which she possessed and which she used to meld them into articulations of her will.

What is meant by 'New Labourism' or Blairism?

This is less easy to define, as Tony Blair was often better on rhetoric and presentation than on clear-cut policy. However, to the extent that he commands an 'ism', he can be said to stand for the following:

• *Selective elements of Thatcherism.* He reinforced item 1 above, by giving independence to the Bank of England shortly after coming to power in 1997, thus removing interest rates from political control. He also accepted as improvements all the privatisations and endorsed the policy, plus number 8 above. He also had much sympathy with items 3 and 5.
• *'Third way'.* This was a belief that the ideologies of the past were outdated and that a new approach by Labour was needed which adapted its traditional values to new conditions, especially the demands of globalisation.

- *Reform of public services.* Blair thought the old structures needed to be 'modernised' in order to become more efficient, though in practice this meant greatly increased public spending, plus the introduction, wherever possible, of market forces and the private sector. This is not far removed from 'Thatcherism' items 3 and 4 above, but has also been described by Professor Steven Fielding as being closer to the 'revisionist' strand of social democracy (Fielding, 1997).
- *Reform of democratic institutions.* This has led to the creation of assemblies in Scotland, Wales and Northern Ireland, directly elected mayors and the reform of the House of Lords.
- *Humanitarian intervention in foreign affairs*, in collaboration, whenever possible, with the United States. This has led to British involvement in Sierra Leone, Bosnia, Kosovo, Afghanistan and, albeit disastrously, Iraq.

Why is Blairism influential in Conservative thinking?

The short answer is that just as Blair absorbed certain key aspects of the Thatcherite status quo, so did the Conservatives, in the form of David Cameron as party leader from 2005 onwards. John Major announced on his accession to power that he sought a nation more 'at ease with itself'. In practice, he largely pursued the policies of his fierce predecessor but in a less fierce way. William Hague and Iain Duncan Smith, the next two leaders of the party, started out by swinging towards the party's liberal tradition, but when poll ratings refused to budge they swung back to the right, in order to 'protect' their ageing core voters by giving them the less diluted Thatcherism they had always wanted. The next leader, Michael Howard, sought to achieve some new synthesis but this too unravelled in May 2005, when Blair's New Labour managed to win a reduced but still safe third majority general election victory. Candidates to replace Howard spanned a wide spectrum but after eight years of Blairism the majority of the party had realised that, given the changed nature of the political culture, a shift leftwards was mandatory if the party was to become electable again. The candidate espousing such a message, the old Etonian David Cameron, won easily and set about dismantling former Conservative tenets and brand images. It soon became clear that Cameron was determined to absorb those elements of Blairism which were now firmly entrenched in the middle ground of politics. The distinguished columnist Simon Jenkins wrote in the *Sunday Times* (3 June 2006) that Cameron and his advisers had 'read Tony Blair as attentively as Blair read Margaret Thatcher. The leadership bloodline holds strong.' Avoiding specific policy commitments, Cameron had succeeded by mid-2006 in:

- distancing the Conservatives from too close a connection with business;
- establishing the Conservatives as very concerned about the environment;
- pledging to maintain sufficient sums to fund public services;

- arguing that social policies should favour the disadvantaged;
- supporting Blair's attempts to introduce market forces into health and education and claiming the Conservatives would do this more effectively;
- persuading women voters – hitherto the preserve of Blair rhetoric – that he had their best interests at heart.

In an admiring article in the *Guardian* (30 May 2006), Max Hastings wrote:

> Cameron refuses to commit a Tory government to abolishing inheritance tax or even cutting taxes at all [this was destined to change in the autumn of 2007]. He declares that the Tories were wrong to oppose university top-up fees. He acknowledges that devolution is 'here to stay', though he wants 'English votes to decide English law'. When criticised for not attacking the government sufficiently vigorously, he says: 'I don't wake up in the morning asking myself "What can I do to destroy the Labour Party?" They're doing that themselves. I ask myself "What can I do to show the people what a Conservative government will be like?"'

By the summer of 2006, Cameron had bested New Labour in the May 2007 local elections and stretched out a lead in the national polls. Previous leaders had fought Blairism and failed; Cameron showed that by embracing it he could also overcome it. The May 2008 local elections were even more successful for Cameron: his party took 44% of the vote to Labour's third-placed 24%. More significantly, the Conservative candidate in the London mayoral election beat the sitting mayor, Ken Livingstone. That summer, the government lost a key by-election in Glasgow East, a rock-solid Labour seat for many years. It was the Scottish National Party which won the contest but Cameron benefited from the resultant weakening of the Labour government.

Has a new consensus emerged?

Given Labour's shunt to the right provided by Blair after his election as party leader in 1994, Labour and the Conservatives began to converge as the 1990s wore on. Until Cameron was elected leader in 2005, the Tories clung on to neo-Thatcherite positions on topics like tax, law and order, the EU and reforming public services. However, the 'modernising' old Etonian reduced the distance substantially by declaring support for public services, a reluctance to cut taxes until the economy justified it, and a softening of lines on the EU and immigration. Cameron even went so far as to support Blair's plan for 'trust schools' free of local authority control, thereby enabling the necessary legislation to be passed in spring 2006. Indeed, a case could be made for the emergence of a 'Blairmeron' consensus, similar to the 'Butskellite' one discerned during the 1950s.

Under Gordon Brown, Prime Minister after June 2007, the consensus was fractured by the 2008 banking crisis, when Tories urged traditional tax and spending cuts while Labour put its faith in borrowing to maintain spending levels.

What is the ideological provenance of the Liberal Democrats?

The Liberal Democrats were formed out of a merger between the Liberals and the Social Democratic Party in 1988, but for the true lineage of their ideology one has to go back to the liberal philosophers of the eighteenth and nineteenth centuries, who were responsible for urging: rationality (John Locke); toleration (also Locke); individual liberty (John Stuart Mill); constitutional checks and balances (the Baron de Montesquieu); and representation (Mill again). It was on the basis of this body of ideas that a new party formed in the mid-nineteenth century, through the drawing together of elements of the Whigs (an aristocratic group of parliamentarians who were nonetheless in favour of reforming the constitution), disaffected Tories and the Manchester Radicals (the creation of the likes of Richard Cobden and John Bright and advocates of classical liberalism).

What is meant by the New Liberalism?

This shift in Liberal opinion arrived towards the end of the nineteenth century, when Liberal belief in equal rights and opportunity shifted from 'negative' freedom (i.e. *from* oppression) to 'positive' freedom (i.e. the freedom *to* develop unhindered by constraints of poverty, education, health or living conditions). A number of Liberal thinkers like T. H. Green, Alfred Marshall and, especially L. T. Hobhouse, began to ascribe to the state a parent-like responsibility to nurture, in the latter's phrase, the 'future citizen'. This provided the starting point of the thinking for old-age pensions, introduced in 1911, and subsequent welfare measures. The definitive statement of this approach was made by William Beveridge in 1942, in his famous report which identified five 'giants' to be slain: idleness, ignorance, disease, squalor and want.

How did the Liberals become the Liberal Democrats?

The answer is found mainly in disputes over ideology. After the fall of David Lloyd George's Liberal–Conservative coalition government in 1922, the great Liberal Party of the nineteenth century lost any chance of becoming the government. In 1924, it gained forty seats; in 1929, fifty-nine seats; in 1935, twenty seats; in 1945, twelve seats; and thereafter for the next three elections only six. There was a brief revival under Jo Grimond but the most the Liberals managed during the 1970s was the Lib–Lab Pact, which helped James Callaghan survive for a while after 1977.

The party saw a lifeline in the early 1980s when senior Labour figures, disillusioned with their party's drift to the left after the election of Margaret Thatcher, set up the Social Democratic Party (SDP). It was immediately apparent that the ideological distance between the Liberals and the new party was not great and eventually the Liberal–SDP Alliance was established, featuring (previously from Labour) Roy Jenkins, Bill Rodgers, Shirley Williams and David Owen, together with David Steel and his colleagues in the Liberal Party. Their initial success in the polls was sensational and in the 1983 general election the grouping won 26% of the vote, though, because of the electoral system, less than 4% of seats. By the 1987, the Alliance's election momentum had been lost, the share of the vote was well down and the stage was set for its winding up and, after a few false turns, the merger of the parties as the Liberal Democrats.

What do the Liberal Democrats stand for?

It would be fair to say that the Liberal Democrats have never quite established a strong sense of what they stand for. Right from the start they have been:

- a kind of 'in between' party, the main question for which, despite vehement protestations to the contrary, was which big party bloc would it support;
- a protest party for which disaffected supporters of the big parties could vote between general elections;
- a local government party, where its hands-on 'community politics' has proved popular and enabled it to do well.

The Thatcher hegemony led the new party to side with Labour under Paddy Ashdown – after all, it did support well funded public services and opposed the general movement to privatisation. Under Charles Kennedy the party offered a less committed 'constructive opposition', though many still perceived more sympathy with Labour than the Conservatives. In 2004, some legacy of the 'revisionist Labour'-inclined Social Democratic Party was evident in the publication of the *Orange Book* of essays, edited by David Laws and Paul Marshall. This collection, written by leading members of the party, offered a surprisingly free market set of answers to a wide range of social problems, including health, pensions, the environment, globalisation and prisons.

The emergence of a renewed Conservative Party under David Cameron and the faltering of Blair after his 2005 election victory raised the prospect of a hung Parliament in which the Liberal Democrats might well hold the balance of power. The party's new leader, Sir Menzies (Ming) Campbell (elected January 2006), declared he would not countenance coalition with either big party, but rumours emerged of a possible alliance between the revived Conservatives and the more market-oriented wing of the Lib Dems.

Box 7.1 How voters perceive themselves, the parties and their leaders

A useful way of comparing political ideas is to ask people where on a left–right spectrum they would place themselves, the parties and the leaders of those parties. Figure 7.1 does exactly that, based on YouGov survey results from 2005. It shows how centrist Tony Blair was seen as being; in fact, he appears a few points to the *right* of the centre. The vast majority of voters consider themselves to be in the centre, with the average self-perception only two points to the left of this.

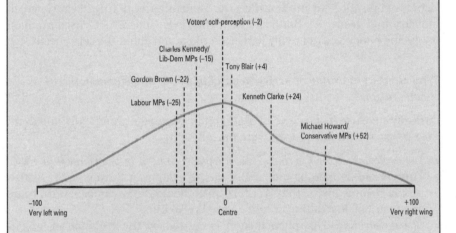

Figure 7.1 *How voters perceive themselves, the parties and their leaders*

Note: Charted here are responses to the following statement from a YouGov survey: 'Some people talk about "left", "right" and "centre" to describe parties and politicians. Where would you place ... on this scale?' Average scores, counting –100 as 'very left wing', 0 as 'centre' and +100 as 'very right wing'. The curve represents the percentage of respondents who see themselves at each point on the left–right scale.

Source: Policy Exchange (2005).

Campbell did not contribute much new thinking to Liberal Democrat policy, although in early June 2006 he did produce a radical suggestion: that of funding a 2p cut in income tax through a levy on cheap air flights and a tougher tax regime for the wealthy. In fact, though, he ran into exactly the sort of criticism he himself aimed at his predecessor, Charles Kennedy, for lack of initiatives and poor performances at Prime Minister's questions in the Commons. In October 2007 he resigned and Nick Clegg was elected leader in his place in January 2008.

What is meant by green thinking?

This is the 'ecological' approach to politics. Such had been people's cavalier attitude to the environment that coherent green approaches to politics have only
been around for three to four decades. Then, in the early 1970s, and especially
after the publication of a 1972 United Nations report *Only One Earth*, a view
emerged which placed the environment at its centre. This is not to say previous
thinkers had not expressed green ideas. William Blake referred to 'those dark
satanic mills' in his famous poem 'Jerusalem' and the early 'utopian' socialist
William Morris, for example, in his *News from Nowhere*, favoured a policy of
'deindustrialisation' in the south-east to reinstate the natural beauty which
industry had destroyed. But apart from this, even socialists focused more on
producing goods and not really bothering too much about the side-effects.

*Why did the environment arrive so quickly as a mainstream political
consideration?*

Basically because its perceived vulnerability became dramatically apparent.
Two key factors in this process were the following:

- *The explosion at the Chernobyl nuclear power station in the Ukraine in 1986.*
  This spread dangerous radioactive dust throughout Europe; most British
  people became aware that Welsh lamb could not be eaten for several years
  as a result of dust falling in rain on the Welsh hills.
- *Global warming.* This phenomenon is caused by the emission of 'greenhouse' gases via human economic activity. These cause the atmosphere to
  retain the sun's heat, with the consequence that the overall temperature of
  the earth has been increasing, causing glaciers to melt and, possibly, more
  hurricanes to form over warmer seas. The fact the scientists had shown
  that the fourteen warmest years on record had occurred in the period
  1992–2008 became reasonably widely known.

What is the distinction between 'dark' and 'light' green thinking?

'Dark' green approaches
These are based on the premise that economic growth is inimical to the survival of the planet, as economic resources are finite and must be preserved
and husbanded with great care. According to this view, people in developed
countries will have to engineer a revolution in their lifestyle:

- eschewing luxuries and extravagances as irresponsible;
- drawing upon local resources rather as those from far away, to avoid the
  associated heavy energy costs and the generation of greenhouse gases;
- drastically cutting down on energy usage, for example by reducing the use
  of cars and aeroplanes;

- being satisfied with 'enough' rather than constantly seeking 'more';
- decentralising economic processes, with the formation of smaller units of production;
- achieving self-reliance rather than being dependent on large agencies.

'Sustainability' or the replacing of what has been used up is a central principle of this purer form of green thinking.

The problem with such a logical set of rules arising from ecological principles is that many people either will fail to appreciate the gravity of the situation or will seek to transfer responsibility to other people. In other words, it may well be the correct way to save the planet for our descendants, but it is very difficult to form a political consensus around such a set of ideas. For this reason, the Green Party, which has tended to advocate dark green approaches, has not won more than a few seats at the local government level though, as a result of public relations successes, it has done better in elections for the European Parliament.

**Box 7.2 How necessary is it for political parties
to subscribe to ideologies?**

The orthodox reply to this question is that it is ideology which provides:

- the motor for the party, in that it enthuses those to whom it appeals, so voters are inclined to listen, absorb and further proselytise the ideological message in order to encourage others to vote for something which is 'right', not just for the sectional group – whether business people, workers or whatever – but for society and the nation as a whole;
- the framework of values and principles which guide the government elected to power (without these, a government might find itself lacking direction, rudderless);
- a body of ideas which can be adapted to new circumstances and provide guidance for the future.

Political scientist Otto Kircheimer, however, has suggested that mass political parties have evolved into organisations dedicated mainly to eliciting votes from coalitions of social groups. This analysis of the 'catch-all' parties suggests that ideology is slowly disappearing as the major thrust of modern political parties. Certainly, though, the Conservative Party has *always* resembled such a creation, in that it has had no real fixed principles apart from holding power to defend those who own property. This foundation requirement has led the party to adopt and then abandon a succession of principles. New Labour has also been criticised for lacking a coherent ideology, in that it abandoned 'Old Labour' 'socialist' tenets like nationalisation and union interest but did not replace them with anything recognisable as an ideology but rather, say the critics, with an expedient collection of transient ideas.

'Light' green approaches

These were the result of the difficulties described above. These concentrate more on reducing pollution and increasing recycling, for example – moderate reformist measures in which most people can participate without feeling they have to abandon their cars and cheap flights. By the late 1990s, perceiving that concerns about the environment had entered the mainstream, most political parties had adorned their policy programmes in a judiciously pale emerald hue.

How 'mainstream' have green ideas become?

This is a matter of judgement, but the fact that David Cameron, concerned to win publicity and support as an innovative leader, chose to emphasise his use of a bicycle to travel to work and made a highly publicised visit to Norway in 2006 to investigate a melting glacier is evidence of how central the message is becoming. Tony Blair regularly polished his own green credentials and the Liberal Democrats claim, with some justification, to be the greenest of all the major parties. Moreover, environmental awareness is now relatively enhanced compared with the late 1990s; recycling is routinely practised by most local governments, carbon emissions are widely perceived to be malign and even restrictions on cheap air travel have been mooted by the Liberal Democrats. As the crisis of the planet's survival intensifies, the locus of green policies adopted by the political parties is moving from the lighter to the darker part of the green spectrum.

Voter backlash and the fringe

Public anger at greedy bankers, who were widely believed to have caused the economic recession of 2008–9, combined with the lack of trust regarding the 'political class', created a febrile atmosphere in which the MPs' expenses scandal broke. The *Daily Telegraph* throughout May 2009 ran a series of revelations regarding the way MPs had used the parliamentary expenses regime to invest in new properties, avoid paying capital gains taxes, hand out favours to partners and family members and generally pay for things – food, gardening, water features, even toilet seats – which most ordinary people have to pay for themselves out of their earnings.

The yawning gap in trust and communication between government and governed threatened to be filled by some of the more raucous voices on the political right. The Greens hoped to benefit as the Euro-elections in June 2009 approached but of more concern to liberal sensibilities was the surge in support for the extreme Eurosceptic United Kingdom Independence Party (UKIP) and the far-right British National Party (BNP), which based its appeal on xenophobia: anti-immigrant and anti-EU. UKIP beat Labour into third place in the Euro-poll. Moreover, the BNP was as jubilant as left-of-centre parties were dismayed when it won two seats in the European Parliament.

References

Fielding, S. (1997) *The Labour Party: 'Socialism' and Society Since 1951*, Manchester University Press.
Laws, D. and Marshall, P. (eds) (2004) *Orange Book: Reclaiming Liberalism*, Profile Books.
Oakeshott, M. (1962) *Rationalism in Politics*, Methuen.
Policy Exchange (2005) *The Case for Change*, Policy Exchange.

Recommended reading

Jones, B., *et al.* (2007) *Politics UK* (6th edition), Pearson: chapters 4–7.
Kavanagh, D., *et al.* (2006) *British Politics* (5th edition), Oxford University Press: chapter 4.
Kingdom, J. (2003) *Government and Politics in Britain: An Introduction* (3rd edition), Polity: chapter 2.
Leach, R., *et al.* (2006) *British Politics*, Palgrave: chapter 6.
Moran, M. (2005) *Politics and Governance in the UK*, Palgrave: chapter 15.

Other texts

Adams, I. (1998) *Ideologies and Politics in Britain Today*, Manchester University Press.
Foote, G. (1997) *The Labour Party's Political Thought*, Manchester University Press.
Giddens, A. (1998) *The Third Way: The Renewal of Social Democracy*, Polity Press.
Gould, P. (1998) *The Unfinished Revolution*, Little, Brown.
Hennessy, P. (2006) *Having It So Good*, Allen Lane.
Heywood, A. (1998) *Political Ideologies*, Macmillan.
Marr, A. (2007) *A History of Modern Britain*, Macmillan.
Tucker, K. (1998) *Anthony Giddens and Modern Social Theory*, Sage.

Websites

Conservative Party, www.conservatives.com.
Green Party, www.greenparty.org.uk.
Labour Party, www.labour.org.uk.
Liberal Democrats, www.libdems.org.uk.

8

The role of pressure groups

The theory of democracy inherited from nineteenth-century Britain tends to focus on individual voters or MPs rather than groups of any kind. In practice, groups figure very highly in the politics of modern democratic states and may be seen as providing a form of 'functional' representation (of social groups or blocks of voters) that is especially important *between* elections.

Definitions

Pressure groups are organised associations that seek to influence policy though not to exercise power. There are two main kinds: economic and cause groups.

Economic groups

These represent different groups in society and can be further subdivided into:

- *trade unions*, which seek to advance the interests of their members in terms of pay and conditions of work;
- *business organisations*, which can be anything from small, privately owned companies to multinational enterprises with publically listed shares, but which all seek to achieve and then maintain the conditions which most suit their activities;
- *professional organisations*, which represent and promote the interests of people with advanced training and qualifications, such as the British Medical Association, the Association of Building Engineers and the Association of Law Teachers.

Cause groups

These can similarly be further subdivided into:

- *sectional groups*, which are concerned with specific groups in society, such as old people (Age Concern), the homeless (Shelter), motorists (the Automobile Association) and so on;
- *attitude groups*, which are committed to certain ideas and seek to advance them in the interests of society as a whole, such as the Howard League for Penal Reform, the Lord's Day Observance Society and Liberty.

In addition we can discern:

- *peak associations*, which are umbrella bodies that coordinate members sharing interests, for example the Trades Union Congress and the Confederation of British Industry;
- *'fire brigade' groups*, which spring up in response to specific problems, such as the nineteenth century Anti-Corn Law League and the Road Traffic Reduction Campaign;
- *episodic groups*, which have members who are normally outside the political fray but who are galvanised by changing events to join it, for example in the form of residents' associations that campaign against new by-passes or airport runways.

Development of pressure groups

Groups have always existed in society but within a democracy organisation is essential if objectives are to be achieved. One of the very first pressure groups was the movement to abolish slavery, led by William Wilberforce – the Committee for the Abolition of the Slave Trade; another, also operating in the early nineteenth century, was the Anti-Corn Law League. Other groups were concerned with philanthropic causes, like the Salvation Army, which did good work among the poor and raised awareness of their plight. In time, government came to recognise such needs existed and began to support and subsidise these groups. Trade unions emerged to defend workers against exploitation by employers and to help them improve wages and working conditions.

In the twentieth century, the extension of government activity into the economy meant 'producer' groups combined to form committees and organisations in order to negotiate and inform government of their interests. After 1945 and the nationalisation of large parts of the British economy, this process accelerated rapidly. Trade unions, of course, were central to this and they came to exercise substantial power by virtue of their control over workers who controlled certain functions, like coal miners, power workers and the like. It followed that, as society became more complex, groups were required to make their organisations more professional, with, for example, press officers and so forth. Groups also began to recruit graduate-entry personnel, who could talk on equal terms with professionals in government and the media.

Civil society and pressure groups

'Civil society' refers to the 'non-political' relationships people have with families, business, church, school and voluntary associations like scouts, guides and sporting clubs. These provide the means whereby young people are socialised into society and absorb its values. They also provide for members some experience in living together, compromising where necessary, taking responsibility and exercising leadership. The existence of groups independent of the state is held by many to be both the foundation and the hallmark of a democratic society. Civil society is the precondition of democracy; it is the soil in which it grows.

Britain has always been famous for its plethora of voluntary societies, and their presence suggests the political culture is healthy. However, while at the middle of the last century the two big parties each had over a million members, membership had slumped to less than 5% of that figure towards the end of the century, according to a 1992 study by Ashford and Timms. Some commentators have discerned a compensating shift of emphasis towards single-issue movements, especially environmental ones: people prefer to invest time and energy in them rather than in the somewhat discredited party system.

But this is not necessarily a symptom of a healthy polity; Robert Putnam (2001), an American political scientist, has shown that voluntary activity over the Atlantic has declined in recent years, while even the groups with huge memberships often merely contain 'passive' members who do little except renew their annual memberships. Explanations for this falling off of activity include the much greater variety of choice people now have to fill their leisure time, though Putnam seems to suggest television watching is the biggest culprit. Peter Hall (1999), studying the British scene, suggests the situation is less worrying over here and the University of Sheffield's 'Citizen Audit' (2001) revealed that, despite the low turn-out in the 2001 general election, British people engaged in a huge range of political activity, from signing petitions to buying or boycotting goods for political reasons (see Pattie *et al.*, 2004).

Chapter 5 looks at civil society in the context of Britain's political culture and Figure 5.1 (p. 42) gives a snapshot of the tendency of British people to volunteer. People in higher-income households are more likely than others to volunteer. In 2001, 57% of adults in England and Wales with gross annual household incomes of £75,000 or more had volunteered formally (such as raising or handling money for a charity or being a member of a committee) in the previous twelve months. They were almost twice as likely to have done so than those living in households with an annual income under £10,000 (29%).

Pressure groups and government

The key relationship of pressure groups, for the political scientist, is with government.

Government point of view

As governments see it, they cannot govern on their own. They need to engage with their citizens to some extent. This is true even in dictatorships: to oppress their citizenry, governments need to recruit and retain at least the loyalty of police or military personnel. In 2007 8, for instance, President Mugabe of Zimbabwe had lost the support of virtually his whole nation as it struggled to feed itself as inflation soared and food supplies disappeared. He ensured his police and army were on side by giving them special access to food and a range of other living privileges. Other dictators find it necessary to keep major business people on side, to ensure access to resources for government purposes. But democracies face much greater imperatives to reach out to groups in society, for the following reasons:

- It is in the interests of government that their people are both employed and prosperous, and economic groups are often key to achieving such objectives.
- Society is composed of employers and employees, and keeping economic groups content makes it likely that the support of both will be gained.
- Economic groups also provide a source of economic support, as governments need to raise revenue via taxation; if they are unhappy, this function might be compromised. Political parties forming governments, moreover, require funds to operate successfully within the political system.
- Citizens have come to accept they have certain basic rights – constitutional as well as free speech and such like – and governments have to be careful not to violate these rights and to keep on reasonable terms with most groups in society.
- Governing well is a function of accurate information and expertise; pressure groups can help provide such essential support, as well as key personnel from time to time. Frank Field, for example, worked in the social voluntary sector before becoming a Labour MP and later a minister.
- When the government is planning new legislation, it needs to establish good relations with the groups involved for two crucial reasons: groups can provide the advice needed to make effective laws; and by endorsing any new law, groups can help maximise its chances of becoming accepted and hence successful.
- Governments have the legitimacy of election victory but a powerful dissenting minority can make life very difficult for even the strongest government. Thatcher's Conservative government in 1984, for example, was forced to take on the miners' union to push through its economic

policy and the result was a year of bitter struggle that any government might have wished to avoid.

Pressure groups' point of view

This is like reversing the telescope and seeing the problem from the other angle. Pressure groups need to be on good terms with government for the following reasons:

- They are concerned that their own interests are going to be recognised and taken into account by government, otherwise those interests might well be damaged.
- If they can, groups will seek to enter the innermost sanctums of policy-making to advance their own causes, or to impede those to which they are hostile.
- Most groups have a common interest with government in achieving basic objectives like employment and prosperity.
- Groups are conscious that governments have huge resources at their disposal and so wish to avoid conflict if at all possible.

To conclude, both government and pressure groups have a common interest in shared political goals and will seek to establish good relations to make their achievement more likely. The word 'pressure' suggests something more conflictual than is the reality, which is that both sides strive to cooperate and avoid any damaging ruptures.

Insider–outsider analysis

Wyn Grant (1989), from the University of Warwick, formulated an influential dichotomy of pressure groups based on their proximity to decision-makers. It assumes that most groups seek 'insider' status, that is, advising government at the highest levels, being on advisory committees and so on. Insider groups can afford to be low key, as their influence is being channelled directly to the key areas. In contrast, 'outsider' groups are those which have not succeeded and consequently often engage in noisy campaigns.

Political methods used

Government methods

- *Consultation status.* Groups like to be recognised by government and flattered by invitations to meetings and respectful attentions. Being given a permanent place on an advisory committee, for example, is a much-prized objective.

- *Public relations.* Government has a large public relations machine at its disposal to counter or discredit messages which go against its interests. Alastair Campbell, for example, in his fight with the BBC in 2003, was ruthless in using every trick in the book to 'win' his side of the battle.
- *The law.* Thatcher's government changed the law so that unions could have their funds sequestered if they transgressed new laws on balloting members before strike action. This proved vital in defeating the miners in 1984–85. Labour also passed laws making certain forms of demonstration against the Iraq war illegal.
- *Force.* Ultimately, government can call upon the police or even the military in clashes with groups at odds with the government. The employment of the police in restraining strikers during the miners' strike was very controversial, as questions of police neutrality were involved.

Pressure group methods

These vary on a scale from wholly peaceful to clearly violent:

- *Petitions, letters.* These can be elicited from members to put pressure on decision-makers.
- *Meetings.* Groups seek to exercise rights of consultation with those who make the decisions, whether they be councillors, employers, MPs, ministers or civil servants.
- *Media campaigns.* These are obvious concomitants of all forms of political pressure, as publicity wins wider awareness and, hopefully, sympathy.
- *Demonstrations.* These can be marches complete with placards and chanting, or specially staged stunts like those undertaken by Fathers 4 Justice, some of which were too extreme for some members (e.g. the use of smoke bombs in the Commons).
- *Violence.* This is a high-risk strategy, as it can lose public sympathy overnight, as the early suffragettes discovered. In the United States, some pro-life groups have taken to assassinating doctors who perform abortions, though without disabling the overall cause especially, it has to be said.

Direct action

Some environmental groups have adopted tactics such as chaining themselves to blocks of concrete to prevent by-passes or runways being built. Interestingly, such campaigns have achieved some kind of legitimacy once middle-class campaigners have joined the struggle. However, the Darley Oaks Farm case illustrated the limits of such direct action. In this instance, in October 2004, animal rights activists stole the remains of Gladys Hammond, the mother-in-law of the owner of a farm that bred guinea pigs for experimentation. This caused a national outrage and middle-class John Ablewhite received little or no sympathy when he was eventually sent down for twelve years.

However, there seems to be a difference in media and public reactions, depending on the issue. The Greenham Common women campaigners against cruise missiles in the 1980s were seen as muddy troublemakers, but if the issue is a green one or animal-related, middle-class support can be influential. Direct action at Brightlingsea in 1997 against the export of live animals involved some middle-aged, middle-class ladies and the coverage was mostly favourable. A similar thing happened in the 1990s with the direct action against a second runway at Manchester airport, when the demonstrators were not anarchistic Marxist types, but nice, idealistic, middle-class kids; one of their leaders, Daniel Hooper ('Swampy'), even became a sort of celebrity for a while.

Pressure points
Groups will aim their messages at any point in the decision-making process which promises to offer some return for the effort:

- *The public at large*. Useful for recruitment and fundraising.
- *Other groups*. Very helpful if interests overlap, as alliances can create more effective campaigning.
- *Parties*. Groups will aim for the major party likely to be well disposed to it (for instance the Campaign for Nuclear Disarmament, CND, 'captured' Labour for a while though never managed to do the same for its official policy in government).
- *Parliament*. Groups will seek out support in the Commons and the Lords and try to involve sympathisers as officers of one kind or another, and will also try to draft bills or amendments for friendly MPs.
- *Ministers and civil servants*. Personal contacts with ministers, even if junior ones, are very valuable and civil servant connections are also, as these people stay in post while politicians are moved on or lose office.
- *The European Union*. As the EU has evolved and assumed more power over British politics, pressure groups have moved into Brussels big time, such that there are now some 3,000 groups applying pressure in the Belgian capital, employing some 10,000 personnel.

Professional lobbying and 'sleaze'

Professional lobbying companies – currently around sixty of them – have sprung up in recent years offering their services, mostly to large companies. They claim to have access to top decision-makers and can either win preferential treatment for clients or prevent their interests being damaged. Often these firms were staffed by former MPs or ministerial aides trading on their contacts book within Whitehall and Westminster. In the mid-1990s there were thirty Conservative MPs on the books of lobbying companies being paid anything up to £10,000 a year or in some cases more. At the start of the 1990s such activity was not thought to be beyond the pale: MPs regularly took up employment outside Parliament and this was thought to be no different. Attitudes changed when reporters from the *Sunday Times*, posing as commercial interests, asked two Tory MPs (Graham Riddick and David Tredinnick) to place parliamentary questions on their behalf.

Being paid to advance business interests rather than representing constituency interests was seen by the public as a dereliction of duty: the word 'sleaze' quickly came to be used to describe such activities. John Major, as Prime Minister, set up a committee on Standards in Public Life under the judge Lord Nolan, which recommended that MPs should not be allowed to table questions and amendments for outside interests and should register all such connections with a new parliamentary commissioner. Sleaze did not disappear once New Labour came to power in 1997 – far from it – but the new measures went some of the way to restoring confidence that MPs were not merely instruments of business interests.

Theoretical perspectives

Pluralism (Robert Dahl)

This is the view that says power should be and largely is distributed throughout a large number of groups and decisions are reached through a process of negotiation. Government often acts, according to this view, as a kind of 'holder of the ring' or referee.

Corporatism (Phillipe Schmitter)

This approach sees groups acting as intermediaries between government and citizen but also sees government 'colonising' groups for its own authoritarian purposes. During the 1970s, for example, it was argued that Labour was pursuing such a course when it made deals with the unions above the heads of their members.

Policy networks (Richardson and Jordan)

This theory says that groups are crucial in the formulation of policy, with departments assembling 'policy communities' basically out of groups. Looser collections – with frequent traffic both in and out – were discerned as 'issue networks'.

Box 8.1   Protests and parliamentary government

On 8 March 2008, *Economist* columnist 'Bagehot' noted the increase in the number of protests launched against Parliament; indeed, a diversion was discerned from parliamentary parties towards single-issue protest groups. Rather than reflecting a failure of Parliament, Bagehot thought it reflected the naivety of the public:

> The basic deal of parliamentary democracy is, or used to be, that on polling day voters make an overall choice among the packages on offer. They can turf out the government at the next election, but until then they have to live with compromise, frequent disappointment and occasional coercion.
>
> That old model seems to be increasingly unsatisfactory to voters accustomed to bespoke treatment in other aspects of their lives. People are right and entitled, of course, to make their views known to their elected representatives; but swelling numbers seem to expect the same sort of service from Westminster as they get from Starbucks – to choose their policies in the same way as they choose the toppings on a cappuccino (a sprinkling of low taxation, please, with a referendum on the side). They demand a kind of personal satisfaction that government, with its conflicting priorities, can't deliver. In places such as California where government has tried to do so, by introducing more direct forms of democracy, the results have been chaotic.

Marxist perspective

This root-and-branch critique perceives democratic structures as 'window dressing' for a control exercised at root by business interests. According to this view, government will be staffed by 'agents' of the bourgeois property owners and unions will be their marginalised dupes. Government officials are also seen as 'agents' who have been brainwashed by being socialised into the bourgeois state by its schools, universities and media.

New right

Margaret Thatcher and her followers saw pressure groups as not entirely legitimate, representing producers rather than consumers and 'short-circuiting' a system which should apply democratic pressures via elected MPs.

References

Ashford, S. and Timms, N. (1992) *What Europe Thinks: A Study of European Values*, Dartmouth.
Grant, W. (1989) *Pressure Groups, Politics and Democracy in Britain*, Phillip Allan.

Hall, P. A. (1999) 'Social capital in Britain', *British Journal of Political Science*, 29(4).
Pattie, C., Seyd, P. and Whiteley, P. (2004) *Citizenship in Britain: Values, Participation and Democracy*, Cambridge University Press.
Putnam, R. (2001) *Bowling Alone: The Collapse and Revival of American Community*, Simon and Schuster.

Recommended reading

Jones, B., *et al.* (2007) *Politics UK* (6th edition), Pearson: chapter 11.
Kavanagh, D., *et al.* (2006) *British Politics* (5th edition), Oxford University Press: chapter 21.
Kingdom, J. (2003) *Government and Politics in Britain: An Introduction* (3rd edition), Polity: chapter 17.
Leach, R., *et al.* (2006) *British Politics*, Palgrave: chapter 8.
Moran, M. (2005) *Politics and Governance in the UK*, Palgrave: chapter 9.

Other texts

Baggott, R. (1995) *Pressure Groups Today*, Manchester University Press.
Giddens, A. (1998) *The Third Way*, Polity Press.
Grant, W. (1989) *Pressure Groups, Politics and Democracy in Britain*, Phillip Allan.
Paxman, J. (1991) *Friends in High Places*, Penguin.
Putnam, R. (2001) *Bowling Alone: The Collapse and Revival of American Community*, Simon and Schuster.
Smith, M. (1993) *Pressure, Power and Policy*, Harvester.

Websites

Countryside Alliance, www.countryside-alliance.org.
Friends of the Earth, www.foe.co.uk.
Greenpeace, www.greenpeace.org.uk.
OneWorld UK, http://uk.oneworld.net.
Trades Union Congress (TUC), www.tuc.org.uk.

9

Political parties

The role of political parties

Political parties are such familiar features of political life that we sometimes fail to appreciate the valuable roles they play in participative democracy. This is especially the case in a modern culture which tends to attribute only malign motives to politicians. In reality, parties are vital to our way of life, for reasons which include the following.

Harmonising differing viewpoints

Given that most sections of society seek to advance the interests of their group, there is a vast array of related viewpoints reflecting economic, regional, ethnic, religious and moral perceived interests. This is made even more complex and intractable by the existence of often opposing views for virtually every opinion one encounters; for example, some people favour the operation of faith schools as a means of allowing religions autonomy within a liberal society, while others oppose them for reinforcing enclaves of difference which have the potential to divide society and, in the light of the London terrorist bombings of July 2005, even to create violent conflict. Parties help put together coalitions of interests and provide coherence to how they articulate their demands, before they are fed into the system.

Recruitment of personnel

Parties provide a means of drawing people into the political system and an elevator to elected office either locally or nationally. David Blunkett, the blind former Cabinet minister, from a deprived and poor background, was initiated into politics, like so many, by campaigning at the local level for the Labour Party. Soon he became an elected local member and rose to be leader of Sheffield council. After demonstrating how completely he had overcome his disability, he moved on to represent Sheffield Brightside and from there he was promoted to some of the highest offices in the land.

Douglas Hurd, by contrast, came from a privileged background of Eton and Cambridge. After a period in the Foreign Office, he served as Edward Heath's private secretary for a while before winning Mid Oxfordshire (later Witney) for the Conservatives. After service in the Cabinet as Home Secretary and Foreign Secretary, he stood for the leadership in 1990 along with John Major and Michael Heseltine. This was a much smoother transition to senior office, perhaps, than Blunkett's but both careers were facilitated and choreographed by the political party of their choice.

Participation and education

Parties rouse voters to be active in democratic politics, something without which democracy could not survive. In the nineteenth century, parties used extensive social activities to attract people in but while this aspect survived into the mid-twentieth century, the dominance in election campaigns of television and other media, not to mention a raft of leisure options, have reduced this aspect of party behaviour to the sidelines. By mobilising activists, parties also contribute substantially to their education in political issues and, indirectly, that of the wider electorate.

Choice

By organising interests into coherent groups and articulating them clearly, parties provide reasonably clear choices for voters at election time.

Accountability

Parties provide not only the personnel and ideas of government but also, in the form of oppositions, alternative governments as well. On election day, the government is held to account by voters for its time in office and if the judgement is negative another party is summoned to try its hand at governing.

Controlling the executive

When a party wins a general election, its leader becomes Prime Minister. He or she then appoints party colleagues as ministers to be in charge of the various departments of state. These ministers represent the line of democratic control bestowed upon the winning party by the electorate; it is assumed they will do the voters' bidding in their stewardship of the departments they run.

Parties are therefore central to the business of democratic government, which could not realistically be carried out without them.

History of party government

Parties emerged as disciplined elements of our national politics – remember, 'democracy' was still in its infancy at that time – only by the end of the nineteenth century:

- The Liberal and Conservative parties shared incumbency of government over the period 1867–1914, with some eighty nationalist Irish MPs complicating the process of government.
- The Labour Party was set up in 1900 as the campaigning reflection of trade unions, socialist societies and working-class voters; by 1924 it was already in power, albeit in a short-lived minority government.
- The Liberal Party, dominant during World War I and immediately afterwards, began to fracture during the 1920s, beginning a decline which continued into the 1950s, when it claimed only six MPs.
- After World War II, the multi-party pattern of the interwar years gave way to two-party dominance; from 1945 to 1997, Labour and the Conservatives won over 90% of seats, with the Conservatives ruling for all but eighteen years of this period.
- In 1981, a number of right-leaning Labour MPs – alarmed by Labour's swing to the left – set up the centrist Social Democratic Party. This merged with the vestigial Liberals and fought two general elections as the Alliance.
- In 1987, the Alliance sundered, following disappointing showings in elections, and the Liberal Democrats were formed out of its constituent elements. That party rallied the centre significantly, winning sixty-two seats in the 2005 general election.

The two-party system has been modified in recent years and it would be fair to say we now have something like a 'two and a half' party system, with the Liberal Democrats hoping, with some justification, to hold the balance of power in a future election. Neither big party now commands anything like a majority of voters' support: in 2005, Labour won a majority of sixty-seven seats on a mere 35.2% of the vote; Conservatives polled 32.4% and the Lib Dems 22.0%.

Conservative Party

This is the traditional 'party of government' in Britain, held to represent the interests of the traditional ruling classes as well as those of property owners and the 'wealthy' in general. In the nineteenth century, Tory Prime Minister Benjamin Disraeli had urged a 'romantic' alliance between the upper classes and the working class and, while commanding the biggest slice of middle-class votes for many years, the party has always been able to attract a crucial proportion of working-class votes too. This is partly because the party has consistently been able to reinvent itself after its fortunes have languished:

- In 1945 it was crushed by a Labour landslide but by 1951 was back in office as a centrist party willing to accept a mixed economy.
- After a period of Labour dominance in the 1960s and 1970s, the Conservatives gave Margaret Thatcher the chance to move the party robustly to the right to attract working-class voters – whose views are often far to the right, even when they vote Labour – as well as alienated former Conservatives.
- After a much longer period in the wilderness subsequent to Labour's 1997 landslide, the Tories finally found a leader who recognised that the Thatcher message had to be adapted for a society which had fundamentally changed since the 1980s. David Cameron, elected in 2005, has managed to resurrect his party by positioning it much closer to the centre and make it seem capable of winning elections again.

Leadership

Election

The Conservative leader used to 'emerge' through confidential soundings until 1965, when Edward Heath was elected via a system some criticised as too complex. Thatcher stood against Heath in 1975 and won but faced her own challenge in 1990 after eleven years as Prime Minister. She narrowly failed to win on the first ballot and, after taking advice from her Cabinet colleagues, agreed to stand down on the grounds that she would have lost the second vote – advice which she and her supporters subsequently questioned for many years, not without bitterness.

John Major took over in 1990, managing a slow decline in the party's fortunes until 1997, when Labour won a massive majority. William Hague won the subsequent leadership election but, after tacking to the centre, returned to the party's right-wing constants and lost the 2001 election disastrously. Similar fates awaited party leaders Iain Duncan Smith in 2001 and then Michael Howard in 2005. With his party in acute crisis – ageing membership in rapid decline, trailing hopelessly in polls and on policy issues – Cameron was elected on a reforming mandate in 2005. So far he has avoided any real pressure to swing to the right once again, though in the wake of the 2009 recession he urged cuts in public spending to reduce government debt.

Constraints

In theory and according to party rules, the Conservative leader is given much authority to lead but in reality he or she has to: avoid policy divisions – crucial as voters punish parties which cannot agree; sustain morale – as it is not easy to maintain leads in the polls when events intervene; keep a balance among the leadership – for example, Thatcher had to compromise with her 'wet' opponents on several occasions; and keep leading figures onside – Thatcher suffered from resignations by key colleagues (Lawson and Howe).

Organisation

1922 Committee
This is a committee of Tory MPs and is independent of the leader. Usually it supports the leader but Major experienced much division within it and related conflict over Britain's membership of the European Union.

Central Office
This is the party bureaucracy and contains some crucial units, like the Research Department, and personnel, like its media managers and advisers. Duncan Smith fought battles over who should do what and critics focused on its undemocratic practices.

Party groups
There are several of these, running from the reforming Bow Group on the left to the No Turning Back Group and Monday Club on the right.

Reforms

- Hague set up a board to run the party's affairs, thus providing more unity to a party with an ancient and fragmented organisation.
- He also introduced a rule that all parliamentary candidates should be chosen by all members of a constituency association.
- Challenging the leader was in future to be made more difficult – following the 'coup' against Thatcher – with, for example, 15% of Tory MPs needed to request a motion of no confidence.
- A new party forum was set up to discuss policy.

Labour Party

Provenance

Unlike the Conservative Party, which originated in Parliament, Labour was a grass-roots party: a 'bottom up' rather than a 'top down' affair. This is reflected in the greater democracy in Labour and more authority in the Conservatives. The party was set up by the trade unions – with the enthusiastic help of various socialist societies – in 1900 to create a 'political wing' to their activities. The unions felt this was necessary once they realised legislative action could be achieved more effectively if they had their own MPs rather than lobbying MPs belonging to other parties. In 1918, the party acquired a socialist constitution and an annual conference with policy-making powers. Throughout its history, Labour has faced the problem of reconciling those in its ranks who favour rapid and far-reaching reform and those who prefer slower but surer, if not safer, progress via established parliamentary methods.

The party conference became a crucial stage on which these battles were carried out.

Leadership

Labour has always seemed distrustful of leadership and intent on collective decision-making as an antidote to a possibly over-powerful leader. Ironically, the party has twice had leaders – Ramsay MacDonald and Tony Blair – who were charismatic and powerful but were subsequently accused of betraying the party's principles.

Power centres in the party

Annual conference

This was set up by the 1918 constitution as the policy-making 'parliament' of the party. Unions were allowed to use the whole of their membership when casting their votes – the 'block vote' – and so dominated the big decisions. Reputations were made by Labour politicians through fiery conference speeches and the conference was always more powerful than the Conservatives' equivalent, which was more a rally of supporters.

National Executive Committee (NEC)

This is voted in at every conference by the membership. As trade unions dominate the membership, the NEC has tended to reflect their choices and moods at the time of voting. At one time, the NEC had a broad policy-making role and in the early 1980s, when the party had swung to the left, it became the focus of left-wing aspirations. Under Blair it lost this function and consequently lost much of its importance.

Trade unions

As we have seen, these were the foundation of the Labour Party and have tended to dominate its key decisions over the years. The fact that unions have contributed (and still contribute) so much money to the party has reinforced this tendency. Block voting, moreover, gave decisive power to unions at conference, until this ability was curbed in the 1990s and the 'blocks' were reduced to one-half of a union's membership.

Parliamentary Labour Party (PLP)

The Conservatives' 1922 Committee was seen as powerful by the Tory Party in the country because of the prestige which membership of Parliament bestowed upon it. However, the PLP has tended to be just one power centre in the history of the party and, since the early 1980s at least, not regarded by party members as having any higher claim to influence than the other power centres.

Power and leadership issues

Conference
The conflict between the conference and the party in government has tended
to be won by the latter. The government has been forced to choose between its
own conference, dominated by activists, and that of the country as a whole.
In the end, it has been Parliament's authority, answerable to all voters and not
just Labour ones, which has been superior to that of the Labour Party's constitution. However, Harold Wilson and James Callaghan, who defied internal
party dissent to do as they thought fit as Labour Prime Ministers, eventually
lost the confidence of party activists, which caused different kinds of problems
during the 1970s and 1980s.

Ideological divisions
Divisions between moderates – often but not always with union backgrounds – and left-wing firebrands caused huge difficulties to the party in the
past. During the 1930s, Labour's pacifism tended to alienate voters, who felt
the country needed to be defended against its enemies, especially Adolf Hitler.
During the 1950s, Nye Bevan's insistence that the party should continue on
a more radical road did the same for voters and Labour faced long periods in
opposition during these years.
     In the 1970s, the pre-eminence of left-wing ideologues seemed to rein-
force the sense of anarchy and decline of the times, and voters were repelled
by a party at war with itself. The result was eighteen years of Conservative
rule, something from which the party learnt a powerful lesson. The disaster
of Michael Foot as party leader also warned party members against being
overly sentimental when seeking power. The result was the careful policy
positioning of Tony Blair's 'New' Labour, which eschewed anything sounding even vaguely like 'socialism', combined with strict party discipline to
ensure everyone was 'on message' with centrist, voter-friendly policies.

Experience of leadership
Ramsay MacDonald, who joined the Conservative-dominated National
Government in the early 1930s, hence 'betraying' his party, may have
indirectly persuaded Labour to choose an exceedingly uncharismatic, but
staunchly reliable, Clement Attlee as leader from the late 1930s onwards.
Subsequent leaders varied from the wily Wilson – also accused by some of
duplicity – to the pro-union Callaghan, the ineffectual Foot, followed by the
talented but ultimately unsuccessful Kinnock. And then it was Blair – much
hated by some in the party but winner of three elections. Gordon Brown, who
took over as premier in June 2007, is certainly less charismatic but is more
closely identified with the party than the privately educated Blair. Yet his poor
judgement over a number of matters has not, at the time of writing, inspired
too much confidence that he can lead the party to victory at the next election.

Liberal Democrats

The Alliance of the Social Democratic Party (SDP) and the Liberals finally came to an end in 1988 when the Social and Liberal Democrats were formed; the present abbreviated title was adopted in 1990. David Owen, former disillusioned Labour Cabinet minister and member of the original 'Gang of Four' who set up the SDP, continued after the merger to attempt to run his own ongoing SDP but in 1990, when his party came seventh behind the joke Monster Raving Loony Party in a by-election, he finally wound up his maverick rump of a party.

Paddy Ashdown became leader of the newly formed Social and Liberal Democrats in March 1988 and, while providing forceful leadership, tended to side with Labour politically. Indeed, Blair was keen to involve the Lib Dems in his government in 1997, but Labour's landslide made such collaboration unacceptable to his party. After Ashdown, Charles Kennedy was less keen on Labour, opposed the Iraq war bitterly and managed to improve his party's representation by some measure. However, his drinking habit eventually caused him to stand down and, after a fairly chaotic contest, Sir Menzies ('Ming') Campbell took over in 2005. After a period in which leading party members felt they had made insufficient progress, Campbell stood down in autumn 2007, and the young and charismatic Nick Clegg became leader in December 2007. The party still suffers from its perennial problem of being insufficiently distinguished from Labour in policy terms.

Devolution and the nationalist parties

As Chapter 12 explains, the 'Celtic fringe' has been achieving independence since the early twentieth century, when Ireland became a sovereign country, with the partitioned northern province bitterly contested by those who passionately wished to remain connected to Britain and those connected to Sinn Fein wishing for a united Ireland. One of the major changes in Britain's political parties has been provided by devolution. From being noisy outsiders clamouring to be heard, nationalist parties have taken their places in government. At the time of writing, the Scottish National Party runs a minority government in Scotland, and Plaid Cymru is in a coalition with Labour in Wales. Yet in terms of Westminster seats, Labour still dominates both these countries, while in England in 2005 the Conservatives actually polled more votes than Labour (yet because of the voting system won fewer seats).

Funding political parties

This has proved an acute problem over the last few decades, for a number of reasons:

- Membership of parties, which was close to 2 million in the early 1950s, plummeted until both major parties had only a couple of hundred thousand members by the end of the century. This meant that neither party could rely any more on subscriptions for a substantial share of its income.
- The decline in respect for politics in general which characterised the latter part of the last century accentuated the problem, with voters disinclined to countenance state funding of parties (as is done in Germany and the Nordic countries).
- Increased reliance on expensive media devices for getting out their messages has increased the cost of running the two main parties to over £20 million a year.
- The consequence of the above has been a greater reliance on big donors by all three of the main parties. This happened earlier with the Tories and they were much criticised for taking money off unsavoury characters who, it was suspected, might seek to use the influence money could buy them for personal ends; Lord Ashcroft, a colourful businessman, has been a major donor to the Tories and accumulated much influence through bankrolling candidates in key marginal seats. However, Labour soon found itself in similar deep waters when it floundered around for campaign money in 2005 and took loans from rich donors who were then linked to possible peerages. The 'cash for peerages' scandal ran throughout Blair's latter years and did much to bring low his own reputation as well as his party's.

Sir Hayden Phillips, a former senior civil servant, was put in charge of an inquiry to find a solution to the problem of party funding. He suggested in autumn 2007 that parties should accept a cap on donations of £50,000. This suited the Conservatives, who could call upon a legion of rich people to donate such sums, but for Labour, the only source would be the unions, the richer ones of which donated much more than this sum. Labour insisted such donations were the aggregate of small individual sums from members, but the Conservatives hotly disputed this and stalemate ensued.

Are political parties dying?

Some commentators have concluded that political parties are on the decline in advanced democracies, especially Britain.

Participation

Simon Jenkins, in the *Sunday Times* (30 September 20007), wrote:

> The collapse of parties in Britain has been spectacular. In the 1950s more than 4m people claimed some affiliation. Today the figure is 0.5m and falling,

having dropped 70% in the past 25 years alone. Even those asserting some political activity amount to a mere 2% of adults, the lowest in any comparable democracy.

The fact is that people now have many more claims on their time than political activity and in consequence democracy is suffering.

Turn-out at elections

Most people are now aware that the decline in party membership and activism is merely a symptom of a wider malaise. In the 1950 general election, turn-out was 80%; during the 1970s it averaged 75% but fell to 71% in 1997; it then plummeted to 59% in 2001, recovering only slightly, to 62%, in 2005.

Funding

As explained above, parties struggle to survive and have become used to living in debt. State funding is opposed by experts who claim it will make our democracy too beholden to government itself. Voters oppose it as they see no reason why politicians should benefit from taxpayers' money in such a way.

Pressure groups as alternatives to parties

These bodies, discussed in Chapter 8, are essential to democracy, just like parties. They have been influenced by public suspicion of parties and now try to keep a distance from them. Moreover, voters are now less interested in seeking action through parties but tend to seek it instead from single-issue pressure groups (see also Box 8.1, p. 80).

The catch-all party as an ideology-free entity

The German political scientist Otto Kircheimer has produced, as we have seen in Chapter 7, the idea of the 'catch all' party, an entity with no real ideology but merely a mobilisation of vote-winning professionals (see Box 7.2, p. 69). But while parties face some daunting problems in Britain, they just about function to the extent that parties are still perceived as the agencies of government and are perhaps only a closely contested election away from a return to high turn-outs and healthier membership numbers.

Recommended reading

The major textbooks deal with political parties as follows:

Jones, B., *et al.* (2007) *Politics UK* (6th edition), Pearson: chapter 12.

Kavanagh, D., *et al.* (2006) *British Politics* (5th edition), Oxford University Press: chapter 18.
Kingdom, J. (2003) *Government and Politics in Britain: An Introduction* (3rd edition), Polity: chapter 10.
Leach, R., *et al.* (2006) *British Politics*, Palgrave: chapter 7.
Moran, M. (2005) *Politics and Governance in the UK*, Palgrave: chapter 15.

Other texts

Crewe, I. and King, A. (1995) *The Birth, Life and Death of the Social Democratic Party*, Oxford University Press.
Garner, R. and Kelly, R. (1998) *Political Parties in Britain Today*, Manchester University Press.
Giddens, A. (1998) *The Third Way: The Renewal of Social Democracy*, Polity.
Kavanagh, D. and Butler, D. (2005) *The British General Election of 2005*, Palgrave.
McKenzie, R. T. (1963) *British Political Parties*, Heinemann.
Rose, R. (1984) *Do Parties Make a Difference?* (2nd edition), Macmillan.

Websites

Conservative Party, www.conservatives.com.
Green Party, www.greenparty.org.uk.
Labour Party, www.labour.org.uk.
Liberal Democrats, www.libdems.org.uk.
Plaid Cymru, www.plaidcymru.org.
Scottish National Party, www.snp.org.

10

Legislature I:
monarchy and the House of Lords

Parliament is the name of the British legislature and it comprises three elements: the monarch, the Lords and the Commons. Of the three, the Commons (Chapter 11) is by far the most important but this is not to say that the Lords and the Queen are of no importance whatsoever.

Monarchy

This institution has been in existence for over 1,000 years, ever since political unity was achieved under Knut (Canute) (994–1035). A council of advisers – the Witenagemot – proved to be the embryo of the modern Parliament; as it developed, it used its ability to grant finance to the King as a lever to acquire influence over law-making and guarantees of fair government. Inevitably, monarchs became exasperated by the need to heed their Parliaments, but when Charles I tried to rule without its authority and support, the Civil War resulted, which led to the King's execution in 1649.

Thereafter, Parliament was always ultimately in command. Later in that century, when James II tried to favour his adopted faith of Catholicism, seven leading public men invited William of Orange to invade. In retrospect, this was an astonishing and treasonable thing to do – but William did invade and did become King, with his wife Mary as Queen. This was the Glorious Revolution of 1689. William agreed that Parliament should have the final say on legislation and throughout the next two centuries the monarchy shuffled gracefully off political centre stage, to become merely influential and then, eventually, mostly ornamental. Now, its functions are largely ceremonial and symbolic but the monarchy retains, therein, some significance. By the 1930s, some royals were dubious as to what role they were now playing. Edward VIII, destined to abdicate in 1936 to live with his mistress, the American divorcee Wallis Simpson, wrote to a friend in the 1920s, before acceding to the throne: 'Who knows how long this monarchy stunt is going to last?' (see Godfrey, 1998).

Democratic legitimacy

Clearly, there is a direct contradiction between democracy and a hereditary, wholly unelected institution but supporters point to the fact that there is a good majority who support the monarchy, even after its travails in the 1980s and 1990s. Over a million people queued to view the Queen Mother's coffin in 2002 and millions poured out their grief when Diana died in 1997. However, critics dismiss such things and go on to point out that: the Queen's personal staff are drawn from the topmost drawer of the aristocratically connected and Eton educated; while her garden parties annually involve a total of 35,000 people, the Queen takes her tea in a tent separate from her guests; and the Diana out-pourings were in some measure critical of the Royal Family, which was seen as dysfunctional and unable to empathise with the woman married to the heir to the throne, let alone understand what the nation itself was feeling.

Choosing the Prime Minister

The academic Peter Hennessy (1995) argues that historians have neglected the 'continuing political influence of the monarchy'; he believes that the mon-arch's power to dissolve Parliament and to appoint a Prime Minister constitute 'anything but marginal activities' and these powers could prove decisive in certain contingencies, as in 1974, when neither of the major parties won sufficient seats to form a government. In these circumstances, the monarch's ability to choose the Prime Minister is accepted as 'active' by the members of the 'golden triangle' at the heart of the constitution: the personal private sec-retary to the Prime Minister, the Cabinet secretary and the personal private secretary to the monarch. Such rules were also accepted as such by party leaders back in 1974 and since. Hennessy quotes Sir Kenneth Stowe, personal private secretary to Wilson and his two successors, in saying that the Queen's government must be carried on and that the Prime Minister appointed by the sovereign must be able to command a majority in the Commons. Hennessy adds that in the event of voting reform, with the adoption of a system of pro-portional representation, such uncertain situations might well become more frequent and the monarch's role further enhanced.

   Andrew Marr (1995) takes the line that the monarchy's real constitu-tional 'muscle' comes into play only in very unusual circumstances: an indecisive election, a parliamentary putsch, or prime ministerial illness gives the monarch 'an umpiring role'. However, Marr saw such monarchi-cal power – if this is what it is – as 'increasingly under threat'. In 1992, the 'golden triangle' considered options in what was anticipated (wrongly) to be an inconclusive general election, but Kinnock was untrusting of the estab-lishment and sought a separate legal opinion.

   Ben Pimlott thought Hennessy exaggerated the monarch's role and potential power, for should she ever seek to exercise her nominal powers they would soon be dismantled; the monarchy's only chance of surviving is if its power is never actually used. Oddly, perhaps, a poll in *The Economist* in the late 1990s revealed that only 19% wished to end the constitutional powers of the monarch, while 62% opposed such a step.

Advising Prime Ministers

According to the nineteenth-century political sage Walter Bagehot, the monarch has 'the right to be consulted, the right to encourage, the right to warn'. The Queen meets the Prime Minister for an hour a week to exercise these celebrated duties; over the years she has advised eleven of them. She also regularly has meetings with members of the Cabinet. Prime Ministers tend to be impressed with her knowledge of current affairs. While she liked meeting early Tory premiers like Churchill and Macmillan, she seems to have got on best with Labour men like Wilson, a particular favourite, and Callaghan. She did not get on with the buttoned up Heath nor the formidable Thatcher (though her mother was a great admirer). Major proved a more acceptable replacement, according to the Queen's biographer, Ben Pimlott. As for Blair, it seems she was more the recipient of advice rather than the source, especially over the best way of handling the crisis caused by Diana's death. The film *The Queen* (2006), starring Helen Mirren, provides an entertaining and revealing version of this episode.

Is her advice valued? Joe Haines, Wilson's press secretary, said his boss thought her advice 'wise' but others, like Heath, seemed to regard the palace meetings as an irritant. Prime Ministers do not lack for advice and the monarch probably comes low down in their ranks in terms of advice likely to be taken. Probably the most typical example of royal influence was the Queen's intervention to prevent Postmaster General Tony Benn removing the Queen's head from postage stamps in 1964.

Head of the armed forces

As the head of the armed forces, the monarch commands an automatic but wholly genuine loyalty from all three arms of the military and constitutional experts maintain that this would act as bulwark against a military coup ever being contemplated, let alone carried out.

Cost

The cost of maintaining the Royal Family has proved contentious, as left-wing critics and sections of the popular press have claimed that the monarchy is excessively expensive. The Civil List, awarded to the Royal Family each year by the Treasury (and reassessed every ten) amounted to £10 million in 2003 but the total state expenditure on the monarchy, including upkeep of houses and palaces and so on, probably works out at not much below £100 million per annum. Since 1993, the Queen has voluntarily paid taxes on personal income.

Defenders of the monarchy point out that it attracts millions of tourists every year, who spend more than the monarchy costs the state, and they argue that a 'bicycling monarchy' as in Scandinavia would not be in the 'splendid monarchy' tradition of Britain. In response, critics argue that tourists would still flock to see the palaces, even if they were empty of royalty.

Symbolism

Bagehot argued that the masses needed a soothing and believable set of symbols to make them feel happy with their government. He felt that the common man – of whom he was no great fan – could relate to the focus of a 'single person doing interesting things' and that the monarch provided a useful symbol of this kind. So the monarchy was one of the many ways, for him, whereby wise men rule foolish subjects.

The superb study of the Queen by Ben Pimlott (1996) suggested the monarchy provided a mirror in which the nation saw itself. The nation needed to see itself and responded well to ceremony which was aimed at the nation as a whole: weddings, birthdays, coronations. The Queen's coronation in 1953 was a massive affair, with troops, carriages, foreign heads of state, parades and national rejoicing.

The fiction of British government is that it is all carried out in the name of the monarch: hence 'Her Majesty's Government' (HMG). Everyone knows this to be untrue but it is conveniently believable in the sense that the Queen represents the nation as a whole: a unified political entity. However, this symbolism was not easily established and is vulnerable. As Bagehot famously asserted in *The English Constitution* (1867): 'Above all our royalty is to be reverenced, and if you begin to poke about in it you cannot reverence it.... Its mystery is its life. We must not let in daylight on magic.' For a long time this secrecy was maintained, and anything potentially damaging about royalty was kept out of the press through a kind of open conspiracy by the ruling class. But in 1969 the Queen's new press secretary – more outgoing than the stiff-upper-lipped Sir John Colville, allowed a fly-on-the-wall television documentary, *The Royal Family*, to be made by Richard Cawston. Rather than satisfy the appetite of the press and public, the programme merely whetted it for a non-deferential age and some say the rot set in at this time. Incrementally the press began to take liberties with the royals, especially after the heir to the throne married the young and beautiful Diana Spencer in 1981. The *Sun* published photographs of a heavily pregnant princess on a beach in the Bahamas. The Queen complained but the next day the *Star* published the same pictures again, without apology. There has been little to stop the press since then, with the Duchess of York, shortly afterwards, having to suffer the indignity of the *Sun* putting on its front page a photograph of her toes being sucked by her Texan millionaire boyfriend.

Moral authority

Traditionally, or at least since Queen Victoria, the Royal Family had been perceived as something of a model, a moral template for the nation. The commonly recognised secrecy served this end, of course. Princess Margaret discovered that her love affair with divorcee Group Captain Peter Townsend had to end for reasons connected, according to the editor of *The Times*, in a thunderous editorial, with the moral health of the nation. But once the veil was lifted in the 1970s, the inevitable ups and downs of the life of the Royal Family were put under the microscope. Unfortunately, the royals proved not just as bad as everyone else but, with the exception of the Queen herself, arguably a little worse, at least regarding fidelity and good parenting. Opinion polls in the 1990s, even before Diana's death, suggested faith in the institution was running perilously low. A poll in the *Observer* on 14 September 1997 revealed that only 12% of respondents were satisfied with the monarchy as it was, while 74% wished it 'modernised'.

Conclusion

Bagehot placed the monarchy in the 'dignified' category of the constitution, as opposed to the 'efficient' or working parts (see p. 49). It is easy to characterise the institution as purely ornamental, something wheeled out for the tourists, ceremonial occasions and for visiting heads of state to enjoy tea and scones with in Buckingham Palace. Political scientist and latterly Labour minister (Lord) Andrew Adonis, however, challenges this judgement:

> Add to its charismatic power the royal family's wealth, its influence over policy and government, its status at the head of the honours system and the hereditary aristocracy, and the monarchy looks every bit as 'efficient' as most departments of state. Indeed, it is a department of state, for the Court and royal household are an enterprise as elaborate and relentless about self promotion as any Whitehall ministry. (Adonis and Pollard, 1998, p. 134)

Another interesting angle on the monarchy is provided by Professor John Gray, of the London School of Economics, who argues that the institution uniquely assists and nurtures the notion of nation and of unity. Reviewing the intractable problems some countries have experienced when establishing their identities, he observed:

> Happily, we do not face in Britain any of the horrors that have accompanied the building of nation-states in other parts of the world. Still, it would be unwise to

take our good fortune too much for granted. The monarchical constitution we have today – a mix of antique survivals and postmodern soap opera – may be absurd, but it enables a diverse society to rub along without too much friction. (*Observer*, 29 July 2007)

The House of Lords

The monarch has always been a key element of the aristocracy – the apex of its power and source of the patronage so eagerly consumed by actual as well as aspirant members ever since the notion of kingship in England emerged. Initially, the King was advised only by close confrères, all ennobled. In time, to the advisers were added representatives of the non-baronial gentry, in order to extend and deepen consent and to elicit finance. But when the crucial conflict between King and country occurred in the mid-seventeenth century, the King and aristocracy split off to fight the forces of Parliament marshalled by Cromwell: 'cavaliers' versus 'roundheads'. This division is sustained – to a degree – to the present day, in that the aristocracy is integrally bound up with the monarchy, which acts effectively as its head.

Lords spiritual and temporal

The Lords grew out of the Anglo-Saxon Witenagemot and the Norman Curia Regis, being gatherings summoned to advise the King. But the assemblage of the leading churchmen of the day plus the earls and barons saw a shift in importance during the middle ages from the former to the latter. As the summons was purely personal and not meant to be representative of any group, the barons assumed it would be repeated for their heirs too; in this way membership became hereditary. This lack of representativeness led to the establishment of the Lower House (the Commons), as a representative chamber, which was therefore perceived as the more legitimate one, and so, after the fourteenth century, it was that house which assumed the right to initiate taxation.

Lords loses ascendancy

As the shift to democracy occurred during the nineteenth century, the Lords further receded in importance, until, in 1911, Lloyd George's epic challenge to its authority succeeded and the Lords thereafter exercised only the power of a two-year delay on legislation, reduced to one year in 1949.

Legislative changes affecting the House of Lords

- The Life Peerages Act 1958 was an attempt to render the upper chamber more acceptable in a democratic age, by making it possible for individuals to be elevated to it for their lifetimes. After this, hereditary peerages were created only by Margaret Thatcher, and then only three.

- The Peerages Act 1963 made it possible for hereditary peers to give up their titles. Lord Home (Alec Douglas-Home), Lord Stansgate (Tony Benn) and Lord Hailsham (Quentin Hogg) were three who did so, the better to pursue their political careers.
- Finally, the House of Lords Act 1999 abolished the hereditary principle and all but ninety-two of such peers, meaning that life peers became the dominant element of the House of Lords.

Present composition

The number of people sitting in the House of Lords (or at least with the right to do so) has been substantially reduced from a figure of over 1,300 in 1999 to well under 800. Table 10.1 shows the composition of the House of Lords at the time of writing.

Table 10.1 *Composition of the House of Lords, January 2009*

Party	Life peers	Hereditary: elected by party[a]	Hereditary: elected office holders[a]	Hereditary: royal office holders[a]	Bishops	Total
Conservative	150	39	9	0	0	198
Labour	212	2	2	0	0	216
Liberal Democrat	67	3	2	0	0	72
Crossbench	173	29	2	2	0	206
Bishops	0	0	0	0	26	26
Other	12	2	0	0	0	14
Total	614	75	15	2	26	732

Note: [a] Ninety-two hereditaries were elected to remain sitting in the Lords by fellow peers for an unspecified transitional period in 1999.
Source: www.parliament.uk.

Functions of the House of Lords

Constitutional
The Upper House can veto any proposal to extend the life of a Parliament beyond the present limit of five years. It can also delay a Bill for a year after its second reading in the Commons, which is a useful weapon, especially in the last year of a parliamentary term.

Useful for the Prime Minister
The present chamber serves a number of useful functions for the Prime Minister.

- *Reward for services rendered.* Patronage is not what it was in the eighteenth and nineteenth centuries but peerages are still greatly valued and Prime Ministers can use them to reward colleagues whom they no longer need in their government (but the 'Cash for Peerages' scandal raised questions as to whether Labour supporters had been awarded peerages in exchange for cash contributions).
- *Adds to government personnel.* According to usual practice, there are two members of the Lords in the Cabinet – the Lord Chancellor and the Leader of the Lords – but there can be more. In addition, there are usually ten to fifteen junior ministers who are members of the Upper House, plus half a dozen whips to look after government party members.
- *Provides a 'backdoor' for non-parliamentary recruits.* John Hoskins, former head of Thatcher's Policy Unit at Number 10, once said that there was not enough talent in the Commons to staff a medium-sized multinational firm. This might seem illogical to outsiders, but to Prime Ministers such a remark would strike a chord, largely because so many politicians are now lacking in experience of the world outside Westminster, having been full-time politicians ever since leaving university. Tony Blair, for example, appointed Lord (Gus) MacDonald, the former television executive, to serve as a junior minister, it was alleged, because he lacked ministers with experience of running large organisations. He later ennobled Andrew Adonis, another former head of the Number 10 Policy Unit, to use him as a schools minister to implement the programme of academy schools.

Deliberative function
The House of Lords holds regular debates on issues of the day. Given the unique mix of experience and expertise in its membership, these debates – according to Lord Dennis Healey for one – are of higher quality than those in the Commons. However, they do not attract anywhere near as much interest, simply because votes in the chamber do not directly affect legislation in the way those in the Lower House do. However, if the vote defeats an important government Bill, it will merit at least a mention in the press. Defenders of the Lords argue that the debates are worth listening to not just because of the expertise but also because peers are not inhibited from speaking their genuine thoughts by any consideration of constituency pressures: as unelected legislators, they are allowed greater licence than members of the Commons.

Legislative function
The Lords 'processes' Bills in a fashion similar to the Commons in terms of readings and amendments. About a quarter of Bills introduced by

government are concerned with finance and so do not concern the Lords, but all others do.

- *Non-controversial legislation.* The Commons is overworked and the Lords usefully relieves some of the pressure by providing an alternative forum for the introduction of legislation, especially those items concerning local government.
- *Revision and amendment.* This is probably the most important function of the upper chamber in the modern day. Much legislation is none too well drafted and arrives in the Lords needing close scrutiny. Given the number of lawyers and semi-retired politicians, there is no shortage of personnel to go over Bills line by line, word by word, so that inconsistencies and loopholes are identified and remedied. Labour often initiates a large body of contentious legislation and so benefits much from such attentions. And during Thatcher's third administration all but a tiny fraction of Lords' amendments were accepted by the Commons. It is fair to say that if the Lords did not perform this function, separate provision for it would need to be made.
- *Select committees.* Few people realise that the Lords has its own select committees as well as the ability to create ad hoc ones relating to contemporary issues. The most important select committee is the European Union Committee, which monitors draft European legislation for any issues with important principle or policy implications. It works through seven sub-committees, each of which contains co-opted members; together they involve over eighty peers. Ad hoc committees have addressed such matters as the Monetary Policy Committee of the Bank of England (reported 2001), stem cell research (2002) and the Constitutional Reform Bill (2004).
- *Private members' legislation.* It is little known that members can introduce their own Bills in the Lords. Most are debated and therefore ventilate the issue involved but this is not a major role and comprises no more than 3% of the Lords' time.

Judicial function

This function relates to the historical role the Lords has assumed as the highest appeal court in the land. Appeals are made when people wish to contest a court's decision. Appeals are heard at the next level up in the hierarchy of courts, so the Lords' role arrives only when a case that has failed in the Court of Appeal is taken further by the party involved. In practice, this role is performed by the twelve law lords (Lords of Appeal in Ordinary) plus peers who have held high judicial office. Hearings involve five to ten of these legal peers in a separate committee room. Legal peers do not normally speak on policy matters in debates in the Lords, in case this compromises them later in a case. A new UK Supreme Court was due to begin operation in October 2009. It will take over most of the judicial functions at present performed by the House of Lords.

Reform

Ever since the nineteenth century, there have been plans for the reform of the upper chamber but, while comprehensive schemes have failed to be adopted, as we have seen, there has been an incremental reduction of its powers. Various attempts to achieve agreement have been essayed and found wanting for one reason or another. In 1969, the Parliament (No. 2) Bill was attacked by Michael Foot for not going far enough and by Enoch Powell for going too far. After that Labour, perhaps, sensed that the public had no sustained interest in changing (let alone abolishing) it, and certainly the Conservatives, with notable exceptions, resisted calls for reform. Most advocates of the Lords accepted that it should not be able to challenge the overall democratic legitimacy of the Commons, as this might cause legislative gridlock, and that it must not impede effective government.

The House of Lords Act 1999 removed all but ninety-two hereditary peers from membership of the House of Lords; the ninety-two would continue until the second stage of the reform, once it was agreed. In January 2000, Lord Wakeham's Royal Commission report, *A House for the Future*, was published. It offered options of: sixty-five members elected on the basis of votes cast regionally in a general election and eighty-seven members directly elected at the time of European elections; or 195 elected by proportional representation, at the time of European elections. Terms of office would be fifteen years and existing life peers would remain as members.

In 2002, a joint committee of both Houses of Parliament produced a report defending the functions of the House of Lords and offered seven options regarding the proportion of members to be elected, from all elected to all appointed. In January 2003, the options were debated in both Houses, with the Lords favouring an all-appointed solution and the Commons failing to endorse any of the options offered. The Labour manifesto in 2005 proposed a reformed House of Lords which would be 'effective, legitimate and representative without challenging the legitimacy of the House of Commons'. But there, to date, the matter of reform rests: yet another unfinished piece of UK constitutional business.

References

Adonis, A. and Pollard, S. (1998) *A Class Act: The Myth of Britain's Classless Society*, Penguin.

Godfrey, R. (1998) *Letters from a Prince: Edward, Prince of Wales to Mrs Freda Dudley Ward, March 1918–January 1921*, Little, Brown.

Hennessy, P. (1995) *The Hidden Wiring*, Gollancz.

Marr, A. (1995) *Ruling Britannia*, Michael Joseph.

Pimlott, B. (1996) *The Queen: Biography of Queen Elizabeth II*, HarperCollins.

Recommended reading

Jones, B., *et al.* (2007) *Politics UK* (6th edition), Pearson: chapter 18.
Kavanagh, D., *et al.* (2006) *British Politics* (5th edition), Oxford University Press: chapter 19.
Kingdom, J. (2003) *Government and Politics in Britain: An Introduction* (3rd edition), Polity: chapter 13.
Leach, R., *et al.* (2006) *British Politics*, Palgrave: chapter 13.
Moran, M. (2005) *Politics and Governance in the UK*, Palgrave: chapter 10.

Other texts

Constitution Unit (1996) *Reform of the House of Lords*, Constitution Unit.
Norton, P. (1993) *Does Parliament Matter?*, Harvester.
Norton, P. (1996) *National Parliaments and the European Union*, Cass.
Rush, M. (2005) *Parliament Today*, Manchester University Press (probably the best short book for students).

Websites

British Monarchy, www.royal.gov.uk.
House of Lords, www.parliament.uk/lords/index.cfm (and see in particular www.parliament.uk/about_lords/what_the_lords_do.cfm).
United Kingdom Parliament, www.parliament.uk.
Unlock Democracy, incorporating Charter 88, www.unlockdemocracy.org.uk.

Anyone wishing to assess the quality of Lords debates can tune into Radio 4, 8.30–9.0 a.m. or 11.30 p.m. weekdays to find out from the edited reports. The Lords also features on the BBC Parliament Channel.

11

Legislature II: the House of Commons

Origins

Parliament emerged through the monarch's need to consult and raise finance for the kingdom's needs. Parliament in its embryonic form was not engaged in 'governing' per se but it subsequently assumed a role in controlling the process of government. This is a role which it still performs in a wholly transformed fashion, a thousand years after Anglo-Saxon English Kings set up their advisory councils. From the fourteenth century, it was the lower, representative chamber which, crucially, set taxation, precipitating the Civil War when Charles I found he could not rule with Parliament, or indeed without it. After the Glorious Revolution in 1688, it was Parliament which exercised the upper hand in determining what kind of government should be in power – in the name of the monarch – and what laws should be passed. But the King and the aristocracy were able to determine a great deal through influence, the astute deployment of patronage and the manipulation of an ancient electoral system. The Great Reform Act of 1832 began the process of establishing the franchise on a genuine electoral basis and by 1884 the franchise had been extended to every adult male citizen; women had to wait until 1928 for the vote to be given to them on the same terms as men.

Some (but by no means all) historians have perceived the mid-nineteenth century as marking the beginning of a 'golden age' of Parliament, characterised by a small electorate, loose party discipline and MPs with independent means. Debates actually determined votes and, as Mackintosh remarked:

> The House sacked Cabinets, it removed individual ministers, it forced the government to disclose information, it set up select committees to carry out investigations and frame bills and it rewrote government bills on the floor of the House. (Mackintosh, 1968, p. 613)

Decline of the Commons

This period of dominance, however, proved short-lived: a century later, Parliament had swung to a position of inferiority in relation to the executive. Why was this? The most important reasons were:

- *Expansion of the electorate and growth of a disciplined party system.* As the number of voters grew, parliamentary parties realised they needed a coherent programme to offer at election times. Once in power, they had to deliver in order to stand a chance of re-election. And to achieve this they needed the guaranteed majority that disciplined parties provided. Individual MPs now took second place to MPs with a clear party allegiance, and parties now appealed directly to voters. Opportunities for free debates disappeared as timetables were rigidly adhered to. Whipped debates became almost wholly predictable as the government's majority of MPs almost always trooped through the lobbies in support of its measures. The real debates now occurred offstage, within the counsels of the governing party. MPs had to accept that without their party label, re-election would not be possible. Party discipline strangled free debates and votes, and with it Parliament's alleged golden age.
- *Growth in the power of the Prime Minister.* Along with their decline in importance came a transfer of interest by MPs in achieving ministerial office. The Prime Minister controlled the allocation of the 100 or so government jobs and so the power of the premier increased accordingly. Independent action by an MP now might win him or her the reputation of being a 'trouble-maker', unfit for office; this was a risk only a few politicians – by nature ambitious – were inclined to take.
- *Extension of government activities and bureaucracy.* As the minimalist view of the state's role declined, it began to intrude into more and more facets of the country's life, with those employed by the state multiplying tenfold, to over half a million by the end of the twentieth century. Given that ministers have not increased in similar proportion, it has been inevitable that civil servants' influence has increased enormously. With such a large number of decisions to make, ministers have come to rely increasingly on appointed employees rather than elected MPs.
- *Loss of control over finance.* The Commons established itself in relation to the monarchy and then the Lords through its ability to control the flow of revenue via taxation. However, as government became the preserve of the party in the Commons with a secure majority, the remainder of MPs became passive bystanders, with little effective input into decisions.
- *Growth of the 'loyal opposition'.* As the majority party became synonymous with government, the second biggest party became a kind of 'government in waiting', ready to fight elections as the 'heir apparent', with a 'shadow' Cabinet ready to slot into positions of control.

- *Growth of pressure-group influence.* More intervention in the life of the nation meant that influencing government increasingly mattered to groups and individuals, whether as part of the economy or as members of groups advocating different causes. The more important groups became vital to the government as sources of information and support when new measures were being formulated. This meant that key decisions were often made by ministers, their civil servant advisers and pressure-group representatives. Parliament, which in theory represented voters, became 'short-circuited' by this new 'triumvirate' of policy-making 'actors'.
- *Increasing influence of the media.* From the early part of the twentieth century, the media have grown in importance and politicians have used the media as their means of communicating with voters. This has meant that the people who control the media – editors, proprietors, journalists, broadcasting executives and presenters – have usurped the role of MPs in holding the executive to account.
- *Membership of the European Union.* Since 1972, Britain has been a member of the European Community and the authority of Parliament has been reduced as laws passed by this multinational body take precedence over laws passed in the UK Parliament.
- *Judicial review.* This procedure is the means whereby an individual or group can challenge whether the government has acted according to its own laws. This has meant that judges have been able to decide the word of the law, rather than Parliament.
- *Referendums.* These were introduced in the early 1970s as a means of deciding constitutional matters of great importance. As they supersede Parliament, they also reduce its authority.

How much has the Commons declined?

It might seem, from the foregoing, that the Commons has retreated to what Bagehot would call one of the 'dignified' rather than the 'efficient' parts of the constitution. Certainly, the House's power and authority were questioned in the 1960s and 1970s, and various suggestions were made to improve its efficacy. It was suggested, for example, that ministers regarded the Commons as something to be outwitted, assisted by clever civil servants and pressure-group personnel. As an extension of this view, the government was seen as presenting ready-made legislation to which the House was merely asked to apply its automatic imprimatur.

In the early 1970s, Professor John Griffith reported that, during the first three sessions of the decade, virtually 100% of government amendments were passed while only 10% of government backbenchers' amendments and 5% of opposition amendments were passed (see Griffith, 1981). Could it be that an institution which evolved from an advisory council into an assembly which beheaded a King and dominated government ever since has been reduced to a rubber stamp? Fortunately for British democracy, the House of Commons has retained many more functions than the above arguments would imply. These are set out in the next section.

Present-day functions of the Commons

Sustaining government

The central fact of British politics is that elections to the Commons determine the political complexion of governments and it is the majority party in that House which provides the government with publicly endorsed support. In February 1979, Parliament voted against the government of the day in a vote of confidence, thus bringing it down and ushering in eighteen years of Conservative rule. And MPs can still defeat governments when they have a mind to, however strong party discipline might be.

Limiting government action

While it is the willingness of the majority party to accept government actions which determines what passes into law, what the party will *not* accept sets the limits to what a government can do. This operates in two ways:

- it prevents totally outlandish suggestions, which might appeal to autocratic rulers for example, from being considered;
- its processes of consultation can adapt measures to the point where they become acceptable (for example, in January 2004 Blair managed to introduce university top-up fees by a margin of only five votes and the measure that was eventually passed into law reflected the compromises that the government had had to make).

A 'sounding board' for the nation

Enoch Powell, MP, a great expert on the constitution, once argued, in a conference at the University of Manchester, that precise representation, for which he accepted the voting system did not allow, is *not* necessary for the House to provide an effective 'sounding board' for the nation: MPs are always better informed on an issue after a debate and every section of society is able to contribute towards it via their MPs. They can make their voices known via a range of devices: question times (see below); major debates on Bills; ten-minute rule Bills (which, albeit minimally, allow a topic to aired); adjournment debates; and private members' Bills.

Legislation

Legislation passes through a well established procedure of:

- first reading (purely explanatory of its aim);
- second reading (a major debate);
- committee stage (clauses examined by a standing committee);
- third reading (Bill reassessed after committee stage);
- then up to the Lords, where a similar process occurs;
- return to the Commons to consider Lords' amendments;
- royal assent.

This extended process allows plenty of time for debate, amendment and re-drafting, although it can be compressed into a few days or even a few hours if necessary.

Influence over finance

After 1971, annual White Papers, debates and the instruction of the Estimates Committee provided more parliamentary scrutiny and influence over finance, though few would argue it amounted to anything like 'control'.

Recruitment and training of ministers

To serve as a minister, a politician has to be an MP, so the Commons provides a socialisation and training period for most aspirant ministers. MPs may serve only a few years or twenty or more before being invited to accept a 'minister's seal' of office from the monarch. During that period, they will have sat through scores of debates, prepared their own speeches and interventions, and sat on countless party and parliamentary committees, all of which help to educate them in the complexities of national issues and to train them in the art of communicating what they have learnt and persuading others of their point of view. Whether such experience trains future ministers sufficiently well in the arts of people and time management is another matter.

Political education

While it is true that some MPs prefer to give interviews to the television outside the Houses of Parliament, and that the introduction of the cameras has diverted some attention to visual images of speakers and away from debates, it remains the case that the Commons is the stage upon which the major events of the day are played out. So Tony Blair made his case for invading Iraq in the Commons in March 2003 and defended his policy on many occasions in the same forum. Few people read *Hansard* reports of parliamentary debates any more, nor do the national dailies provide wide coverage of what went on in the chamber the night before. But the weekly Prime Minister's Questions and the big speeches in important debates get good coverage and when the chamber is in summer recess there is nothing much for the media to find a purchase on for political reporting. Instead, 'silly season' stories appear.

Redressing private grievances

On average, MPs receive some 200 letters a week from constituents, as well as telephone calls and emails. These communications can concern a huge range of problems, from immigration and benefit claims to lobbying for special causes and campaigns to prevent supermarkets being built in residential areas. MPs have to respond to such requests and even without the ambition which drives them to higher things, MPs have a full-time job just being a good constituency MP. They will advance such grievances via letters to ministers, raising matters via questions and, sometimes, on adjournment motions (at 10 p.m.). If the matter relates to maladministration, the MP will refer it to the Parliamentary Commissioner for Administration, or 'Ombudsman'.

Legitimising decisions

Most societies adopt some way of showing that a law has been passed, often through a degree of ceremony and ritual. The centuries-old procedures of the Commons, culminating in the monarch's signature, provide such a function admirably. However, many claim such procedures and their antique language now need to be modernised.

Scrutiny of the executive

This takes place in a number of ways:

Question time
Prime Minister's Questions occur once a week (Blair reduced this from twice a week in 1997) on Wednesdays. It is scarcely an effective check on the government but it is probably the most watched Commons event of the week. The Prime Minister faces questions on all aspects of government activity for thirty minutes. The Leader of the Opposition is allowed three or four supplementary questions and the leader of the next biggest party a mere two. Often the questions are bland enquiries about the Prime Minister's schedule, the purpose being to deliver the allowed rejoinder as the real question (called a 'supplementary'), for which the Prime Minister is unlikely to be prepared. In reality, the Prime Minister is briefed exhaustively – usually for two hours or so – on possible supplementary questions and usually has a good idea of what they might be. However, the element of risk that the Prime Minister will be caught out, plus a full house and a television audience, makes this event a stage on which

party leaders seek to show their debating skills, their ability to retain complex information and their quickness of wit in aiming ridicule at opponents. Maybe this is not much of a check on the executive, but it is a valued occasion for the testing of leaders and the raising of party morale. The Prime Minister is always a skilled parliamentarian and, with proper briefing, usually wins the day, especially as the benches behind contain the majority of MPs.

Most ministers similarly face their own question time, according to a rota, Monday–Thursday, for thirty minutes. Again, a good minister, well briefed by civil servants, will take on all comers with confidence.

Select committees
These have a remit to investigate some aspect of policy and have power to collect evidence and summon witnesses. There used to be only a few of these but in 1979 they were overhauled and transformed into a series of departmental committees, shadowing each major department. A third of all MPs are involved in them. The most powerful is the Public Accounts Committee, which examines how government money has been spent and reports any inefficiency or malpractice by civil servants. In addition, there are a number of internal and procedural committees but none of them has the kind of power allocated to US Congressional committees; select committees submit reports but the government is not obliged to debate them, let alone act upon them (though it may do so). Since these committees have been televised, their status has grown and their chairs can assume considerable prestige and influence; backbench Labour MP Chris Mullin (himself a one-time junior minister), in his diaries, argues such chairs have more influence than junior ministers (Mullin, 2009).

Party committees
All parties have a wide range of committees on virtually every departmental topic. There are also a number of all-party committees and ad hoc ones on specific topics. These are useful for MPs wishing to advance a constituency matter – for example, lobbying for a local hospital on the health committee – or simply to learn the ropes of a new speciality with a view to promotion in the future.

The power of the Commons

While the Commons has lost a huge amount of its power to influence policy, it is still the defining forum of the nation's politics, providing the colour, the atmosphere, the drama of the crucial decisions which shape the nation's destiny. It lost power up to the 1970s but has enjoyed something of a renaissance since. Major's small majority after 1992 made many votes cliff-hanging events and Blair's growing band of rebels did the same for him as his policies on the welfare state and then Iraq earned the enmity of a good third of his parliamentary party, who did not hesitate to vote against their own government when they felt they had no other option. But while the chamber has increased its power vis-à-vis the executive, it is still very much in the subservient position. And this despite two decades of reform.

Reform of the Commons

In 1978, the Select Committee on Procedure reported that the relationship between the Commons and the government 'is now so weighted in favour of the government to a degree which arouses widespread anxiety and is inimical to the proper working of our parliamentary democracy'. Since then, a sea change has occurred in MPs' attitudes towards the legislature, which has helped propel a number of reforms. Some reforms are structural and have had a major impact, while others are minor and only procedural. A number have occurred since the late 1980s:

- *Devolution.* Since 1999, this has removed many matters relating to Scotland and Wales from consideration by the Commons, as they are now dealt with by the devolved assemblies. Devolution has also created the 'West Lothian question', the complaint by English MPs that while Scottish and Welsh MPs can vote on matters relating to England, English MPs are not able to repay the compliment.
- *House of Commons Commission.* Set up in 1978, this body gave the House more political and financial control over its own administration and personnel.
- *National Audit Office (NAO) and Public Accounts Commission.* The NAO replaced the Exchequer and Audit Department of the Comptroller and Auditor General – the official entrusted with the task of ensuring government funds have been disbursed as intended. Now the Comptroller and Auditor General acts independently of Treasury control and on the basis of formal statutory authority, not convention as before.
- *'Special' standing committees.* These used only to scrutinise the clauses of Bills but after 1980 some were allowed to hold hearings into the subject matter of the Bills and to hear from witnesses.
- *Opposition days.* Twenty-nine days used to be set aside for the opposition to choose topics for debate. In 1981, 'supply days' (as these opposition debating days are called) were reduced to nineteen but in 1985 they were increased to twenty and three were given to the second largest opposition party – usually the Liberal Democrats.
- *Televising Parliament.* In 1966, a proposal to televise the Commons was defeated – it was felt by traditionalists that the Commons in session had a unique, almost mystical quality, which the cameras would ruin.

Box 11.1 The MPs' expenses scandal of spring 2009

Exploiting the generous allowances given to MPs was not unknown before 2009; Derek Conway's payment of his two sons as 'researchers' when they did little or no work for their taxpayer-funded salaries, for instance, had caused much trouble for the Conservative Party in January 2008.

The leaking of all expenses claims made by MPs over the previous four years to the *Daily Telegraph* in the spring of 2009 caused a minor earthquake in the political system; the newspaper thereafter released daily bulletins of what MPs had claimed.

MPs receive a salary of £64,000 a year, almost three times the national average, though compared with many professional salaries, relatively modest. Pressure by MPs to receive pay increases were often resisted by governments in the past, but they allowed expenses to increase by way of compensation. Former MP and Mayor of London Ken Livingstone argues that the rot set in when MPs voted in July 2001 to allow themselves a 40% increase in their 'second homes' allowance, taking it up to over £24,000 annually.

The most controversial allowance was for this 'second home', which MPs outside central London may need to do their jobs in both constituencies and the Commons. Expenses could cover mortgage payments and furnishings up to a high-quality level. Claims were allowed on second homes but it seemed some MPs 'flipped' the designation of their main and second homes so as to be able to make claims on one and then the other. It was also possible seemingly to profit from the sale of these properties after their improvement at tax payers' expense. Others used their 'ability to flip' to avoid paying capital gains tax and still others claimed for absurd items like toilet seats, 'duck islands' and 'moat cleaning'. Still others made arguably fraudulent claims for mortgages which had already been paid off.

Expenses up to £250 could be claimed without receipts. In order to claim, MPs had only to declare such expenses had been incurred in the course of parliamentary duties and most claims were paid by a fees office without question, as it tended to accept MPs were 'honourable'.

Public reaction to these revelations was explosive, with MPs vilified for claiming for things which hard-pressed voters had to pay for out of their own (generally much smaller) salaries. MPs guilty of particularly egregious claims were shamed into paying money back and in some cases stepping down as MPs at the 2010 election. Speaker Michael Martin received particular criticism for seeking to block information about MPs' expenses and he was eventually forced to step down, followed by a number of MPs from both sides of the House. Cameron and Clegg took the lead in being very hard on transgressors, while Prime Minister Brown seemed leaden footed by comparison.

The mood of the public was such that radical constitutional changes were seriously discussed, like the introduction of proportional representation voting, fixed parliamentary terms, more power to the Commons via select committees and less power for the whips. Just how much comes of all this ferment remains to be seen, although proportional representation seems an unlikely outcome.

Successive votes in the 1970s similarly rejected the proposal, but slowly opinion was changing. In 1989, television was finally allowed its first shy peep and the world continued to turn as before, despite the earlier dire predictions. People have become familiar with the Commons in a way not possible before, through the regular clips which appear on news bulletins; the famous chamber has never been more viewed. But television is a cruel master; MPs now prefer to queue up to speak to the cameras on the green outside the Houses of Parliament, on the grounds that they will be seen by millions on the 'telly' but only by a few MPs if they deliver their views in the chamber.

Brown's planned reforms

Soon after entering Number 10 in June 2007, Gordon Brown issued a consultation paper on British governance. It was welcomed by reformers in all sections of the party system, as it promised:

- *A review of voting systems in Britain.* This is bound to highlight the anomaly of having proportional representation for the devolved assemblies and certain local elections while the Commons persists with the unrepresentative first-past-the-post system.
- *Abolition of the royal prerogative.* This ability to act without parliamentary approval enabled the monarch – and then the Prime Minister, when the government adopted these powers – to appoint bishops, judges and senior officials to deploy troops abroad and to ratify international treaties.
- *A pre-Queen's speech* consultative process on the proposed legislative programme.

Whether such a sweeping set of suggestions is implemented is of course another question. Blair, for example, asked Roy Jenkins to chair an inquiry into the electoral system, which advocated a system of proportional representation for the UK, but then he decided to 'kick it into the long grass', as the saying goes, and little more was heard about it.

Social background of MPs

Some claim that MPs should mirror the society they represent; others are content merely that they represent at all. Certainly, the membership of the House of Commons does not offer anything like a mirror image. In fact, MPs are predominantly white, middle-aged, privately educated and male (Tables 11.1–11.5).

Table 11.1 *Age of MPs elected at the 2005 general election, by party*

	Number	Average age (years)	Under 40	41–59	60+
Labour	355	52.2	10%	71%	19%
Conservative	198	49.3	17%	65%	18%
Liberal Democrat	62	46.0	31%	60%	10%
Other	31	50.8	13%	77%	10%
All	646	50.6	14%	68%	18%

Source: Social background of MPs, House of Commons Library, www.parliament.uk.

Table 11.2 *Numbers of women MPs by party, 1987–2005 (% of party total)*

	Labour	Conservative	Liberal Democrat	Other
1987	21 (9%)	17 (5%)	1 (5%)	2 (9%)
1992	37 (14%)	20 (6%)	2 (10%)	1 (4%)
1997	101 (24%)	13 (8%)	3 (7%)	3 (10%)
2001	94 (23%)	14 (8%)	5 (10%)	5 (17%)
2005	98 (28%)	17 (9%)	10 (16%)	3 (10%)

Source: Social background of MPs, House of Commons Library, www.parliament.uk.

Table 11.3 *Education of MPs elected in 2005 (three main parties)*

	Labour	Conservative	Liberal Democrat
Fee-paying school	63 (18%)	118 (60%)	24 (39%)
University	226 (64%)	160 (81%)	49 (79%)
of which, Oxford and Cambridge	58 (16%)	86 (43%)	19 (31%)

Source: Dennis Kavanagh and David Butler, *The British General Election of 2005* (Palgrave Macmillan, 2005), table 10.5. Reproduced with permission.

Table 11.4 MPs' occupations, 1987–2005: number (%) of all from main parties (Conservative, Labour, Liberal Democrat)

	1987	1992	1997	2001	2005
Professions	262 (41.7%)	258 (41.1%)	272 (43.2%)	270 (42.9%)	242 (39.3%)
Barrister	57 (9.1%)	53 (8.5%)	36 (5.7%)	33 (5.2%)	34 (5.5%)
Solicitor	31 (4.9%)	30 (4.8%)	28 (4.5%)	35 (5.6%)	38 (6.2%)
Doctor	5 (0.8%)	6 (1.0%)	9 (1.4%)	8 (1.3%)	6 (1.0%)
Civil service/local government	22 (3.5%)	26 (4.1%)	37 (5.9%)	35 (5.6%)	28 (4.6%)
University/college teachers:	36 (5.7%)	45 (7.2%)	61 (9.7%)	53 (8.4%)	44 (7.2%)
School teachers	48 (7.6%)	57 (9.1%)	65 (10.3%)	64 (10.2%)	47 (7.6%)
Business	161 (25.6%)	152 (24.2%)	113 (18.0%)	107 (17.0%)	118 (19.2%)
Miscellaneous	133 (21.1%)	154 (24.6%)	188 (29.9%)	200 (31.7%)	217 (35.3%)
White collar	27 (4.3%)	46 (7.3%)	72 (11.4%)	76 (12.1%)	78 (12.7%)
Politician/political organiser	34 (5.4%)	46 (7.3%)	60 (9.5%)	66 (10.5%)	87 (14.1%)
Publisher/journalist	42 (6.7%)	44 (7.0%)	47 (7.5%)	50 (7.9%)	43 (7.0%)
Manual workers	73 (11.6%)	63 (10.0%)	56 (8.9%)	53 (8.4%)	38 (6.2%)
Miner	17 (2.7%)	13 (2.1%)	13 (2.1%)	12 (1.9%)	11 (1.8%)
Total	629 (100.0%)	627 (100.0%)	529 (100.0%)	630 (100.0%)	615 (100.0%)

Source: Dennis Kavanagh and David Butler, The British General Election of 2005 and earlier editions (Palgrave Macmillan, 2005). Reproduced with permission.

Table 11.5 *Ethnicity of MPs elected at general elections, 1992–2005*

	1992	1997	2001	2005
White				
Labour	266	409	400	342
Conservative	335	165	166	196
Liberal Democrat	20	46	52	62
Other	24	30	29	31
Total	645	650	647	631
Non-white				
Labour	5	9	12	13
Conservative	1	0	0	2
Liberal Democrat	0	0	0	0
Other	0	0	0	0
Total	6	9	12	15
Total				
Labour	271	418	412	355
Conservative	336	165	166	198
Liberal Democrat	20	46	52	62
Other	24	30	29	31
Total	651	659	659	646

Sources: Dod on Disk; Dennis Kavanagh and David Butler, *The British General Election of 1997* (Palgrave Macmillan, 1997); Operation Black Vote; House of Commons Library Research Paper 05/33.

References

Griffith, J. A. G. (1981) *The Politics of the Judiciary* (2nd edition), Fontana.
Mackintosh, J. P. (1968) *Cabinet Government*, Stevens.
Mullin, C. (2009) *A View from the Foothills: The Diaries of Chris Mullin*, Profile Books.

Recommended reading

Most of the big texts treat Parliament in one chapter, though Jones allocates two (ch. 18 on the Lords):

Jones, B., *et al.* (2007) *Politics UK* (6th edition), Pearson: chapter 17.
Kavanagh, D., *et al.* (2006) *British Politics* (5th edition), Oxford University Press: chapter 19.

Kingdom, J. (2003) *Government and Politics in Britain: An Introduction* (3rd edition), Polity: chapter 13.
Leach, R., *et al.* (2006) *British Politics*, Palgrave: chapter 13.
Moran, M. (2005) *Politics and Governance in the UK*, Palgrave: chapter 10.

Other texts

Blackburn, R. and Kennon, A. (2003) *Griffith and Ryle on Parliament: Functions, Practice and Procedure*, Sweet and Maxwell.
Cracknell, R. (2005) *Social Background of MPs*, House of Commons Library (available online).
Norton, P. (2005) *Parliament in British Politics*, Palgrave.
Rush, M. (2005) *Parliament Today*, Manchester University Press (this is the best student book).
St John Stevas, N. (ed.) (1974) *Walter Bagehot, The English Constitution: Collected Works*, Economist.

Websites

Directories of MPs, www.parliament.uk/directories/directories.cfm.
Hansard Society for Parliamentary Government, www.hansard-society.org.uk.
Parliament, www.parliament.uk.

12

Devolution

Towards the end of the twentieth century, pressure built for sweeping constitutional change regarding: the voting system, the House of Lords and the nature of the Union, which had been set in something like stone by the Acts of Union in 1536 (Wales), 1707 (Scotland) and 1800 (Ireland). Forces had been in motion for several decades which had eroded the strength of this union.

Rise of nationalism

It is often forgotten that the origins of nationalism in the constituent parts of the UK date back to when they were independent political entities: Wales was a Celtic stronghold which the Anglo-Saxons found hard to penetrate; Scotland had its own distinctive government for centuries; and Ireland had a history dating back more than a thousand years. The senses of identity which preceded the Acts of Union survived surprisingly intact; it only needed a little breath on their coals to cause them to glow and the flames to burst forth.

Scotland was never 'defeated' by England; rather, it was Scotland's James VI who became James I of both countries in 1603 (Mary Queen of Scots provided the heir which her cousin, Elizabeth I, had failed to produce). The 1707 Union to some degree was strategic, in that it pre-empted a possible French alliance with Scotland, but substantial autonomy remained even after the Act. This was not the case with Wales, which had been virtually defeated by Edward I in the thirteenth century; it was forced to accept English criminal law and finally annexed under Henry VIII. The fact that the Welsh language was proscribed caused particular bitterness; indeed, it was an issue on which the twentieth-century Prime Minister David Lloyd George felt particularly strongly when growing up in Wales. This difference in history meant that when nationalism emerged in both these countries, it was in significantly different forms.

Modern Scottish nationalism

Modern Scottish nationalism was founded in 1934 by John MacCormick, in the form of the Scottish National Party (SNP). From the outset it claimed Scotland could raise its own taxes and pay its own way; it had no need of its neighbour to the south. Economic arguments became even more passionate after the discovery of North Sea oil, which the SNP asserted was 'Scottish oil'. As this coincided with a steep economic decline in Scotland's traditional industries, the message had particular resonance. The SNP won its first seat in 1967 and thereafter eleven in 1974.

Plaid Cymru (Party of Wales)

This was established in 1925 by John Saunders Lewis; its early emphasis was on creating a bilingual society and promoting the Welsh language but by the 1930s home rule had been added to the party's objectives. In 1962 Saunders Lewis, the party's President, gave a radio talk entitled 'The fate of the language', which promoted the formation of the Welsh Language Society. Gwynfor Evans won Plaid's first seat in 1966; another two were added in 1974.

Kilbrandon report

Evidence of political support for national autonomy prompted the setting up in 1969 of a royal commission on the constitution; its voluminous report was submitted in October 1973 and recommended separate elected assemblies for Scotland and Wales. Alternatives considered, including independence and a federal structure, had been rejected in favour of a solution which, it had been hoped, would satisfy demand for autonomy while drawing the sting of the nationalists' demands. Consequently, a Bill was drafted and passed, not without difficulty. The referendum for a Welsh assembly, however, was defeated by a four-to-one majority and the Scottish one, subject to an amendment won by opponents during the passing of the Bill that the majority had to exceed 40% of the electorate, was passed by too small a margin. Devolution then languished during the decade when Margaret Thatcher was Prime Minister. Her brand of ultra-Conservatism, combined with her haughty Home Counties manner, however, managed to restoke the fires of nationalism and, by 1997, with the help of constitutional reform group Charter 88, it was poised to have its day.

Ireland and devolution

For very different reasons, 'devolution' had occurred much earlier in Ireland, though without much initial success. The 1800 Act of Union had been born, as partly in the case of Scotland a century earlier, of an English fear that

France might exploit the less than fraternal relationship England had with its Celtic cousins. English rule in Ireland since Henry II invaded in the twelfth century had not been well received, characterised as it was by absentee landlordism, effective 'ethnic cleansing' of Catholics from the better land by Protestant settlers, and periodic brutal suppressions of dissent during the seventeenth and eighteenth centuries.

Ireland, which had had its own Parliament until 1800, was given seats in the Commons and eventually filled them with advocates of home rule, who made much trouble for British government during the nineteenth century. William Gladstone, passionately concerned to solve the 'Irish problem', in time became converted to the need for home rule but never managed to deliver it. World War I delayed any chance of home rule and the Protestant minority proved so troublesome in their own right that they won the concession of a partition, whereby they retained six northern counties as their 'homeland'; meanwhile, the other twenty-six counties formed a new independent country, which, ambiguous towards Britain during the war against Hitler, in 1949 left the Commonwealth for a distinctly separate existence.

Northern Ireland was governed by a devolved assembly, sitting in Stormont Castle. But the Protestant majority was concerned to minimise the role played by the one-third Catholic minority in the province: they were marginalised in the workplace and excluded from political power. By the 1960s, a civil rights movement had emerged to fight for the Catholic cause; by the end of the decade, internecine fighting broke out and two paramilitary forces – the Ulster Defence Association (UDA) and the revived Irish Republican Army (IRA) – engaged in the most bitter of civil conflicts. 'The Troubles' persisted for the next two decades, with several attempts at power-sharing between the two antagonistic groups foundering on the rock of suspicion and distrust.

Scottish, Welsh and Northern Ireland Offices

With some nationalist grumblings for ministerial representation, awareness grew of the need to delegate certain functions away from London. The first was the Scottish Office, set up in 1885; it lasted until 1999, when most of its functions were transferred to the new Scottish Executive. The Welsh Office appeared in 1965, like the Scottish Office, headed by a Cabinet minister. Also like that office, its major functions were eventually transferred to the new Welsh Executive in Cardiff. The Northern Ireland Office was created in the wake of 'the Troubles', in 1972, when the functions of Stormont were transferred to Westminster. As in the other two cases, most of its functions were later transferred to an executive, but the suspension of that body meant that the Northern Ireland Office has, of necessity, been maintained in existence. However, in the light of the 2007 settlement it is to be hoped that all the residual functions will be transferred to the Northern Ireland Executive in Belfast.

Devolution and Labour after 1997

Labour leader John Smith had been a firm advocate of constitutional devolution but Tony Blair, who took over on Smith's death in 1994, was not so keen. Other major figures, however, including Robin Cook, Gordon Brown and Donald Dewar, were convinced of the need for such measures and the enabling Acts were duly passed.

Scotland

To pre-empt any accusation of 'imposing' a new Parliament, Tony Blair introduced a referendum in September 1997, which endorsed the idea by a three-to-one majority, and the notion of giving the Parliament tax-raising powers was endorsed by a slightly smaller majority (Table 12.1). In the first election, in May 1999, to the 129-member Parliament, using the new partially proportional voting system (see Box 12.2, p. 124), Labour won fifty-six seats, the Conservatives eighteen, the SNP thirty-five, the Liberal Democrats seventeen and others three. Labour thereupon struck, not without difficulty, a deal with the Lib Dems and ruled in coalition, with Donald Dewar as First Minister. The Scottish Parliament at Holyrood has powers delegated to it for passing *primary legislation*; this means it has jurisdiction over most domestic matters – education, health, agriculture, fisheries, local government and justice – but final sovereignty lies with Westminster, where retained responsibilities include foreign policy, abortion law, broadcasting, defence, security, energy policy and overall economic strategy.

In the 2003 elections, Labour lost six seats but the coalition with the Lib Dems survived; the SNP was very disappointed to lose eight seats. The 2007 elections, however, created a sensation when the SNP, under its new leader Alex Salmond, made a storming come-back, winning forty-seven seats to Labour's forty-six, the Liberal Democrats' seventeen, the Conservatives'

Table 12.1 *The 1997 Scottish referendum results*

	% of turn-out	% of electorate
Should there be a Scottish Parliament?		
Yes	74.3	44.87
No	25.7	15.53
Should a Scottish Parliament have tax-raising powers?		
Yes	63.5	38.24
No	36.5	22.00

Source: www.scottish.parliament.uk.

sixteen and the Greens' two. After much discussion, the SNP took over as a minority government and Alex Salmond became First Minister. In August 2007, buoyed by good opinion polls on his first few weeks in power, he launched a document proposing that Scotland become an independent country – a bold move but optimistic, in that polls showed only a third of Scots voters favoured such a course. In August Scottish Labour chose Wendy Alexander as leader. She surprised many when she challenged Labour leader Gordon Brown in May 2008 by calling for a referendum on independence; her idea was that voters, on poll evidence, would reject the idea, to the disadvantage of the SNP. She was forced to resign in June 2009.

Wales

In marked contrast to Scotland, initial enthusiasm for devolution in Wales was muted. The referendum in September 1997, on a turn-out barely above 50%, posted 50.3% in favour and 49.7% opposed. Support was strongest in

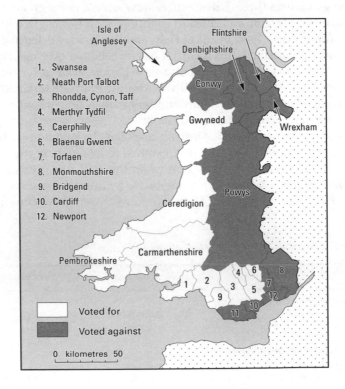

Figure 12.1 *Support for Welsh devolution*
Source: Daily Telegraph, 20 September 1997. © Copyright of Telegraph Group Limited 1997, reproduced with permission.

the north and west and weakest in the eastern areas (i.e. adjoining England) (see Figure 12.1). The popularity of the new arrangements was scarcely advanced by the fate of their architect, Labour's Ron Davies, who resigned after an unlikely episode in a gay cruising area on Clapham Common. Rather than accept Rhodri Morgan as the popular choice as his successor, Blair belied his stated aim of fostering democracy by seeking to impose the more malleable (and indeed Blairite) Alun Michael as Welsh leader.

In 1999, Labour took power in the new Welsh Assembly with twenty-eight seats; the Conservatives won nine, the Liberal Democrats six and Plaid seventeen. A year later, Michael was forced to resign and in October 2000 Morgan took over as First Minister. In 2003, Labour improved to thirty seats, with Conservatives eleven, Liberal Democrats six and Plaid twelve. In the 2007 elections, Labour lost some ground, along with the Liberal Democrats, but managed to stay in power, assisted by a new 'red–green' coalition with Plaid Cymru, agreed on 27 June between Morgan and the Plaid leader, Ieuan Wyn Jones. The proposed 'rainbow coalition' between the Lib Dems, Conservatives and Plaid, unsurprisingly perhaps, failed to get off the ground.

Northern Ireland

Shortly after Blair's arrival in Downing Street, the Good Friday Agreement was signed, in 1998. This landmark agreement set up the Northern Ireland Assembly and after the first elections to it, in June of the same year, the Ulster Unionists emerged as the biggest party and its leader, David Trimble, became First Minister, with Sinn Fein's Martin McGuinness serving as Education Minister. However, the Ulster Unionists were under great pressure from their

---

Box 12.1 The European Union connection

The EU connects with British government at a variety of levels and devolution has intensified connections, especially at the sub-national level. At the national level, though, there is a problem for Scotland, in that, while its shores provide over half of the UK's fish catch, it is the London-based government which negotiates within the framework of the EU's Common Fisheries Policy on its behalf. The same is true – and for Wales as well – over the choice of needy areas qualifying for EU assistance grants.

Scotland was quicker off the mark in adapting to the EU, and was the first to have a permanent office in Brussels, but Wales and Northern Ireland soon followed suit. For the nationalists, the EU is a useful reference point. They can point to the fact that Europe has many smaller states – such as the Baltic States, Luxembourg, Malta – and that they can bypass London to deal direct with Brussels, centre of a huge market, source of economic assistance, a common currency and, maybe, eventually, a source of foreign policy leadership and protection.

Box 12.2 Powers of the devolved assemblies

Scottish Parliament

This was established in 1999 at Holyrood. There is a four-year term. Members of the Scottish Parliament (MSPs) are elected using 'mixed member proportional representation', sometimes known as the 'amended additional member system', which is based on the German system. This allocates two votes to each voter. One vote goes to elect seventy-three MSPs from geographical constituencies on a first-past-the-post basis, while the other goes to elect another fifty-six from a 'top-up' pool to achieve the proportionality first-past-the-post seldom delivers. Proportionality is achieved via party lists, with seats allocated to parties according to the percentage support they achieve. So voters vote for a *person* with one vote and a *party* with the other.

- *Powers devolved to Edinburgh.* Parliament has the right to pass primary legislation on: home affairs and the judiciary, health, housing and local government, farming and fishing, social services, and the implementation of EU directives. It also has the option of adjusting income tax by ±3%.
- *Powers reserved by London.* These include employment law, economic and monetary policy, social security benefits and pensions, passports and immigration, dealings with the EU and foreign policy.

National Assembly for Wales

This has sixty members (Assembly Members, or AMs) who sit in the Senedd, in Cardiff.

- *Elections.* Forty AMs are elected from single-member constituencies and the other twenty are from regional lists, on the same basis as in Scotland.
- *Powers.* The Welsh Assembly lacks the ability to pass primary legislation but can pass secondary legislation, which can amend the former. Supporters of the Assembly campaign for the same powers as Scotland. In practice, however, certain important financial adjustments have been made: prescription charges have been abolished; tuition fees for Welsh students studying in Wales have been reduced; and more generous provision is made for nursing care.
- *Powers devolved to Cardiff.* The Assembly has responsibility for agriculture, fire services, economic development, environment, food, health, transport, local government, sport, and town and country planning.

---

members and Ian Paisley's Democratic Unionist Party (DUP) to insist that the IRA properly disarm itself. The IRA, immersed in its own history of struggle, refused to do more than pay ambiguous lip service to such 'decommissioning' and it was not long before the new government was suspended, in 2002.

The elections of November 2003 saw the fading away of the Ulster Unionists and the strengthening of the extremes, in the form of several

- *The Government of Wales Act 2006*. This became law on 25 July 2006. It gave the Assembly powers similar to the other devolved legislatures. However, Assembly Order-in-Council requests – a form of direct government fiat – are subject to veto by the Secretary of State for Wales and the House of Commons or the House of Lords.

Northern Ireland Assembly

This was established following the 1998 Good Friday Agreement. Its meeting place is Stormont Castle. It has 108 members, elected according to the single transferable vote system of proportional representation, chosen for its ability to fully represent all the communities in the province. Members are known as Members of the Legislative Assembly, or MLAs. The Assembly has the power to appoint the Executive. The Executive had been suspended, with authority handed back to the Northern Ireland Office in London, on more than one occasion, but full power was restored on 8 May 2007.

The First Minister and Deputy First Minister are elected by a cross-community vote; all other ministers are appointed to parties in accordance with their elected strengths. The powers which Westminster retains are divided into 'excepted matters', which are permanently excluded from the Assembly, and 'reserved' matters, which may be transferred at some future date.

Laws which are in conflict with the powers of the Assembly, EU law or the European Convention on Human Rights can be struck down and if the Secretary of State for Northern Ireland judges that a bill which has passed through the Assembly violates its constitutional powers, he or she can refuse to pass it upwards for royal assent.

- *Transferred matters*. These include education, health, agriculture, enterprise, trade and investment, environment, regional development (including transport), employment, finance, social development, culture, arts and leisure.
- *Reserved matters*. These are criminal law, police, navigation and civil aviation, international trade and financial markets, telecommunications/postage, the foreshore and sea bed, disqualification from Assembly membership, consumer safety and intellectual property.
- *Excepted matters*. These are royal succession, international relations, defence and armed forces, nationality, immigration and asylum, taxes levied across the UK as a whole, appointment of senior judges, all elections held in Northern Ireland, currency and the conferring of honours.

more seats for the DUP and Sinn Fein. Oddly, the close interface between the implacable foe of Catholicism, Paisley, with the leaders of Sinn Fein seemed to generate a new understanding and, to much astonishment, the eighty-year-old Paisley, after background work by Irish premier Bertie Ahern, Blair and Northern Ireland Secretary Peter Hain, emerged as First Minister on 8 May 2007. Few denied that Blair's tireless pursuit of peace in the province had finally provided him (it is to be hoped) with a genuine legacy, one which had eluded every British Prime Minister since William Gladstone.

Devolution problems considered

Advocates of delegating legislative authority to Scotland, Wales and Northern Ireland were concerned to reduce the centralisation of control in London and to allow citizens in the areas affected to have a bigger say in running their own affairs. As we saw earlier, mainstream party leaders also sought to reduce the appeal of national independence in Wales and Scotland by offering the 'compromise' of substantial delegated autonomy. But plans in politics seldom succeed in the way intended and a number of problems have been highlighted as a result of Labour's constitutional changes:

- *West Lothian question.* The most famous question concerning devolution was asked in 1977 by Tam Dalyell, MP (representing the West Lothian constituency at that time): is it fair that MPs elected to Westminster cannot have a say in the affairs of West Lothian yet possible for MPs elected from Scotland still to have a say in the affairs of West Bromwich? Moreover, goes the argument, Labour is often dependent for its majority in the Commons on Scottish MPs, as in 1964 and 1974. Scottish MPs are therefore doubly empowered and English MPs reduced to a lesser status. Similar points can be made about Welsh MPs. Some defenders of devolution argue that this same problem was present when Ulster MPs represented their province at Westminster while Stormont had domestic jurisdiction. The whole anomaly, they argue, was then (and is still) simply ignored.
- *Cabinet responsibility.* With First Ministers in Belfast, Edinburgh and Cardiff it seems unnecessary and confusing to retain Secretaries of State in London. Yet these residual titles are allocated to existing Cabinet ministers, often with a close connection to the countries concerned. So Peter Hain, an MP for a Welsh constituency, retained the title along with his job as Work and Pensions Minister (and then when he resigned in January 2008 he was replaced by Paul Murphy MP, though he was a full-time and not part-time Secretary of State) and Des Browne, the Defence Minister, doubled up as 'part-time' Secretary of State for his own home-land: Scotland.
- *Proportional representation.* The proportional voting systems for the devolved assemblies has greatly benefited the smaller parties (and also the Conservatives in Celtic areas) and implicitly posed the question of why Westminster remains elected by a first-past-the-post system. Paradoxically, some Labour politicians, angry that their traditional hegemonies in the Celtic regions have been ended, are now hotly opposed to extending similar voting reform to Westminster.

- *Pressure for equal powers for Wales.* While the Scottish Parliament can pass legislation through three stages and receive the royal assent as well as adjust taxation, the Welsh equivalent can do neither.
- *Nationalists in power?* It is reasonable to suppose that in a democracy the opposition nationalists might one day win an outright majority, as the SNP virtually did in 2007. This poses the question of whether devolution – framed to a degree to pre-empt independence – might have provided a route whereby it will eventually be achieved.
- *Ministerial anomalies.* When Labour's John Reid became Secretary of State for Health, it was pointed out by critics that, even though he was a Scottish MP, he had no jurisdiction over health in his own country and was effectively only a Minister of Health for England.
- *'Control freak' danger.* Blair's attempt to exclude Rhodri Morgan in favour of the compliant Alun Michael reveals that devolution had an Achilles' heel: as in the case of Ken Livingstone and the London mayoralty (see below), Blair could give power away in theory but not in reality.
- *Different treatment.* The fact that Scottish denizens received 22% more public expenditure per head and Welsh 13% more than English ones (2006 figures) has fuelled resentment in England against the devolved settlement (see Barnett formula, below).

English nationalism

Many English people like to delude themselves that they are immune from anything so vulgar as nationalism but the facts suggest otherwise. Throughout earlier centuries, England was the motor for 'British' imperialism, absorbing the Celtic periphery before taking on the wider world. Shakespeare's plays indicate that even in the seventeenth century ('Cry "God for Harry, England and Saint George!"' – *Henry V*) the notion of patriotism was warmly embraced and the growth of empire nourished that sense of worldly superiority which has so annoyed some of England's neighbours. But this was more a passive than a proactive sentiment: English people seldom showed their colours unless threatened, as by the Kaiser and Hitler in World Wars I and II. Since then, patriotism has been more commonly displayed in international football matches, often in an ugly fashion too. Another form of national feeling is reflected in attitudes to the disproportionate shares of public expenditure Scotland and Wales receive compared with England.

Barnett formula

This somewhat obscure ratio provides the reason why England receives a smaller per capita share of public expenditure than its Celtic neighbours. The formula originated with the then Chief Secretary of the Treasury, Joel

Barnett, who, calculating block grants to the regions, sought to compensate what were then less economically prosperous areas of the UK. He expected the 'formula' to last a year, but four decades later it is still in operation; in 2004 he confessed that, given the reductions in inequality which have since occurred, it was 'an embarrassment to have my name attached to so unfair a system' (*Manchester Evening News*, 6 February 2004).

Spending allocations for 2006 per capita in the four UK countries was as follows:

- Northern Ireland   £8,898
- Scotland   £8,096
- Wales   £7,509
- England   £6,623

Government spending in Northern Ireland is not so surprising but the near £1,500 difference between Scotland and England is glaring; the discrepancy between Wales and England is less, but still considerable at nearly £1,000.

England and its regions

The EU's emphasis on regional development led John Major to encourage it in England so that the UK government could fit more neatly into EU structures. In 1994, nine areas were set up to provide Euro-constituencies: Greater London, South East, South West, West Midlands, East Midlands, North West, North East, Yorkshire and Humberside, and East of England. In addition, each region was endowed with an assembly, not elected, but appointed by county and borough councils. These assemblies have no executive power but can have influence on certain matters, for example planning proposals. It is this domestic 'democratic deficit' which reformers would like to rectify with elected regional councils so that devolved regional agencies are accountable to elected bodies.

Regional development agencies

The Kilbrandon Commission recommended the setting up of elected regional assemblies to provide accountability for those regional functions already administratively devolved (see p. 119). Given the failure of the foray into devolution in the 1970s, this aspect of the Royal Commission's plan sank along with its main proposals. But the idea was exhumed when Tony Blair came to power in 1997, determined to devolve authority where it seemed possible. In 1999, regional development agencies (RDAs) were set up to coordinate regional plans with relevant government departments and agencies.

The main aim of the RDAs was to reduce differences between the rich south and the generally poorer northern regions. However, survey evidence revealed that 'regional consciousness' varied markedly across the country, from strong in the north-east to weak (very weak) in the south-east; many respondents, moreover, did not think any additional layer of government at regional level would do much good – even though the government had plans to remove one layer of local government (county or district) to compensate. A White Paper of May 2002 proposed referendums in areas where support for regional assemblies seemed to merit such a move.

John Prescott, the deputy Prime Minister and the most enthusiastic Cabinet member on the issue, led the campaign for an assembly in the north-east, allegedly the region most resentful of the power wielded by the Scottish Parliament and the Welsh Assembly. In the event, the referendum gave a huge black eye to Prescott, with a more than three-to-one majority against the proposal; in mitigation, he hoped the idea would gestate and grow to fruition at some later date – as indeed devolution itself had done after the debacle of the 1970s.

Greater London government

It is a moot point whether Greater London is part of local or regional government, but as it covers a wide area – 609 square miles – which is heavily populated – containing 7.5 million people (much more than either Scotland or Wales) – and has a distinctive new system of government, it is perhaps best considered under the latter heading.

The original London County Council was set up in 1889, but even then urban overspill exceeded its boundaries. Plans considered throughout the early years of the twentieth century were eventually implemented in 1965 on the basis of the 1960 Herbert report (and the subsequent London Government Act 1963), when the Greater London Council was set up, eliminating the old counties of London and Middlesex and absorbing parts of Kent, Surrey and Essex.

This was a two-tier arrangement, with thirty-two boroughs plus the unchanged City of London authority. Margaret Thatcher targeted the larger Labour-dominated metropolitan counties, created by the Local Government Act 1974, and abolished them in March 1986, despite a spirited rearguard action by the then leader of the Greater London Council, Ken Livingstone. The absence of any specific government authority for the London region attracted criticism across the political spectrum and, in opposition, Labour resolved to remedy the situation and was influenced, as was Conservative Michael Heseltine, by the American model of the elected mayor. In 1998, Labour, now in power, published a White Paper entitled *A Mayor and Assembly for London*. The following year, the Greater London Authority Act was passed following a positive referendum verdict on the proposed changes.

Tony Blair attracted opprobrium for seeking to veto Ken Livingstone's candidacy for Mayor but Livingstone defiantly left the Labour Party, stood

---

Box 12.3 Elections for the London Assembly and Mayor

The London Assembly is led by a directly elected Mayor, who serves a four-year term. In addition to the Mayor's powers over budgeting, strategic planning, transport and so on further powers were granted in 2006 over planning, waste, culture, sports, climate change and appointments to the functional bodies controlling the police and so forth.

To stand as a candidate in the Mayoral election requires a deposit of £10,000 (which is lost if the candidate polls less than 5% of the vote). The 'supplementary vote' system is used, whereby voters mark their first and second preferences. If no candidate receives over half the vote, second preferences are counted until the margin is reached. The Mayor's annual salary in 2007 was £137,579. Candidates for the Mayoralty tend to be a bit unusual, relative outsiders, maybe, like Ken Livingstone. In 2000, the Conservatives gambled with another outsider, the novelist Lord (Jeffrey) Archer, but his candidacy was ended when he was tried and convicted of perjury. In 2008, Boris Johnson's victory seemed to reinforce the impression that 'outsiders' do well.

The Assembly, which has twenty-five members, is also elected for a four-year term, on the same day as the Mayoral election, via an amended 'additional member' system (as used in German elections and in Scotland and Wales), whereby each voter has two votes, one for a constituency member and one for a regional party list. The party list seats are allocated on the basis of the percentages of the vote won by each party, with a qualifying limit of 5%. There are fourteen constituencies, returning one member each, and eleven members are returned from the party list; it follows that, to be sure of being returned, candidates need to be placed high up on the party list, but the advantage of the system is that it produces a more proportional end result than the first-past-the-post method. In 2008, there were eleven Conservative members of the Assembly, eight Labour, three Liberal Democrats, two Greens and one member of the British National Party (BNP).

---

as an independent in May 2000 and won an easy victory to become the first directly elected Mayor in the UK. As Mayor, he had responsibility for transport, fire services, police, culture and economic development (see Box 12.3). He won again in 2004 – this time as a Labour candidate, having been allowed back into the party – winning on second preferences (which come into play if no candidate attracts more than 50% of the vote on first preferences). On 1 May 2008 the maverick Conservative MP Boris Johnson beat Livingstone as he attempted to win a third term.

The London Assembly was also elected (see Box 12.3), a body which oversees the work of the Mayor, although the only real power it has is to veto the Mayor's annual budget by a two-thirds majority. One of Livingstone's main achievements in his first term was the introduction in 2003 of a 'congestion charge', an electronic toll which succeeded in reducing traffic by (a not un-disputed) 17%. His attempt to improve the London Underground was not so straightforward, as he clashed with Chancellor Gordon Brown on the best way of financing improvements, with the latter imposing a public–private partnership in preference to the Mayor's plan to raise the funds through floating public bonds. During his second term, he made climate change a priority and set up the London Climate Change Agency and related bodies.

Impact of devolution

There can be little doubt that devolution has proved to be a major constitu-tional measure, the implications of which are still being worked out. However, a number of things can already be identified which have been significant:

1 The dominant pattern of one-party government has been broken in British politics, with coalitions becoming quite normal in Scotland and Wales.
2 There is more transparency in the devolved assemblies, with the minutes of Cabinet meetings being published almost immediately on the web, in contrast to the usual thirty-year delay in the case of Westminster.
3 Business in the devolved assemblies is not conducted in the archaic form of Westminster but is direct and modern in style.
4 Fixed-term parliaments have strengthened calls for similar innovations for the London-based UK government.
5 The above is also true of proportional representation, as the present means of electing the Commons now seems an anomaly.
6 Two classes of MP have been created at Westminster: those Celtic members who have the ability to legislate on their own affairs and on those of England; and those English ones who can legislate only on the domestic matters of their own country and not those of Scotland or Wales.
7 Some practical measures have improved life for certain groups of people (albeit courtesy of the archaic Barnett formula): elderly Scots have free per-sonal care; students in Scotland receive university tuition free of charge; Welsh people under the age of twenty-five years receive free prescriptions and dental treatment; Welsh pensioners receive free bus travel.
8 The devolved assemblies have developed some interesting innovations. For example, in Scotland, peripatetic committees travel around consult-ing widely on proposed legislation. In Wales, subject committees meet, comprising the Cabinet minister, members from all parties, plus civil serv-ants; while their status is merely advisory, they meet frequently and some predict their influence will grow.
9 The Scottish Parliament had passed some sixty bills into law by 2004, many with far-reaching effects (as point 7 above affirms).

10 The Welsh Assembly has also proved itself a regular part of Welsh life and its importance can only continue to grow.
11 Even the often-suspended Northern Ireland devolved administration managed to abolish the 'eleven plus' exams, to introduce free bus fares for the elderly and to abolish school league tables.
12 Devolution has seen the early stirrings of what may become a more robust form of English nationalism as the treatment of Scotland and Wales begins to be perceived as unfairly generous.

Recommended reading

Jones, B., *et al.* (2007) *Politics UK* (6th edition), Pearson: chapter 14.
Kavanagh, D., *et al.* (2006) *British Politics* (5th edition), Oxford University Press: chapter 6.
Kingdom, J. (2003) *Government and Politics in Britain: An Introduction* (3rd edition), Polity: chapter 6.
Leach, R., *et al.* (2006) *British Politics*, Palgrave: chapter 16.
Moran, M. (2005) *Politics and Governance in the UK*, Palgrave: chapter 11.

Other texts

Bogdanor, V. (1999) *Devolution in the United Kingdom*, Oxford University Press.
Bulpitt, J. (1983) *Territory and Power in the United Kingdom*, Manchester University Press.
Deacon, R. (2006) *Devolution in Britain Today*, Manchester University Press.
Gamble, A. (2003) *Between Europe and America*, Palgrave.
Kumar, K. (2003) *The Making of English National Identity*, Cambridge University Press.
Marr, A. (2000) *The Day Britain Died*, Profile.
Pilkington, C. (2002) *Devolution in Britain Today*, Manchester University Press.

Websites

London Assembly, www.london.gov.uk/assembly.
London Mayor, www.london.gov.uk/mayor.
Northern Ireland Assembly, www.niassembly.gov.uk.
Scottish Parliament, www.scottish.parliament.uk.
Welsh Assembly, www.wales.gov.uk.

13

The executive I: Cabinet, Prime Minister and the 'core executive'

Prime Minister and Cabinet, as key features of British government, emerged around the late seventeenth and early eighteenth centuries. The monarch originally looked to the Privy Council for advice on matters of state but Charles II found it too large and so invited a smaller group to meet with him in his 'cabinet' or private rooms. Under Queen Anne it became an official title and the Cabinet still remains, formally, a committee of the Privy Council. As Parliament had won supremacy over the monarch in the Glorious Revolution of 1688–89, this senior committee of ministers became the most important in the land. When Anne failed to produce an heir, the Hanoverians were imported, with George I their first king. As he was not so interested in matters of state and his English was poor, he nominated the First Lord of the Treasury to be his intermediary and this minister soon became the 'Prime Minister'. It is interesting to speculate whether, if George had been a better linguist, the office of Prime Minister would have developed in the way it did.

To some extent the roles of Prime Minister and Cabinet, both at the very centre of major decisions, have been in conflict. For this reason it is not always easy to separate them for analysis but, allowing for that, the Cabinet is examined first.

Cabinet

By the nineteenth century this body comprised all the major portfolios and took all the major decisions. By the end of the century the Prime Minister was more than 'first among equals', as he was initially seen, and from then on the office acquired more prestige and power. But the Cabinet, too, was enhanced by more authority and prestige, which made it the key body to belong to and the pool of talent from which Prime Ministers were drawn.

Size and composition

Cabinet usually comprises twenty to twenty-four ministers but during the two World Wars 'War Cabinets' were a quarter of that size. In normal times of peace, they include all the major ministers – Chancellor, Home Secretary, Foreign Secretary, Health, Work and Pensions Ministers, and so forth – but also included are those with the more specialist jobs of Leader of the House, Chief Whip, Leader in the Lords, Attorney General and Lord Chancellor, plus the occasional 'all purpose' and archaic portfolios of Lord Privy Seal or Lord President of the Council, who often chair Cabinet committees or perform specific tasks for the Prime Minister. Non-Cabinet ministers also attend by invitation.

Collective responsibility

This long-established principle of British government is that once Cabinet has taken a decision, all ministers, including non-Cabinet ones, are obliged to support it even if they personally have reservations about it. As the rule is codified in *Questions of Procedure for Ministers* (now known as the *Ministerial Code*), Cabinet decisions are 'binding on all members of the government'. Anyone wishing publicly to oppose such a decision or policy is obliged to resign or will be sacked by the Prime Minister. In 1975, Cabinet ministers opposed to Britain's continued membership of the European Community were allowed, owing to the special circumstances, to dissent from government policy on this course of action. However, more typical was Robin Cook's resignation over Tony Blair's policy of invading Iraq in 2003, together with the usual explanatory speech to the Commons, in his case an especially powerful one.

Functions of the Cabinet

The Cabinet has the following functions:

- *Determining policy*. Cabinet discusses all the major issues, takes advice and then decisions. Sometimes these will be on issues which have not been resolved within departments and Cabinet sub-committees and have been referred up for wider discussion and resolution.
- *Planning the business of Parliament*. Cabinet decides on major debates and who will lead for the government.
- *Providing leadership*, along with the Prime Minister, for the party in Parliament and for the government as a whole.
- *Controlling the executive arm of government*. This is the most powerful committee in the country, staffed as it is by the heads of all major government departments and chaired by the Prime Minister.
- *Coordinating government departments and arbitration of disputes between them*. Cabinet is assisted in this work by the Cabinet Office (see below).

Cabinet committees

The weight of government business is such that much of it has to be delegated to smaller committees and sub-committees. When there is full agreement, these committees have the authority of a full Cabinet decision but where there is not, Cabinet may be called upon to resolve the matter. The work of such committees used to be secret (for no obvious reason) but in recent decades their numbers and responsibilities have been made public. There were 400 of them in the early 1970s but Callaghan halved them and Thatcher reduced them to just over 100. There is always an economic policy committee, a future legislation committee and a domestic affairs one (which when chaired by John Prescott had nine sub-committees), as well as a number of ad hoc committees on current problems.

Cabinet business

Typically, Cabinet meetings will involve the presentation of a series of reports – on foreign affairs, Europe, home affairs, parliamentary business from the Leader of the House. Contentious items of the day will also be discussed, possibly based on papers submitted by the lead minister involved. Until recent decades, Cabinet papers were regularly discussed at length and Cabinet meetings lasted several hours; however, Thatcher and Blair were less patient and wanted to short-circuit too much verbal interchange; consequently, the frequency and length of Cabinet meetings (they used to be weekly on Thursdays but Brown changed the day to Tuesday) and the number of papers discussed were all reduced. Blair's meetings often lasted less than an hour and mostly comprised a reporting of decisions taken elsewhere.

Cabinet Office

Founded in 1916 by Lloyd George, and first headed by Sir Maurice Hankey, the Cabinet Office has grown into a high-powered body which coordinates briefings to the Cabinet on the top policy issues, such as security and intelligence and foreign policy. It provides management of the civil service and is entrusted with ensuring its efficiency. In addition, it organises appointments in the Prime Minister's gift and the not always easy disbursement of honours. Staffed by around 1,000 people, including many high-flyers in Whitehall, it also follows up decisions and monitors whether they have been implemented. It operates through several secretariats, including: Economic, Overseas and Defence, European, Science and Technology plus Security and Intelligence. In addition, it has seen the invention of several new units, including the Social Exclusion Unit, the Policy and Innovation Unit and the Future Strategy Unit. The British executive lacks the kind of staffing the US President enjoys but the Cabinet Office provides, in effect, something not very dissimilar to the person at the pinnacle of British government.

Cabinet Secretary

The Cabinet Secretary heads the Cabinet Office and is officially head of the civil service. The post is always held by someone who has already pursued a successful career within a department. Since Hankey, a number of outstanding civil servants have held the job of Cabinet Secretary, including Sir Norman Brook, Sir John Hunt, Sir Robin Butler, Sir Andrew Turnbull, Sir Richard Wilson and (since 2005) Sir Gus O'Donnell. This post is the most important public office in the country – Sir Burke Trend, from Harold Wilson's time in 1964, described it, accurately, as 'the Prime Minister's permanent secretary'. Possibly this was why Butler rather resented Blair's appointed aides, especially Alastair Campbell, as the Communications Chief at Number 10, who usurped this hitherto umbilical link between the Prime Minister and the head of the civil service. Campbell, together with Jonathan Powell, Blair's Chief of Staff, had also, to Butler's distaste, been granted authority over civil servants by a special dispensation embodied in the arcane device of an Order in Council.

Prime Minister

How did the office of Prime Minister gather such power in the twentieth century? There were a number of factors:

- The requirements of wartime in the first half of the twentieth century placed a huge focus upon the premier, who became the national leader, shouldering the weight of reverses but enjoying the political fruits of victory in terms of the nation's gratitude. Lloyd George became synonymous with Britain's victory in World War I and Churchill with that in World War II. Resisting the same formidable enemy bestowed upon the occupant of Number 10 a new importance as national leader and first citizen, which usurped that of the monarch.
- The responsibility for taking momentous wartime decisions led to a number of changes. The Cabinet was reduced greatly in size and a streamlined bureaucracy was established to do the Prime Minister's and Cabinet's bidding.
- The electronic media in particular have turned the head of government into a household figure nationwide; in the nineteenth century, the Prime Minister might have been well known but few would have heard him speak – as the nation heard Baldwin in his regular broadcasts or Churchill during the war – or indeed have seen him; in contrast, the nation regularly saw Margaret Thatcher and Tony Blair at Prime Minister's Questions and while traversing the world on diplomatic business. Even if they resisted the idea, the media have made Prime Ministers better-known than the biggest film stars; their lives, actions and even families are scrutinised and dissected by reporters and commentators every minute of the day. Even

if Prime Ministers were not wholly in charge of their governments, their media profile generally made it appear as if they were.
- The phenomenon of powerful Prime Ministers in the latter part of the twentieth century pushed forward the limits of prime ministerial power to an even greater extent. Margaret Thatcher and Tony Blair are the two most obvious examples (see below on their styles of governing).

What roles does the Prime Minister perform?

Any Prime Minister has to take on a variety of roles in an exhausting job (see Table 13.1). Note, though, that despite being the main driving force of policy and, in Blair's case, the person who took the country to war on several occasions, the Prime Minister is not the Commander in Chief of the armed forces, as the US President is.

Head of the executive
- Like the US President, Prime Ministers have to head up the government of the day. They have to appoint members of Cabinet and other ministers. Unlike the President, they are limited in this recruitment to the pool of Members of both Houses of Parliament. Likewise, they have to remove members when necessary and 'reshuffle the pack' to maintain freshness and competence in the Cabinet team.

Table 13.1 *The Prime Minister's roles*

Function	Supporting office
Head of the executive	Cabinet secretariat Private office
Head of government policy	Policy Unit Press Office (communication)
Party leader	Political secretary (party outside Parliament) Parliamentary private secretary
Head appointing officer	Appointments Secretary (crown appointments) Cabinet Secretary (senior civil service) Principal private secretary (ministers)
Leader of party in Parliament	Parliamentary private secretary Private secretary – parliamentary affairs
Senior British representative overseas	Cabinet Secretary (Commonwealth) Principal private secretary Private secretary – foreign affairs

- The Prime Minister has to chair Cabinet meetings.
- The Prime Minister also oversees the civil service and various government agencies.

Chief policy-maker
- While government departments generate most of the volume of policy initiatives, it is the Prime Minister who sets the tone and the context in which that policy is made. For example, Thatcher advocated less government, lower taxes and more market forces and these tenets both provided the framework in which lesser policy was framed and reflected the aims of fellow MPs and party members. Before Thatcher, Edward Heath had sought to operate within the context of the postwar consensus, which basically accepted the status quo which Thatcher wanted to change.
- In the same way, Blair wanted to haul Labour away from the left-wing end of the spectrum and into the electable middle ground once again. While accepting the tenets of Thatcher's economic policies, he wanted to distance the party from its closeness to the trade unions, its 'tax and spend' policies and its perceived 'softness' on both law and order and defence. Both Prime Ministers took these powerful policy objectives into Number 10 – Thatcher's aims, it has to be said, being clearer than Blair's – and they provided the outline of their governments' respective directions.
- To criticise and to some extent resist departmental influences, Prime Ministers since Wilson have established their own Policy Unit. The first, in 1974, was headed by Bernard, now Lord, Donoughue and Thatcher found it convenient to continue the practice with businessman John Hoskyns as her head. John Major employed Sarah Hogg in this capacity. Tony Blair appointed David Miliband before he entered the Commons as an MP and then minister (and later Cabinet minister). Such appointees usually attended meetings with their appropriate departmental staff and on occasions their ideas are preferred to those of the department. For example, the controversial decision to increase tuition fees for university students was allegedly designed and advanced by Andrew Adonis, in Blair's Policy Unit.

Party leader
Given that Britain has a system based on parliamentary majorities, the party is all important. The Prime Minister is the leader and in this media age, the brand leader, to an extent he/she *is* the party as far as the voter is concerned.

In the Commons, the Prime Minister has to rally and lead a band of MPs, in collaboration with the Chief Whip, who advises on how MPs are feeling and on such matters as appointments and ministerial reshuffles. This means that the Prime Minister is expected to lead important debates and generally set the tone of the government on the important issues of the day. Prime Minister's questions (PMQs) are a noisy weekly sideshow which often is no better than a parliamentary knock-about. Voters take little notice of how good the protagonists are – William Hague, for example, was brilliant against Blair, but it did little for his standing in the polls. However, a good performance helps maintain the support on the backbenches on which every Prime Minister ultimately depends. Lacklustre displays by Iain Duncan Smith when Leader of the Opposition contributed in no small way to his demise as Conservative leader in 2003. The same thing happened to Menzies Campbell as leader of the Liberal Democrats (2006–7).

In the country, the Prime Minister is also the flag waver for the party during election campaigns. In the media age, party membership is not as important as once it was, but, as research from Sheffield University has shown, low party membership and effort during elections are closely related to poor performance on election day (Whitely and Seyd, 2002).

Senior UK representative
The premier is not the head of state but is clearly more important politically than the Queen. While overseas dignitaries might visit Buckingham Palace, the real work will be done in Downing Street. Blair took this role to a new height by establishing warm personal relations with other government heads, notably José María Aznar in Spain, and Gerhard Schroeder and later Angela Merkel in Germany. Most controversially he holidayed in the luxury villa of Silvio Berlusconi, the right-wing media magnate and Italian Prime Minister. His close relationship with Bill Clinton, a Democratic President, was thought quite natural, as both parties are left of centre, but his subsequent very close connection to Republican George Bush was criticised within his own party.

Head of patronage
The Prime Minister not only hires and fires ministers but also doles out recommendations for honours, from MBEs to peerages. This has proved a difficult role for some premiers; Wilson was criticised for his 'lavender list' of highly personal appointees to honours when he left office; and Blair was questioned by police in the 'cash for honours' scandal in 2006–7.

First citizen
This is a new role which the media spotlight has bestowed upon Prime Ministers when their behaviour or that of their families is judged appropriate or not.

To some extent the Royal Family used to fulfil this role but as their salience as national figures declined, the role of Prime Ministers and their families has strengthened. Some anticipation of it was discernible in Thatcher's period in power when her personal behaviour – thrifty, energetic, litter-clearing – won attention. Her family also won some of the spotlight, with husband Dennis seen as loyal and supportive but nevertheless something of a joke figure. Her children tended to be ignored until Mark won attention through various escapades and then when it seemed he was using his mother to advance business interests.

John Major was such a grey figure his home life was largely ignored except for his love of cricket and the occasional amorous activities of his son, James. If the media had gained even a sniff of his long-standing affair with Tory MP and minister Edwina Currie he would have become the focus for the most intense scrutiny and probably have been forced to resign, but this only emerged years later, via Currie's memoirs.

It was the fate of Blair to occupy a near permanent position in the media spotlight, because he was a relatively youthful, handsome, rather glamorous figure with a pretty wife and young family. It was also a consequence of his open wooing of the media, with photo-shoots and deliberate attempts to exploit media coverage. His speech on the death of Princess Diana, in which he found words to express the nation's grief, raised Blair above the partisan and made him something of a national spokesman and his family a model to which the nation looked for some kind of guidance or at least example – hence the criticism when his behaviour appeared to fall below the expected level.

How do prime ministerial styles of governing differ?

Every person is unique, so it follows that a contrast of styles is found in the various postwar Prime Ministers. A selection is made below to illustrate.

Clement Attlee
Clement Attlee was a public-school-educated Oxbridge graduate who fought in World War I and rose to become a major. He went on to become leader of the Labour Party, almost by default, and by a somewhat similar process became Deputy Prime Minister to Churchill during the war. While Winston indulged in colourful rhetoric and caused Cabinet meetings to drag on, Attlee, when chairing Cabinet in Churchill's absence, provided a complete contrast, ticking off agenda items with military efficiency. This provided the template for his conduct as Prime Minister after 1945. The various items in Labour's 1945 manifesto were ticked off the list one by one until almost all were fulfilled: nationalisation, the National Health Service, independence for India and so forth. After four years in office he was able to indicate how most of the pledges had been achieved. In Cabinet he was rather devoid of charisma but very brusque and businesslike. One unfortunate minister whom Attlee sacked was summoned into Attlee's office to be told the sad news. After the minister entered, Attlee continued writing something but noticed his former minister was still there, waiting. 'Might I ask why my services are no longer required?' he stammered. Attlee seemed surprised by the question: 'Oh, you're no good.'

Harold Macmillan
Macmillan offered a great contrast. He was given to more reflective exposition than Attlee, though much less so than Churchill. He was subtle and

diplomatic, eliciting opinion, leading the debate and then drawing conclusions which reflected the weight of agreement.

Margaret Thatcher

Thatcher was quintessentially a one-off. Early in the 1970s she herself did not think she would see a woman Prime Minister in her lifetime. But she realised that her convictions coincided with a time of crisis which made her views highly relevant. Rallying the right wing to her standard, she exploited the dire difficulties of Callaghan's Labour government and came to power in 1979. Her early years proved difficult and rebellions against her tough line on withdrawing government funding for ailing industries, reducing over-staffing and curbing the power of the unions made enemies in her own party let alone the Labour movement.

The big switch occurred when she led the nation to war against Argentina over the Falkland Islands. Tempered by the drama of that conflict and its need for considerable steadiness of nerve, she emerged with her reputation hugely enhanced. It was a brave or reckless colleague who challenged the mighty war leader, Thatcher, from the middle of the 1980s onwards.

She tended not to be a good chairperson in the accepted sense. She found it hard not to lead with her own opinions, daring other Cabinet members to disagree with her. She was always amazingly well briefed on issues led by other colleagues and could be ruthless if errors were made. She was determined to be the boss of her Cabinet and brooked no opposition. The slightest disloyalty was noted and the offender often reshuffled in quick time.

She was also capable of being crushingly dismissive – as she was repeatedly to Geoffrey Howe, who took his mistreatment calmly until November 1990, when he decided he could take no more and delivered the resignation speech which eventually sent her on her way out of Number 10. So her imperious style in Cabinet eventually became an issue in itself, which contributed to her demise. Another aspect of her style which annoyed her colleagues was her habit of seeing ministers and civil servants plus advisers in small groups out of Cabinet to agree policy in advance – Cabinets sometime found themselves faced with *faits accomplis* with no discussion allowed on matters she had already decided to sort out in her own way.

John Major

Following the formidably controlling Thatcher, it was inevitable that Major should occupy a less assertive role as Prime Minister. Perhaps it was also part of his nature to consult and invite comment before making decisions in Cabinet but these characteristics became features of his period in power. At first he won plaudits for being more collegiate and democratic than his predecessor, but this changed once his government hit troubled times. He began his 1992 ministry with a majority of only twenty-one and when around a dozen of his party, egged on by the retired Thatcher, began to rebel over the issue of Europe, Major's government began to wobble. When several members of his Cabinet virtually echoed this Euro-sceptical opposition, his inclusive style suddenly began to seem not democratic but weak and easily deflected. This impression gradually grew during the middle of the 1990s and, shortly before his defeat in 1997, even his former colleagues were, with little justification, dismissing his leadership skills as non-existent.

Tony Blair

From the start, Blair's style of government was more informal than that under previous Prime Ministers – in Cabinet, everyone was on first name terms, for example – but was also tightly centralised and controlled and the accusation of 'control freak' was soon made. More so even than Thatcher, Blair was impatient with formal structures and wished to cut through to the result he wanted. Consequently, he reduced the number of Cabinet meetings and shortened their typical length from a couple of hours or so to little more than an hour or even 30 minutes. Moreover, Cabinet became more of a reporting forum rather than a debating one. The habit of circulating prepared papers on key issues tended to be sidelined and Blair put into practice the style for which he became notorious – 'sofa' government. This entailed the Prime Minister, plus his press secretary, maybe another minister or two and a couple of civil servants sitting in conclave to sort out issues, often without any formal minute of the meeting being taken. In his report of 2004 (on the decision to go to war with Iraq), Robin Butler issued a magisterial rebuke, since repeated in public several times:

> However, we are concerned that the informality and circumscribed character
> of the Government's procedures which we saw in the content of policy-making
> towards Iraq risks reducing the scope for informed collective political judge-
> ment. (p. 160)

Blair also used his political aides to help make policy (for example, Jonathan Powell over Northern Ireland).

It is often noted that more traditional Prime Ministers tend to follow the more powerful, innovative ones – hence Major followed Thatcher – but the impact of Thatcher and Blair may well have transformed the office and raised it to another level of power and influence. After Blair, it is quite possible that a more formal style was reintroduced by Brown but the pattern of a high-profile Prime Minister, constantly in the eye of the media and manipulating this fact for the government's ends, is likely to become a permanent feature. Certainly Brown aspired and appeared to be more traditional, though there was often criticism that he too had made policy independently, for example his proposals on MPs' expenses in April 2009.

Prime Minister or President?

As the power of Prime Minister has increased, a number of academics have perceived the evolution of the office into something much more like a presidency:

- making decisions individually, or in small groups, or with unelected aides rather than in Cabinet, as traditionally;
- being the centre of the media spotlight at all times (including family members);
- being so dominant in Cabinet that other members defer to what is believed to be the Prime Minister's judgement (as in the case of the Millennium Dome, when the Cabinet did 'what Tony wants' even though he had left the meeting and several members were opposed);
- usurping the role of the monarch as the head of state, above party (Thatcher used to visit the injured in hospital and Blair delivered the speech on the death of Princess Diana, which many would have thought more appropriate coming from the Queen);
- having a substantial body of advisers (Number 10 staff plus the Cabinet Office now amounts to a virtual Prime Minister's Department, not unlike, though smaller than, the White House staff);
- jetting around the world, performing an international rather than national role (Blair seemed to relish this part of being Prime Minister and received much criticism for neglecting home affairs).

Against this it can be argued that:

- Prime Ministers are the leaders of their parties and are elected via them, not individually and for a fixed term as in the United States.
- If a premier's party loses faith in him or her, then all is lost, while a US President can serve out a term with impunity (Blair, for example, was virtually forced out before his term was up, as a result of party pressures).
- The Prime Minister is ultimately subject to party and Cabinet accountability. Thatcher was challenged for the leadership in 1990 and was eventually forced out when her Cabinet refused to support her. She condemned this as 'treachery' but it can be argued that it was merely the checks in the system making themselves felt.

The office of Prime Minister is substantially different from a presidency – at least a US one – in terms of constitutional arrangements, but it is a flexible institution and tends to accrete power, depending on who is in office and what they wish to achieve. Premiers like Callaghan and Major were relatively traditional in their perceptions, chairing Cabinet, circulating papers and accepting the majority view. However, Thatcher took the idea of Prime Minister to another level and, especially after her Falklands victory, seemed to evolve into a 'super' version of Number 10's incumbent, or even a president. Blair, too, followed the same road, elevating himself above party and acquiring a distinctly presidential style. In his book *The Hubris Syndrome* (2007), Lord Owen suggests that both politicians had succumbed to a 'syndrome' or form of 'illness' whereby they believed their judgement superior to that of all others, even close advisers. He argues that Blair effectively undermined the system of Cabinet government and substituted personal rule, especially on foreign affairs.

Deputy Prime Minister

There is no constitutional basis for this post but several Prime Ministers have found it useful to invent it, usually for party political reasons. Geoffrey Howe was made Deputy Prime Minister in 1989, though this was possibly to compensate him losing his beloved Foreign Office. Michael Heseltine was also so elevated, though probably as a reward for supporting Major during his 1995 're-election' episode. John Prescott, as Blair's Deputy, was seen as the key link with 'Old Labour' and the unions but he was also given his own department with a range of planning and local government functions. There are no established functions, however, as the post does not officially exist unless called into being by the Prime Minister. In the event of a Prime Minister dying, the Deputy would take over until a new premier was elected.

The core executive

What is meant by the 'core executive'?

This term has become popular in recent years as a more accurate description of how decisions are made at the centre of government. Moran (2005) considers it an improvement on the more traditional 'pyramidal' notion of the Prime Minister and senior ministers at the top, applying downward democratic control over the government machine and guiding it in desired directions. Moran observes that, at the top level, the distinction between administration and policy is not really relevant: politicians and mandarins confer on virtually an equal basis. Moran also dismisses the idea that departments are similarly pyramidal. He sees them rather as 'a series of tribes', with their own recognised territory, cultures and policies. The Treasury is clearly the dominant tribe, as it controls the flows of finance on which government depends. Often, government at the highest level involves bargaining between the tribes.

Moran discerns four characteristics of the core executive:

- It removes the policy/administration distinction, as explained above.
- It emphasises interdependence and coordination. Policies stream into Number 10 from the departments and they have to be reconciled so that

they do not conflict and can be made to appear to be part of an overall drive in a given direction – usually the main lines of the election manifesto.

- It also emphasises roles rather than structures. Members of the core executive will have multiple roles and so may slip into its inner workings and then out, perhaps to attend to departmental business. Mere structures will not explain a great deal about the workings of government; roles explain more.
- It focuses on decisions. The members of the core executive are engaged in managing events and a stream of often conflicting policies. There are no fixed boundaries, as developments in politics happen so quickly that resources have to be suddenly focused to deal with what are often unforeseen problems – for example, the abduction of the BBC's Gaza correspondent Alan Johnston in the spring of 2007 and the substantial outcry which resulted from the Corporation and from media sources all over the world.

What does the core executive comprise?

It comprises a collection of policy-making units and 'actors' at the centre of government (Figure 13.1). (Most have been detailed earlier in this chapter.)

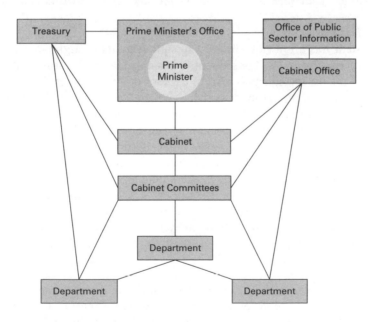

The core executive

Figure 13.1 *The wiring of the core executive*
Source: Michael Moran, *Politics and Governance in the UK* (Palgrave Macmillan, 2005), p. 118, figure 7.1.

- Prime Minister's Office and related units – the Prime Minister's Parliamentary Private Secretary, Chief of Staff, foreign policy adviser, EU adviser, Forward Strategy Unit, Director of Communications and Strategy, Office of Public Service Reform, Delivery Unit. Prime Ministers regularly tweak this machinery, creating and merging units as the need arises.
- Cabinet.
- Cabinet Office.
- Cabinet Secretary.
- Cabinet committees.
- Departmental heads. The permanent secretaries of government departments are also included in the network called the core executive; they will spend much of their time within their departments but will be drawn into the 'core' from time to time according to the topic and the unfolding of events.

How is the core executive's policy presented?

Presentation is an essential part of government; some critics of Tony Blair argued that he saw it as most, sometimes *all* of government, rather than a mere aspect. We can judge only on the basis of what we know and how we come to know things about politics is therefore a contested area, sometimes bitterly so.

Regular briefings
Government has an obvious interest in signalling its thoughts to the public on a very regular basis. Consequently, briefing is more or less continuous. Teams of media specialists (partisan experts or 'spin doctors') now organise this aspect of government activity, which had formerly been done by government information officers. The personnel within the core executive associated with directing press relations have tended to have a relatively high profile, especially Thatcher's press secretary, Bernard Ingham, then Labour's Communication Director Peter Mandelson and finally the most powerful of them all, Alastair Campbell, Tony Blair's media chief and highly influential guru (often called ironically the 'Deputy PM'). Briefings used to be secretive and 'off the record' but are now more open and attributable, with the Prime Minister holding a monthly press conference and agreeing to be questioned by a committee comprising the chairs of all the select committees.

Print journalism
This is less important than television but still has a great role in terms of setting the political agenda and feeding in crucial information. Core executive media operatives ensure they know the editors of the national newspapers so that influence can be applied more effectively. It is also the case that newspaper personnel are often recruited into government – witness Campbell himself and the 2007 appointment of Ian Coulson, former editor of the *News of the World*, as David Cameron's media chief.

Broadcasting

The broadcast media are used a great deal by members of the core executive to convey their messages, defend the government when attacked and generally to advance its solidity and competence. The Prime Minister's Press Secretary will be on first-name terms with all the main news editors of television companies and constantly on the phone to seek slots whereby trusted ministers can be allowed to speak on news bulletins or current affairs shows. Often, if the government is feeling vulnerable on a topic, broadcasters will not be able to persuade ministers to come and speak; this risks appearing shifty at best or at worst allowing the opposition an open goal.

References

Butler, R. (chairman) (2004) *Review of Intelligence on Weapons of Mass Destruction: Report of a Committee of Privy Councillors*, The Stationery Office.

Moran, M. (2005) *Politics and Governance in the UK*, Palgrave: chapter 7.

Owen, D. (2007) *The Hubris Syndrome: Bush, Blair and the Intoxication of Power*, Politicos.

Whitely P. and Seyd, P. (2002) *High-Intensity Participation: The Dynamics of Party Activism in Britain*, University of Michigan Press.

Recommended reading

Jones, B., *et al.* (2007) *Politics UK* (6th edition), Pearson: chapter 19.

Kavanagh, D., *et al.* (2006) *British Politics* (5th edition), Oxford University Press: chapter 11.

Kingdom, J. (2003) *Government and Politics in Britain: An Introduction* (3rd edition), Polity: chapter 14.

Leach, R., *et al.* (2006) *British Politics*, Palgrave: chapter 11.

Moran, M. (2005) *Politics and Governance in the UK*, Palgrave: chapter 7.

Other texts

Foley, M. (2000) *The British Presidency*, Manchester University Press.

Hennessey, P. (1986) *Cabinet*, Blackwell.

James, S. (1999) *British Cabinet Government*, Routledge.

Kavanagh, D. and Seldon, A. (1999) *The Powers Behind the Prime Minister*, Harper Collins.

King, A. (ed 1985) *The British Prime Minister*, Macmillan.

Mackintosh, J. M. (1962) *Cabinet Government*, Stevens.

Seldon, A. (2005) *Blair*, Little, Brown.

Seldon, A. (2007) *Blair Unbound*, Simon and Schuster.

Smith, M. (1999) *The Core Executive in Britain*, Palgrave.

Websites

Cabinet Office, www.cabinetoffice.gov.uk.

Number 10 (official site of the Prime Minister's Office), www.number-10.gov.uk.

14

The executive II:
ministers and the civil service

Ministers

While Cabinet members discuss matters of high policy, back in their departments they deal with more bread-and-butter matters – day-to-day administration, devising new policy to meet new challenges, meeting targets and the like. Cabinet ministers usually have a team of junior ministers to assist them (see below) and all ministers have usually one or two advisers plus armies of civil servants.

Legally, a minister is very important in British government; as Norton points out (2006, p. 514), it is in the minister's name that authority is granted by an Act of Parliament. Ministers are also crucial within the theory of democracy, in that they are the voters' representatives in controlling government (see below). Senior ministers will usually be called Secretaries of State, after the original single Secretary of State (so named at the end of Elizabeth I's reign) appointed to serve the monarch.

Big departments are headed up by Cabinet ministers but they are almost always supported by a team of junior ministers. For example, in August 2007 the Secretary of State for Defence was Des Browne. He was assisted by: Minister of State for the Armed Forces, Bob Ainsworth MP; Minister of State for Defence Procurement and Support (promoted to Secretary of State in June 2009), Lord Drayson; and Under-Secretary of State for Defence and War Veterans, Stephen Twigg MP. At the Department for Children, Schools and Families, Cabinet representation was provided by Ed Balls, with: Jim Knight MP, Minister of State for Schools and Learners; Beverley Hughes MP, Minister of State for Children, Young People and Families; Lord Adonis, Parliamentary Under-Secretary of State for Schools and Learners (promoted to Cabinet in charge of transport in June 2009); and Kevin Barron, Parliamentary Under-Secretary of State for Children, Young People and Families.

This reveals that: members of the Lords are often given junior ministerial briefs (Adonis is a noted educational specialist but Drayson was a businessman before being given a peerage by Tony Blair, a few months after giving Labour half a million pounds); junior ministers usually take care of a specific area of departmental business; and there are two main grades of junior minister – Minister of State and Parliamentary Under-Secretary. In addition, there is the unpaid role of Parliamentary Private Secretary (PPS), when MPs become, in effect, aides to ministers, acting as a conduit for backbench contact with the minister – very important for any ambitious minister who wants to maximise support within the party – and learning the ropes and gaining the first rung on the ministerial promotion ladder. That first step is often made through personal contacts with a more senior minister (whose personal grouping the MP has joined).

Junior ministers are usually keen to become senior ministers. Promotion is likely to depend on them showing their paces, usually in the Commons, by: demonstrating expertise in the business of their department; speaking well in debates and committees; and, when required, defending and advancing the department's cause via the media.

Very rarely are ministers appointed directly into the Cabinet, unless a party has long been in opposition, like Labour in 1945, 1964 and 1997. Usually, there is a period of apprenticeship and it could be that an MP will never make it beyond junior minister but will return to the backbenches after two or three years. Often such reshuffles cause resentment (because they will always involve sackings) and the ranks of former ministers in the government party often provide fertile ground for rebellions and plots of various kinds. It is possible, however, for sacked ministers to retain loyalty, keep working for the party and be given office again: Harriet Harman was a good case in point in Labour governments after 1997, and Mike O'Brien another.

A typology of senior ministers

Philip Norton (2006) has discerned five types of senior ministers, based on a 2000 study:

1 *Team player.* This type of minister prefers collective decision-making and being part of a team; few ministers fall into this category.
2 *Commander.* These are ministers who enter office with a clear idea of what they wish to achieve and set about doing so.
3 *Ideologue.* This is someone who is driven by a clear philosophical vision of what they want to achieve. Examples include Thatcherites Sir Keith Joseph and Nicholas Ridley.
4 *Manager.* This kind of minister is not driven by anything in particular but merely wishes to do a decent job for the party, weighing the evidence and taking balanced decisions. Norton identifies Douglas Hurd in Conservative Cabinets and Margaret Beckett in Labour ones.
5 *Agent.* There are two subtypes of 'agent' minister. 'Prime ministerial' are those the Prime Minister places in post for a specific purpose, for example

Andrew Adonis to look after the 'Academy Programme' or Alan Johnson to resolve employee problems in the National Health Service in 2007. The 'civil service' kind of 'agent' minister merely accedes to the will of the department – what Gerald Kaufman, in a masterful little book, calls, perhaps unimaginatively, 'departmentalitis' (Kaufman, 1980). Senior civil servants are clever and persuasive and it is not difficult for some ministers to passively accept the advice and become, in effect, an 'agent' for departmental interests.

Ministerial responsibility

It is a fundamental of the British constitution that ministers are individually responsible to Parliament for the work of their department. (Historically, responsibility was to the monarch but when Parliament moved into the ascendant, so did the location of the responsibility.) In theory, this means that a minister carries responsibility for every aspect of the department, whether he or she knows about it or not. Civil servants, on the other hand, do not carry that burden and they can to some extent 'hide' behind their minister. The price they pay is that they become anonymous, politically neutral and without publicly expressed opinions: by convention, they do not speak of anything relating to their advisory work with ministers and recognise a professional vow of silence on such matters. In this way there is an elected minister to answer to the people via Parliament for every aspect of government activity. It follows that civil servants who have achieved unusual success often have to stand back and watch the minister take all the credit; alternatively, they can take a back seat when things go wrong and leave it to the minister to stand up to the consequent slings and arrows. However, civil servants do not wholly escape adverse consequences when they mess up: they can expect their careers to suffer at the very least.

The doctrine is arguably not as sternly recognised now as it was in the past. Huge administrative catastrophes occurred during Blair's years in power, from debacles with the introduction of information technology to prisoners being released into the community who should have been deported, but no one resigned and no civil servant was held up as responsible. Furthermore, the civil service 'omerta' seems to have diminished or even disappeared, with former ambassadors, like Christopher Meyer, writing memoirs which gave accounts of highly confidential meetings between British ministers and US officials, not to mention diaries being published by former Number 10 aides like Alastair Campbell.

Civil service

This began in the form of the secretariats, various offices of the crown set up during the Middle Ages. As the British Empire and trade began to expand in the eighteenth century, the secretariats expanded into offices with several employees. Often employment was established via contacts, through patronage or by straightforward purchase by the employee. During the eighteenth century, the use of influence to acquire government 'sinecures' was a well established means of raising income by the upper and middle classes. By the nineteenth century, the system was not 'fit for purpose' (to use the phrase used by John Reid in May 2006 to describe the Home Office when he was appointed to run it). However, in 1806 the East India Company, which had virtually colonised India for Britain, did something unorthodox for the age: it set up a training college for its employees. This was the result of a recommendation by someone who had worked in China and had observed the methods of training used there for public servants. This meritocratic model influenced the historic Northcote-Trevelyan report into the civil service.

Northcote-Trevelyan report, 1854

This report, which came some time after the need for good administration had been recognised as crucial, advocated a politically neutral service with appointments made on merit, with a clear distinction made between 'administrative' staff, who advised ministers and implemented decisions, and routine, 'mechanical' employees, who served their superiors in a variety of ways. The Civil Service Commission was set up in 1855 to provide for recruitment and put an end to the debilitating practice of patronage. For 100 years this system served the government well, with British civil servants – frequently called 'mandarins' because of the Chinese connection – gaining a worldwide reputation for competence, hard work and political neutrality. In practice, there were three grades in the civil service: an administrative 'officer' class to advise ministers and provide the elite; an executive 'NCO' class to do the everyday tasks; and a clerical 'other ranks' class to do the really boring jobs. (Table 14.1 sets out the senior rankings of civil servants.) Yet the military-style caste system worked reasonably well, with not much informality between classes but provision for 'class to class' promotion for those with genuine talent. Strains began to appear, however, by the middle of the twentieth century.

Fulton report, 1968

The service had been criticised for being too 'generalist'; the Treasury, for example, had only nineteen trained economists in 1963. It was also felt that the mandarins were recruited from too narrow a middle-class base (typically educated at public school, Oxbridge – only 3% of the administrative class were working class in the 1960s), making them remote from the everyday life of the nation they were helping to govern. Comparisons were made with France's famous Ecole Nationale d'Administration (ENA), which produced specialist

Table 14.1 *Senior grades in the civil service*

Very old title	Old title	Now often known as:
Cabinet Secretary and Head of the civil service		
Permanent Secretary – permanent head of a government department		
Deputy Secretary	Grade 2	Director General
Under-Secretary	Grade 3	Director
Assistant-Secretary	Grade 5	Director or assistant director
Senior principal and principal	Grades 6 and 7	Deputy director, assistant director, team leader, policy manager etc.

Table 14.2 *Principal central departments, 2009*

Departments	Ministries	Offices	Others
Education and Employment	Agriculture	Cabinet	HM Treasury (includes Her Majesty's Revenue and Customs)
Environment	Defence	Foreign and Commonwealth	
Health		Home	
Lord Chancellor's		Northern Ireland	
National Heritage		Scottish	
Social Security		Welsh	
Trade and Industry			
Transport			

administrators rather than generalists. In theory, the generalists, with their degree in classics, PPE (philosophy, politics and economics) or history from Oxbridge could do any job in government.

Fulton reformed this caste system and set up a Civil Service College (now known as the National School of Government), as well as the Central Policy Review Staff (known as Number 10's 'think-tank') to advise the Prime Minister. However, Fulton's other 150 or so recommendations were either ignored or squashed by senior mandarins, worried that their traditional arm lock on ministerial advice might be broken.

Reform during the Thatcher era

After 1979, the Conservatives under their charismatic female Prime Minister began to wield their new broom. They believed civil servants tended to support the postwar consensus (built around a mixed economy and the welfare state) and to automatically defend their bureaucratic empires as well as extend them. So Thatcher set about reducing their number, from 732,000 to 594,000 by 1986. She also famously believed the private sector to be efficient and the public sector not. So she appointed former businessmen to help reform the public service. For example, Derek Raynor from Marks and Spencer was invited to set up and run an Efficiency Unit; in the Ministry of Defence Michael Heseltine pioneered his MINIS system, a kind of corporate and business planning method which was copied by many other ministries. And Sir Robin Ibbs – formerly of ICI – produced the *Next Steps* report in 1988. This last was something of a revolution, as it effectively separated routine civil service functions from the more cerebral business of advising ministers. Within a few years, scores of 'executive agencies' were set up, on the lines of the Driver and Vehicle Licensing Agency in Swansea, the Benefits Agency and the Training Agency. By 1997, about 80% of all civil servants were employed in some 200 such agencies. Tony Blair accepted the philosophy of the agencies and set up a few of his own but did not solve the problem which many critics noted – their lack of accountability, positioned as they were at arm's length from ministers in Whitehall and far away from parliamentary scrutiny.

Privatisation

Thatcher was determined to reduce the size of the public sector and the number of civil servants it employed; her prime target was the nationalised industries. First up for treatment was British Telecom, in 1984. This was originally the General Post Office but it converted into a public corporation before being floated on the Stock Exchange with great success and considerable profit to the government. Critics who said such a process was tantamount to selling something back to the person who owned it, or to 'selling off the family silver' as former Prime Minister Harold Macmillan (then Lord Stockton) put it, were ignored as the bonanza for the Treasury continued: coal, gas, steel, forestry, electricity, water and (the ill-fated) railways. By the mid-1990s, virtually all the enterprises nationalised after the war were back in private hands, at huge financial benefit to the Exchequer. While criticisms continued, the consensus on both sides of the political divide was that the return to the private sector had reduced costs to the taxpayer, raised money for the public purse, improved efficiency and helped spread share ownership. Significantly, Blair did not reverse privatisations as Labour had promised each time they occurred.

Reform of the civil service under New Labour

Blair tended to adopt most of the practices and precepts of his predecessors, for example executive agencies and the notion that the private sector was better. Consequently, huge sums were given to consultants to advise and sometimes run innovations, and private firms were brought in to run major new information technology projects, like the US firm EDS, which now directs most of the new projects and is responsible, according to critics, for the relative failure of many of them.

Civil service personnel

The senior civil service (Table 14.1, p. 152) is reckoned to number over 3,000 officials, all helping to run the departments of state.

Permanent Secretary

This person is at the head of the departmental hierarchy. Usually, the Permanent Secretary will be a career official and will have spent all of that career in one department, with possible periods in the Cabinet Office if spotted as a high-flyer. Kevin Theakston's 1995 study of Permanent Secretaries revealed a group predominantly privately and then Oxbridge educated; contrary to the spirit of Fulton, most were generalists rather than specialists.

A Permanent Secretary acts as the top manager of a huge enterprise, often with thousands of employees (the Ministry of Defence, for example, employs some 40,000 people), and answers directly to the minister. However, the Permanent Secretary is also answerable directly to Parliament via the Public Accounts Committee, which ensures that money voted to the department by Parliament has been spent appropriately.

Gender balance and open competition

Few women are found in the very highest reaches of the service, possibly because time out for children hinders their ascent through the ranks. However, in recent decades more women have been recruited and so will soon feature among in the topmost positions; already in 2005 the figure of nearly 30% women had improved on the 18% in 1999.

As Norton points out (2006, p. 520), almost a third of senior positions are now open to public competition from people outside the civil service – from jobs in industry or elsewhere in the public sector; this is especially true for the heads of executive agencies.

There has also been a new emphasis on managerial expertise – assisted by the Centre for Policy and Management Studies – and a more flexible approach to advising ministers, with a wider range of advice than that previously provided by tight cabals of senior mandarins.

Political advisers

This group – outside the official civil service – became very controversial during the Blair years. Advisers to premiers and ministers have always existed in one form or another, but began to be appointed more frequently during the 1970s, when Jack Straw was attached to Barbara Castle and Bernard Donoughue to Harold Wilson and then Jim Callaghan. Margaret Thatcher was keen on eliciting advice from confidants like right-wing journalists Woodrow Wyatt and Simon Heffer. Major employed thirty-two advisers when in power. Blair outdid this easily, appointing seventy-eight during his time in Number 10, including his Chief of Staff, Jonathan Powell, and his formidable spin doctor, Alastair Campbell, to both of whom he gave authority – via the device of Orders in Council – over civil servants. Robin Butler, former Cabinet Secretary, was especially displeased by this arrangement. When the Blair era ended, one of Gordon Brown's first actions was to rescind this particular Order in Council, suggesting he was about to revert to a more traditional style of governing (it is generally believed he did not).

Many of these advisers entered politics as researchers to politicians or were childhood friends, as Anji Hunter was of Tony Blair. Many also had political ambitions; for example, after the 2001 election, David Miliband, James Purnell and Andy Burnham all gave up their adviser jobs and became MPs and later ministers. Andrew Adonis followed sometime later via the House of Lords.

Who makes policy – minister or civil servant?

This is a traditional question in political science and, as with all complex problems, the answer is not straightforward.

Ministers have the authority to make decisions but it is easy to believe the plot of the hugely successful sit-com *Yes Minister*, that naïve, *temporary*

Box 14.1 Civil servants and ministers: how they attempt to get their own way

David Blunkett, three times a Cabinet minister in Blair governments, published his diaries in 2006. In them, he describes how civil servants brief ministers in such a way that the course they favour is adopted:

March 2002
The civil service has a particular line that they've developed well over the years.
First, if they don't want you to do something, they produce the lengthiest, most obscurantist document, with no clear recommendations but in the text itself all of the so-called pluses and minuses, except with the minuses (which avoid them having to do what it is they do not wish to do) highlighted. The second element is to put up costings that make it impossible even to consider arguing with the Treasury, so everything is inflated beyond belief....

Source: David Blunkett, *The Blunkett Tapes* (Bloomsbury, 2006), p. 763. Reproduced with permission.

Box 14.2 The 'generalist' in the civil service

The 1968 Fulton report criticised the tradition of the generalist in the civil service. Unlike the French Ecole Nationale d'Administration (ENA), many senior civil servants (or 'mandarins' as they are called) have been educated in subjects like classics, history or PPE, not economics, statistics or, perhaps most importantly, law. Defenders of the 'generalist' argue that:

- The people recruited are among the cleverest of their generation, coming, as they do, from the best universities.
- Public administration is complex, even unique, and so it is hard to prepare anyone for its demands. Years doing the job are usually thought to be superior to the education in any particular subject years before.
- Ministers themselves are 'generalists', as few have specialised skills. The senior mandarin is therefore the public servant mirror image to the elected minister in charge. Together they decide what is best for the national community.

Against this the following arguments can be made.

- Local government has no problems in vesting authority in specialised architects, planners, engineers and the like. Why should the highest advice to ministers be less expert?
- French officials, with their specialised training, show that it can be worthwhile: the so-called 'enarchs', who graduate from the ENA, are famed for their ability and populate the highest ranks of administration in just about every walk of French public administration.
- There have been so many government failures in terms of information technology disasters, inadequate equipment for soldiers serving abroad and a welter of other incompetence (like the loss of bank details for some 25 million people in autumn 2007), surely, say critics, better-trained civil servants would reduce the depressing catalogue of government failures.

---

ministers (few serve more than two years in a post) are easily outwitted by smooth, devious, *permanent* civil servants (Box 14.1). However, in practice, most of the evidence suggests it does not work that way. In the first place, ministers are usually strong personalities who understand power very well. They will mostly know what they want and will not allow even the most silky-voiced mandarins to lead them astray.

Secondly, civil servants are socialised all their careers to play according to the rules and they are democratic ones: the minister represents the people's will and is the 'master' of the mandarins, however clever and senior they might be. So even if they complain about their minister – which they frequently do – civil servants will usually do everything they can to fulfil their remit within a representative democracy. The only area where civil

servants might resort to delaying tactics and the rest is if civil service interests are involved; this might explain why the recommendations of the Fulton
report (see Box 14.2) were mostly 'kicked into the long grass'. Also, if a minister is constantly undecided, civil servants are tempted to step in, if only to
keep the wheels of the department turning.

Relationships between ministers and civil servants are usually characterised by mutual respect and cooperation. Ministers need to achieve the aims of
the government, and civil servants need to keep their departments running
smoothly and effectively.

Finally, on this vexed question, any minister who cannot impose his or
her will on the departmental staff will not be a minister for long.

Norton (2006) explains in more detail the various theories of minister–
civil servant relationships.

References

Blunkett, D. (2006) *The Blunkett Tapes: My Life in the Bear Pit*, Bloomsbury.
Campbell, A. (2007) *The Blair Years*, Random House.
Kaufman, G. (1980) *How To Be a Minister*, Faber and Faber.
Meyer, C. (2005) *DC Confidential*, Weidenfeld and Nicolson.
Norton, P. (2006) 'Minister's, departments and civil servants', in B. Jones (ed.), *Politics UK*, Pearson Education.

Recommended reading

Jones, B., *et al.* (2007) *Politics UK* (6th edition), Pearson: chapters 20, 21.
Kavanagh, D., *et al.* (2006) *British Politics* (5th edition), Oxford University Press: chapter 12.
Kingdom, J. (2003) *Government and Politics in Britain: An Introduction* (3rd edition), Polity: chapter 15.
Leach, R., *et al.* (2006) *British Politics*, Palgrave: chapter 12.
Moran, M. (2005) *Politics and Governance in the UK*, Palgrave: chapter 8.

Other texts

Barberis, P. (ed.) (1997) *The Civil Service in an Era of Change*, Dartmouth
Barnett, J. (1982) *Inside the Treasury*, Deutsch.
Brazier, R. (1997) *Ministers of the Crown*, Clarendon.
Burnham, J. and Pyper, R. (2008) *Britain's Modernised Civil Service*, Palgrave.
Hennessey, P. (2001) *Whitehall*, Pimlico.
Hurd, D. (2003) *Memoirs*, Little Brown.
Kaufman, G. (1997) *How To Be a Minister*, Faber.
Lawson, N. (1992) *The View from Number 11*, Bantam.

Pyper, R. (1995) *The British Civil Service*, Prentice Hall.
Rhodes, R. (1997) *Understanding Governance*, Open University Press.
Theakston K. (1995) *The Civil Service Since 1945*, Blackwell.

Websites

Cabinet Office, civil service reform, www.cabinetoffice.gov.uk/civil_service_reform.aspx.
Civil service, www.civilservice.gov.uk.
National School of Government, www.nationalschool.gov.uk/index.asp.

15

The media in British politics I: the 'mainstream' media

The role of the media in modern politics is one of the most discussed and contested topics in democratic debate. This chapter examines the provenance of political communication and the ways in which it currently impacts on the political system. The media may not initiate specific measures but they help create the atmosphere, or 'political culture' (Chapter 5), in which such things can happen.

What are the media?

'The media' is a collective term for all of the various means of communicating information. There are many kinds of media and their relative importance has varied over time. The most important currently (the 'mainstream' media) are the newspapers, radio and television, and these are what most people would understand by the term. However, there are other media. Authors like Charles Dickens in the nineteenth century helped awaken the British middle classes to the evils of poverty and John Steinbeck's book *The Grapes of Wrath* drew dramatic attention to the privations of poor families migrating to the American west during the 1930s Depression.

In addition, theatre can carry a powerful political message – witness the left-wing plays of Bertolt Brecht (1898–1956) – and artists, too, can be the vehicle for political messages, as evidenced by the 'socialist realism' approach used in former communist countries.

Film is more obviously suited to delivering a strong message. Politically motivated film-makers are legion. The films of Rainer Werner Fassbinder (1946–82), for example, advanced a generally left-wing critique of German society and Ken Loach (1936–) has done the same for British society.

What impact did printing have on political communication?

Printing presses

The first printing press appeared in China in the eleventh century, invented by Bi Sheng, but in Europe it was the German goldsmith Gutenberg who obliged around 1450. In 1476 William Caxton opened the first press in Britain, where a printing industry was built up around Oxford. Hitherto, books had been hand-copied onto vellum and lavishly illustrated, mostly by monks in monasteries; now several hundred could be reproduced by a handful of people in a matter of a few years or even months. But in an age when religion was married to politics, different versions of the Bible or religious writings could be the source of political tensions. The translation of the Bible into English, for example, encouraged dissident movements like the Lollards in the fourteenth and fifteenth centuries.

A couple of centuries on, pamphlets were a major element in the English Civil War, with both monarchists and parliamentarians disseminating their ideas through this medium. During this time another dissident movement, the Levellers, led by Gerrard Winstanley (1609–76), advocated a form of Christian communism which they sought to advance through preaching, discussion and printed pamphlets.

In the eighteenth century, political ideas underwent a transformation as revolution began to shake the foundations of established regimes throughout Europe. Books and pamphlets abounded, especially among those wishing for change.

Tom Paine (1737–1809) was a great populariser of liberal and revolutionary ideas. His work *Common Sense*, advocating independence for the American colonies, was said to have sold 120,000 copies. Later, he had even greater success with *The Rights of Man*, which helped to support the ideas behind the French Revolution. Indeed, the spread of ideas through publications helped strengthen the movement for democratic reform during the nineteenth century, the Chartist movement in particular benefiting from such early propagandising.

Newspapers

By this time, however, the newspapers – the first appeared in 1605 – were selling daily. *The Times* was founded in 1785 and the first Sunday paper, the *Observer*, in 1791. By the end of the nineteenth century, the mass publication of the story-book 'penny dreadfuls' was accompanied by the popular newspapers: the *Daily Mail* in 1896, the *Daily Express* in 1900, the *Daily Mirror* in 1903 and the *Daily Sketch* in 1909. As these news-sheets contained political news and editorial opinions, the press emerged as a power to be reckoned with, and became known as the 'fourth estate'.

How important were/are the press barons?

Those energetic entrepreneurs who founded and ran newspapers became almost instantly known as 'press barons' as their political influence began to be reflected in the honours handed out by politicians keen to curry favour with these powerful men. Foremost among them were Lord Beaverbrook (1879–1964) – the Canadian magnate who became an intimate of Churchill – and Lord Northcliffe (Arthur Harmsworth, 1866–1922) and his brother Harold, who became Lord Rothermere (1868–1940). These men became national figures, courted by Prime Ministers and occasionally given jobs in government; for example, Lloyd George gave Northcliffe – often described, by virtue of his newspapers, as 'the most powerful man in Britain' – a job as head of anti-German propaganda in World War I and Beaverbrook served in Churchill's War Cabinet. While indisputably powerful in terms of their own businesses, few press barons, however, ever exercised any major political influence, such as to change things substantially.

Subsequent press magnates have been as important – for example Robert Maxwell (1923–91) and the Canadian Lord Black (1944–) – but the role of the Australian turned American citizen Rupert Murdoch (1931–) probably exceeds in importance any of those mentioned hitherto.

How important is the press in the present day?

The press is declining in influence as circulation figures dip in Britain, as in the United States and other western countries (see Table 15.1). Newspapers saw a one-fifth loss of sales over the period 1990–2002. This is because young people do not seem to be acquiring the habit of reading newspapers regularly. They tend to be bored by politics – witness the low voting turn-out for the younger cohort – or to use new media to obtain their information and comment (see Chapter 16). For this reason, advertisers are now moving their resources to the internet and thus further weakening the power of the press.

But the press still exerts considerable influence, in the following ways.

- It helps set the agenda of what people discuss in the media and this has a bearing on the political climate at any one time. For example, many of the items discussed on Radio 4's *Today* programme take their purchase from the morning papers. (Table 15.2 lists the main political topics covered across the mainstream media in 2001 and 2005.)
- The press helps influence voters considering how to cast their vote, especially over a longer period of time.
- It can inject energy into campaigns. In 1992, for example, the Conservative Party treasurer attributed his party's surprise victory to the vigour and attack of the tabloid press; the *Sun* agreed, leading with the headline, 'It's The Sun Wot Won It'. Other subsequent studies suggested the tabloids had indeed been a major factor in delivering victory to John Major.

Table 15.1 *Circulation (in millions) of national newspapers, 2001 and 2005*

	2001		2005	
	Political leaning	Circulation	Political leaning	Circulation
Daily press				
Guardian	Labour	0.40	Labour	0.34
Independent	Anti-Conservative	0.23	Liberal Democrat	0.23
Times	Labour	0.71	Labour	0.65
Telegraph	Conservative	1.02	Conservative	0.87
Financial Times	Labour	0.49	Labour	0.38
Daily Express	Labour	0.96	Conservative	0.87
Daily Mail	Anti-Labour	2.40	Conservative	2.30
Sun	Labour	3.45	Labour	3.26
Mirror	Labour	2.79	Labour	2.29
Star	Labour	0.60	None	0.85
Sunday press				
Observer	Labour	0.45	Labour	0.42
Independent on Sunday	Anti-Labour landslide	0.25	Liberal Democrat	0.18
Sunday Times	Labour	1.37	Conservative	1.35
Sunday Telegraph	Conservative	0.79	Conservative	0.65
Mail on Sunday	Conservative	2.33	Anti-Labour	2.37
Sunday Express	Labour	0.90	Conservative	0.84
Sunday Mirror	Labour	1.87	Labour	1.53
News of the World	Labour	3.90	Labour	3.64
People	Labour	1.37	Labour	0.94
Star on Sunday	–	–	None	0.46

Source: Guardian, 2 May 2005. © Copyright of Guardian News and Media Ltd 2005, reproduced with permission.

Table 15.2 *The issue agenda: top ten themes in national media coverage, 2001 and 2005*

2001	Prominence (%)	2005	Prominence (%)
Labour	39	Electoral process	44
Europe	9	Political impropriety	8
Health	6	Iraq	8
Politicians' conduct	6	Asylum and immigration	7
Taxation	6	Taxation	5
Crime	4	Health	4
Education	4	Crime	4
Public services	4	Economy	4
Social security	3	Education	3
Other	19	Other	13

Source: Loughborough University Communication Research Centre, *Guardian*, 2 May 2005.
© Copyright of Guardian News and Media Ltd 2005, reproduced with permission.

- The press also exerts influence through its *perceived* strength. The influence of individual newspapers varies immensely but three examples rebut any idea that the press is of no consequence politically. First, Tony Blair was known to believe the *Daily Mail* generally expressed the views of 'Middle England', the voters whom Blair knew he had to attract to deliver New Labour majorities. Consequently, he placed great store by what that paper covered and commented on. Second, Blair also had enormous respect for press magnate Rupert Murdoch. To this end, he agreed to address the staff of the News Corporation in 1997 and shortly afterwards was rewarded by the *Sun's* conversion to his cause. It has even been suggested that Murdoch was a 'silent' member of Blair's Cabinet, in that he could veto any policy – especially on the European Union – to which he felt opposed. Third, in the summer of 2006, newly appointed Home Secretary John Reid was accused of adjusting policy on the hoof in response to tabloid campaigns and even participating in a police raid to pander to them.

How important is radio broadcasting in politics?

Radio was the first broadcast medium and was skilfully exploited by a number of people:

- Adolf Hitler used broadcasts of his speeches to electrify the German nation, especially during the interwar period.
- Stanley Baldwin, the Conservative Prime Minister, used to charm the nation with his 'fireside chats', which managed to make people feel good about themselves during difficult times in the 1930s.

- Franklyn Roosevelt, the US President, also used the radio rather like Baldwin and had a microphone installed in his White House Oval Office.
- Churchill was probably the greatest political exploiter of the medium, utilising his wartime broadcasts to rally the nation in a way which is incalculable but must have been worth several armies of soldiers. (At the same time, Ed Murrow's reports from Blitz-affected London during the war roused sympathy for the beleaguered Brits and helped swing the United States into joining the fight against Hitler.)

In the present day, radio still has an important role to play. BBC's Radio 4 maintains a constant output of news-based programmes, which help inform the station's primarily middle-class, educated audience. Foremost is the *Today* programme, which runs from 6.00 a.m. to 9.00 a.m. every weekday and features nationally known presenters like John Humphrys and James Naughtie. Because it attracts an audience of over a million decision-makers, there is a queue of politicians, pressure group leaders and anyone wishing to influence the news agenda for the day (not to mention the nation's political anoraks). The programme is highly influential and controversial to boot. Margaret Thatcher once famously rang up during the 1980s to interject her own views into one discussion.

How did television develop in relation to politics during the latter part of the twentieth century?

Britain may have been up to a decade behind the United States regarding television, where, as early as 1952, Richard Nixon bought half an hour of television time to clear his name when alleged financial wrong-doing threatened to force him off the vice presidential ticket for the upcoming election. Sweaty, apparently unshaven and pale, Nixon appealed to Republicans to accept that his wife, Pat, had no fur coat but a 'Republican cloth' one. He also said that someone had sent his youngest child a puppy, which they had called Checkers, and that he did not care what 'they' might say, 'we're not going to send it back'. In contrast to the derision with which the politically sophisticated greeted his broadcast, most viewers were moved by this apparently wrongly accused honest man; he received massive support and stayed on the ticket to become Vice President and later President. Politicians all over the world noted how this shamelessly schmaltzy emotional appeal had worked a treat.

In the mid-1950s, British political parties began to use the 'box' to sell their messages. Macmillan even induced President Eisenhower, in August 1959, to stage an apparently relaxed televised conversation with him in order to improve the Conservatives' electoral chances in a few weeks' time. For its part, Labour employed the precocious talents of Anthony Wedgwood (later 'Tony') Benn to incorporate television into its campaign.

By the 1960s, television was becoming essential to parties as the principal vehicle by which their messages were communicated. Party political broadcasts (PPBs) were given free of charge to parties on the basis of their electoral strength – unlike in the United States, where parties with big war-chests could exploit the medium to the limit of their resources. But PPBs were not generally viewed widely or taken seriously; it was more the discussion programmes, interviews and coverage on news bulletins which helped to form voters' image of what was on offer.

During the 1960s, three further developments in television had political significance:

- *Satirical attacks.* Such attacks on politicians became even more a part of British political culture, requiring politicians to handle them with good grace or lose face. *That Was The Week That Was* (*TW3*) was the first major satirical show but there were many others, including the puppet show *Spitting Image* and later the Rory Bremner shows also starring John Bird and John Fortune.
- *The political documentary.* Granada Television created *World in Action* during the 1960s to match the BBC's weekly *Panorama* programme. Both delved into areas of political sensitivity and potential embarrassment and were duly criticised by politicians of both main parties. This was never more the case than during the 1980s, when Thatcher's governments seemed to regard suspicion and criticism of the BBC as a litmus test of Conservative orthodoxy.
- *The confrontational political interview.* Some interviewers eschewed any deference and grilled their 'victims' mercilessly. The progenitor of this style was Robin Day, who moved the tone of interviewing Prime Ministers quickly away from the deferential 'Sir' to a challenging 'Prime Minister!' The major political interview became a feature of political life and the means whereby voters could see policies tested under continuous and well informed interrogation – much more so than in the House of Commons – as well as learning more about their rulers. Day's success and popularity spawned many imitators and the style developed during the latter part of the twentieth century, perhaps reaching its apogee in the person of Jeremy Paxman, the fiercely combative anchor of BBC 2's late-night current affairs flagship, *Newsnight*. Michael Howard, when Home Secretary in May 1997, refused to answer a question on the prison service fourteen times and established Paxman as the man politicians most feared as their interviewer (official papers subsequently revealed that Howard was not guilty of Paxman's accusation). Paxman was later much criticised for unjustifiable intrusion when he insisted on asking Charles Kennedy, leader of the Liberal Democrats, in July 2002, whether he had a drinking problem. Kennedy denied it emphatically, though Paxman's supporters claimed final justification when Kennedy admitted having just such a problem before being forced to stand down as leader in January 2006.

Is aggressive questioning of politicians on television justified?

Occasionally, interviewers do over-reach themselves. Robin Day was frequently taken to task by politicians, but the better debaters among them respected him for his sharpness and forensic skill; Harold Wilson once said he enjoyed the 'swordplay' of an interview with him and Margaret Thatcher clearly had a soft spot for him, despite the tough time he often gave her. Probably the interviewer who is most criticised, even more than Paxman, is John Humphrys of the *Today* programme. Both Tories and Labour have defined a 'Humphrys problem' where arguably none existed except their concern not to be put under too much interrogative pressure. Not for nothing has the Welsh interrogator been compared to a Rottweiler.

Paxman once said that, in the back of his mind, during interviews he held the question posed by a veteran journalist from *The Times*, Louis Heren: 'Why is this lying bastard lying to me?' Many prominent politicians, as well as John Birt, when Director-General of the BBC, expressed reservations over an approach which seemed to assume bad faith from the outset. There can be no doubt that many politicians are genuinely sincere and committed servants of society: unfortunately, they do not always remain so and experience proves that the temptations of political life to further personal interests are hard to resist.

Many argue that an assertive media help to keep politicians on the straight and narrow and make them accountable to the public. As politicians are highly skilled in verbal evasion and plausible explanation, it is argued that a tenacious interviewer not only provides better television but also better serves the ends of democracy.

What are the criteria used by news editors when deciding what to run in their papers or programmes?

It is often suggested that the 'news agenda' for the day is set by the newspapers. This may be a breaking news story resulting from an investigation, a leak or an interview; or it might just reflect a judgement on what deserves a headline in their publications. But what exactly *is* the basis on which items are included or discarded from a newspaper or television or radio programme? Inevitably such criteria reflect the facts that the chief aim of editors is to increase circulation or ratings and that most people are not very interested in the contents let alone the minutiae of politics. Bearing this in mind, it seems fairly clear that 'news values' are something like the following:

- *A focus on personalities.* Voters may have yawned at the details of Conservative disputes over the European Union, but they were glued to their sets when the famously 'grey' John Major launched his 'put up or shut up' fightback against his enemies in July 1995. Further, leadership contests attract much attention – sometimes too much for parties when the fur starts to fly – and interest as personalities are engaged in colourful competition.

- *Revelations regarding transgressions.* While government policy on planning applications will not sell many papers, stories involving scandal – sexual or financial – or politicians who have broken important rules will be more likely to quicken the blood.

- *Violations of the law or social values.* These stories – murders, robberies, muggings of older people – often bedeck tabloid pages as the law-abiding have a fascination with the law-breakers – part righteous indignation, part maybe a bit morbid – and are guaranteed to push boring political stories down the news priority list.

- *Major misfortunes and disasters.* The human psyche, perhaps understand-ably, is fascinated by the dangers which can threaten the human race. We are all concerned to avoid danger but have a perverse interest in those who become its victims. For this reason, accidents, especially those involving famous people like Princess Diana in August 1997, attract a morbid inter-est. It seems to follow that the bigger the scale of the accident, the bigger the interest, hence the wall-to-wall coverage of the tsunami disaster of Boxing Day 2004.

- *Celebrity involvement.* A feature of modern society is a peculiar obsession with famous people. Celebrity gossip comprises substantial sections of both the popular press and specialist magazines like *Hello* and *Heat*. Further, the public extends its obsessive concern to those who want to become famous, hence the coverage given to participants in reality shows like *Big Brother*, in addition to the celebrity variants of reality programmes.

How useful are 'news values' for advancing democratic government?

Probably, not very. Ideally, in a democracy, news broadcasts would contain all the information people need to make judgements on the issues of the day, for example the economy, the European Union, public services and their funding, civil rights and the need to tighten security against terrorists.

The problem with delivering such content is twofold: first, many or even most voters would find it hard to understand such complex issues – after all, skilled economists cannot agree on what would be the nation's best econ-omic policies; and second, most voters prefer entertainment – sport, drama, soaps – to dry current affairs programmes.

How useful are different media in meeting this democratic purpose?

It all depends on the medium and who it is aimed at. Table 15.3 summarises the 'democrativeness' of the main media in Britain today.

Table 15.3 *'Democrativeness' of media elements*

Democratic criteria	Broad-sheets	Tab-loids	BBC radio	Com-mercial radio	BBC tele-vision	Com-mercial television
Easily accessible to target audience	+	+	+	+	+	+
Varied and plentiful	+	+	+	+	+	+
Concentration of ownership	−	−	+	−	+	−
Reliable factually	+	−	+	−	+	+
High-value political content	+	−	0	+	+	−
Tendency to facilitate democracy	+	−	+	+	+	−
Accountability of medium to public	−	−	−	−	−	−
Low bias	0	−	+	+	0	0

+ = high tendency to encourage democracy.
− = low tendency to encourage democracy.
0 = neutral effect (i.e. 0 is given to BBC radio as, apart from Radio 4 and 5 Live, it is largely music-based, and to the broadsheets regarding bias because they tend to give space to alternative opinions).
Source: Extended version of table published in B. Jones, 'Media and government', in R. Pyper and L. Robins (eds), *United Kingdom Governance* (Palgrave Macmillan, 2000). Reproduced with permission.

Printed press

Tabloids
Because they are aimed at less well educated readers (the average reading age of *Sun* readers is calculated at ten years), tabloids tend to contain minimal serious news coverage. Long feature articles on issues like funding the Health Service, or the politics of the Middle East, tend to give way to short, pithy articles on more accessible subjects like resignations and scandals affecting politicians. More often, political news is eschewed altogether in favour of stories about acting or sports celebrities. However, during election campaigns tabloids take sides with great passion and urge readers to vote in a particular way. Their shorter length and written style suit negative stories, where the alleged faults and shortcomings of politicians and their parties are asserted.

Broadsheets
These newspapers take their role seriously and seek to provide readers with as much information about current issues as they can read. Their editorials seek

genuinely to influence decision-makers as well as the mass of voters. By any standard, broadsheet newspapers fulfil the requirements of a mature democracy. But the problem is, as with all serious political education, readers of such newspapers are a minority: fewer than 3 million of the 13 million readers of daily papers and an even smaller proportion of the Sunday papers.

Broadcasting

Radio

Rather like the printed press, radio stations aim at discrete audiences. BBC Radio 1 seeks to satisfy the demand for non-stop popular music, mostly among younger people. News bulletins occur regularly but they are short, are often accompanied by background music, and have a distinct tabloid feel. Commercial radio tends to be even more unhelpful to those who seek information about the issues of the day.

BBC Radio 3 and Radio 4 are the 'serious' channels which embody, more than any other broadcast services, the ideas of John Reith (the famous first Director-General of the BBC) of informing and educating. While Radio 3 concentrates on classical music, Radio 4 offers a rich diet of current affairs, extended news programmes and serious discussions. The target audience is unashamedly middle class and educated; it scores highly as a democratic educator.

Radio 5 Live is a relatively recent addition to the BBC portfolio of radio channels; it offers a mix of sport, news and phone-ins.

Television

BBC 1 and 3 offer a varied programme of entertainment for the broad body of the nation but do include regular national and regional news bulletins, as well as occasional documentaries on current affairs.

BBC 2 and 4 are more serious channels, with more political documentaries and regular programmes like BBC 2's *Newsnight*, the flagship news and discussion programme, sometimes hosted by the formidable interrogator (discussed above) Jeremy Paxman.

The ITV channels vary across the country and aim their products mainly in competition with BBC 1.

Channel 4 is aimed at smaller audiences and has a self-conscious public interest in political programmes, including documentaries and the excellent *Channel 4 News*; on balance, it is an asset to democratic debate.

Rolling news programmes include BBC 24 and Sky News, both high-quality, round-the-clock services which have helped make the news today truly a global, 24-hour industry, able to break news at any time, from any place in the world. These channels are slowly beginning to attract a regular following; they must be good for strengthening democracy.

Recommended reading

Jones, B., *et al.* (2007) *Politics UK* (6th edition), Pearson: chapter 10.
Kavanagh, D., *et al.* (2006) *British Politics* (5th edition), Oxford University Press: chapter 25.
Kingdom, J. (2003) *Government and Politics in Britain: An Introduction* (3rd edition), Polity: chapter 8.
Leach, R., *et al.* (2006) *British Politics*, Palgrave: chapter 9.
Moran, M. (2005) *Politics and Governance in the UK*, Palgrave: chapter 16.

Other texts

Blumler, J. and Gurevitch, M. (1995) *The Crisis in Public Communication*, Routledge.
Blumler, J. and McQuail, D. (1967) *Television in Politics*, Faber.
Bruce, B. (1992) *Images of Power*, Kogan Page.
Chippendale, P. and Orrie, C. (1992) *Stick It Up Your Punter*, Mandarin.
Cockerell, M. (1988) *Live from Number Ten*, Faber.
Franklin, B. (1999) *Tough on Sound-Bites, Tough on the Causes of Sound-Bites*, Catalyst.
Jones, B. (1993) 'The pitiless probing eye: politicians and the broadcast political interview', *Parliamentary Affairs*, January.
Wring, D. and Deacon, D. (2005) 'The election unspun', in A. Geddes and J. Tonge (eds), *Britain Decides*, Palgrave.

Websites

BBC, www.bbc.co.uk.
Economist, www.economist.com.
Guardian, www.guardian.co.uk.
Independent, www.independent.co.uk.
Telegraph, www.telegraph.co.uk.
The Times, www.timesonline.co.uk.

16

The media in British politics II:
influence, bias and the new media

The media have become more complex, with new actors (e.g. spin doctors and marketing people) and a whole new dimension with the internet. This chapter analyses these developments, with brief discussion of bias, voting and language in politics.

How important have advertising agencies become in British politics?

Until the 1970s, neither of the two big parties bothered with advertising in the professional sense. Propagating political messages via the media was thought to be a job for the specialists: politicians. However, the Conservatives began to use advertising agencies in the 1970s under Margaret Thatcher; when the leading firm Saatchi and Saatchi was hired it had a major impact with the 'Labour isn't working' campaign. The Conservatives continued using the agency for several years. In 1983, Labour, used to regarding such things as part of the capitalist system it wished to eradicate, also employed an advertising agency – though to little effect, given the Tory landslide of that year. Michael Foot vetoed one advertisement as overly negative during that campaign and both parties made similar decisions during elections in the 1990s. The 1997 Conservative 'demon eyes' campaign, depicting a satanic-ally masked Blair with burning red eyes, was thought to have been badly received by voters, who felt Blair was anything but satanic. A film during the same campaign showing a Faustian Blair selling his soul to the Devil ('Just *say* you'll not raise taxes' persuades the Devil) in exchange for votes was pulled by John Major, for fear of a similar voter reaction. Marketing experts argue that such attacks will not work if there is no genuine point of purchase in them. Marketing and advertising people – Phillip Gould, Stephen Carter, Steve Hilton – are now regularly employed by the big parties and their participation in elections has become commonplace.

Box 16.1 Personality politics

On 22 January 2007, Lord Roy Hattersley suggested in the *Guardian* that British voters had had their fill of 'personality politics', under Tony Blair, with its spin, extravagance, untruths and superficiality, and that they were now ready for some austere, serious leadership from Gordon Brown. This gives rise to an interesting question:

Why don't many voters take their electoral responsibility more seriously?

- *Political ignorance and apathy.* Most voters are bored by political news and are not motivated to acquire the knowledge needed to create a mature, well functioning democracy. They are not responsive therefore to the messages such 'serious' politicians might send out via the media.
- *Image.* Many, or even most, voters are influenced in their choices by irrational factors like appearance, voice, charm. Politicians who are well briefed are often ignored because their plentiful detail quickly bores voters.
- *Spin.* Given the ignorance of voters and their vulnerability to possibly vacuous charm, it is possible for politicians to win elections on the basis of clever media presentation and manifestos carefully calibrated to meet voters' needs as measured by opinion polls and focus groups. Experience suggests that even though voters are aware that politicians promise unachievable goals, they still seem to fall for the same trick again and again.

The above analysis suggests that we have the worst of two worlds: we have come to view politicians, often unfairly, as duplicitous and self-seeking, yet serious politicians, who might be more likely to deliver what they promise, tend to bore us during election campaigns.

How important have 'spin doctors' become?

Spin doctors are actually probably less important than they are frequently alleged to be by conspiracy theorists, but certainly they now exert substantial influence.

The term 'spin doctor' originated across the Atlantic, when advisers sought to tell the media what their political masters *really* meant to say in their speeches or press conferences. The word 'spin' relates to baseball – though it could as easily apply to cricket – where the pitcher can apply spin to make the ball elude or otherwise confuse the batsman.

Politicians in the United States and, though to a lesser extent, Britain employ staff to assist them in their work and efforts to get re-elected. Some Congressmen have dozens of specialist staff, several of whom might be concerned with dealing with the media, producing press releases, networking with key media personnel, writing articles for the local press on behalf of their boss, advising him or her on media presentation and so forth. In Britain, such large staffs do not exist except for the party leaders, but for them advisers have become of key and controversial importance: Tony Blair had Peter Mandelson and Alastair Campbell while David Cameron currently has Andy Coulson.

Tony Blair and the dominance of spin

Why was Labour under Blair accused of depending too much on 'spin'? Labour's penchant for media management dates back to the 1980s, when the right-wing press regularly made mincemeat of Labour's attempts to convey its messages. Michael Foot, for example, who unexpectedly won the leadership election in 1981, was portrayed as a senile old ideologue with no dress sense nor any leadership ability. Thatcher's press secretary, Bernard Ingham, was effective in centralising the government's media output while Gordon Reece ensured she looked perfect on the television and in addition sounded word perfect. Labour was thrashed in the 1983 election, again in 1987 and more narrowly in 1992. People like Neil Kinnock, not to mention the then rising young MPs Tony Blair and Gordon Brown, felt that, in a twenty-four-hour media world, a slick operation was the basic requirement for any political party seeking to move from opposition into government. Peter Mandelson, Labour's former television producer and formidably well connected Communications Director, was the spearhead of a determined revival of Labour, effected via the media.

Labour's formidable media operation helped deliver the landslide in 1997 but commentators noted that, even after victory, the tight group of advisers – Gould, Campbell, Mandelson – was still closest to the prime ministerial ear. Media sources complained that the government in power was managing them with the same ruthless zeal the party had demonstrated in opposition. Something akin to a cult of personality was created around Tony Blair, based on his good looks, his attractive family, his brilliantly media-friendly personality and his almost occult sense of what the nation was feeling. Nowhere were these qualities better applied than in the aftermath of the death of Princess Diana. Using a phrase coined by Campbell, Blair delivered a moving, apparently extempore speech, mourning 'The People's Princess', which perfectly expressed the mood of the nation. The film *The Queen* (2005) probably exaggerated the extent to which Blair helped the monarchy survive this difficult period, but there can be no doubt that his role was valuable.

The problem with appearing to be so all-conquering was that Blair, after a couple of years, became a target for the media, irritated as it was by the government's tightly controlled spin machine. His mistakes now attracted extended attention and his wife, too, was seen as fair game for newspaper hatchet jobs. The press was delighted therefore to gloat over the memo leaked from Number 10 in April 2000 in which Blair suggested: 'We need two or three eye-catching initiatives that are entirely conventional in terms of their attitude to the family.... I should be personally associated with as much of this as possible.'

Blair's association with 'spin' was by now well established. Writing in March 2003, Thatcher's former Press Secretary, Sir Bernard Ingham, declared that 'spin is everywhere' and that 'Blair has forfeited the trust of the nation'. Certainly, polls indicated that the public did not trust the

---

Box 16.2 Manipulative populism

Writing in the *Observer* on 19 April 2009, Peter Oborne warned of the dangers to democracy of 'celebrity Prime Ministers'. He recalled that Stanley Baldwin and Clem Attlee were Prime Ministers who worked through their ministers – who are the people who actually wield the legal power of government – and Parliament. It followed that the Chief Whip was the person on whom the Prime Minister relied most heavily for support in political battles. But no more: the arrival of the 'celebrity Prime Minister', by which Oborne seemed to mean Tony Blair and by implication Thatcher, has seen the emphasis shift to the chief spin doctor. He illustrates this by reference to the eclipse of the fictional Francis Urquhart – the epicene Chief Whip villain of Dobbs' *House of Cards* – by the fictional Malcolm Tucker, the foul-mouthed hero-villain of Armando Ianucci's *The Thick of It* and the film *In the Loop*:

> All the same blacks arts are at work; however, the battlefield has changed. Urquhart applied himself to parliament, Tucker bypassed the traditional institutions of the state and was only concerned with the media and its other methods of control: access, favouritism, information and the creation of an elite corps of client journalists.

Oborne recalls Brown's 2007 promise:

> [to] bring back cabinet government, respect civil service impartiality, restore the primacy of parliament and to abandon the dark political arts at which the team of political assassins around Blair had so excelled.

However, Brown did none of these things and Cameron's appointment of former *News of the World* editor Andy Coulson as his chief spin doctor suggests there will not be any real change if Cameron heads up a new regime.

Oborne also explains that the elevation of Tucker, Campbell or Coulson is due not necessarily to mere media strategies, but to the new nature of the media. It is now so all-encompassing, such a constant and demanding presence that it has become the instrument of a new kind of politics. Parliament is supposed to be the body which ultimately determines policy and decisions but the media are now so powerful they can apply a range of influences: certainly delays, sometimes vetoes as well as urging courses of action. Oborne cites the vivid phrase coined by Anthony Barnett to describe this new way in which we are governed: 'manipulative populism'.

Prime Minister's word. Even the Speaker of the House of Commons, Michael Martin, weighed in (in January 2003) with criticism of spin doctors, whom he described as 'an absolute nuisance', and former Speaker Betty Boothroyd agreed. Worse was to come.

- Once the war in Iraq was joined, Blair ran into two major credibility problems. First, his claims that 'weapons of mass destruction' were being stored by Saddam Hussein soon looked thin when intensive searches failed to find them. And second, claims that he had made exaggerations within the September 2002 dossier – allegedly based on authoritative military intelligence – in order to persuade Parliament to support the Bush initiative led to the suicide of a respected defence scientist, Dr David Kelly – the alleged source of insider suggestions of Blair's embellishments made to the BBC. There were accusations that the government was to blame and Lord Hutton was called in to investigate. His report exonerated the government but the evidence revealed, to the satisfaction of many, that Number 10 staff had indeed intervened to make the language of the dossier more persuasive.
- Despite the retirement of Alastair Campbell in September 2003, it was well known that he continued to assist Blair (and later Brown) with advice, especially during the campaign for the 2005 general election.

Do the mass media influence voting behaviour?

Clearly, the media must exercise some influence, but the question is, how much?

Some students of the media argue that they do not have a huge influence, as people tend to select those items which fit in with their ideas and tend to forget or overlook those which do not. For example, most readers choose the newspaper which they feel speaks for them, so Conservatives will tend to read the *Daily Telegraph*, as this has loyally supported their political cause for many years. Psephologist David Denver, from Lancaster University, is fond, on this point, of quoting the line from Simon and Garfunkel's song 'The Boxer': 'A man hears what he wants to hear and disregards the rest'.

Some research suggests that media campaigns do not influence voters that much even during elections (the results of which sometimes merely replicate opinion poll party support registered at the beginning of the campaign). In 1992, for instance, 80% of respondents in one poll said they had voted in accordance with their position before the campaign even started.

Nonetheless, even if most people decide how they will vote months before an election, they must have been influenced by information filtered through the mass media. For example, some 4 million voters deserted the Conservatives in 1997 compared with 1992, and at each election key groups, maybe not very numerous overall, decide the outcome. Short-term exposure to an element of the media – say a newspaper – may not decide how someone votes but over time the regular ingestion of news mediated through partisan conduits is bound to have an effect, just as children more often than not end up espousing the same ideas and prejudices as their parents.

Moreover, even though it may seem that support for the parties in a campaign is static, Ivor Crewe has pointed out that, underneath the surface, significant 'churning' is taking place, as people who shift from one party to another are cancelled out by those moving the other way. He calculates that up to 30% of voters can change their voting intention during a campaign.

Why do politicians accuse the media of being biased?

The answer to this question reaches to the heart of what makes politicians the people they are.

- During the 1960s, Harold Wilson liked to say that, while the print press was in the same camp as the Tories, television was 'our' medium (although he was convinced that the BBC was also Conservatively inclined). Maybe both feelings helped to explain his rage in 1971 when a BBC film profile of Labour was broadcast entitled *Yesterday's Men*, in which presenter David Dimbleby asked Wilson how much money he had made out of his memoirs. Wilson was furious and peppered the BBC with complaints.
- During the 1980s, with Margaret Thatcher in power, the Conservatives tended to see the BBC, in the colourful words of Norman Tebbit, as 'that insufferable, smug, sanctimonious, naïve, guilt-ridden, wet, pink, orthodoxy of that sunset home of that third-rate decade, the 1960s'. Tebbit became Thatcher's 'enforcer' regarding the Corporation, applying pressure as election campaigns approached, but the situation reversed once Labour was in power after 1997.
- In 1999, the Conservatives complained loudly when Greg Dyke, a well known Labour donor, was made Director-General of the BBC. It was inevitable perhaps that, with a government so obsessed with presentation, even a Labour inclined Director-General should fall out with the party leadership. Following David Kelly's suicide (see above), the Hutton report into the incident blamed the BBC for inadequate journalism and Dyke eventually and reluctantly had to resign.
- One target, already mentioned, who attracted fire from both parties, was John Humphrys, presenter of Radio 4's *Today* programme. His relentless forensic style proved problematic for both Thatcher and Blair.
- The problem with politicians is that they tend to think they are always right and that people who fail to agree with them may be biased against them. As a result, they have a natural desire to exert control over the means whereby voters receive their information: via the media. Thatcher once said she would like to have four hours of airtime on her own to get

---

Box 16.3 How accurate is John Lloyd's critique of the media?

An influential critique of the media was made by John Lloyd in *What the Media Are Doing to Our Politics* (2004). Lloyd, himself a journalist on broadsheet newspapers, argued that the media have 'decided that politics is a dirty game, played by devious people who tell an essentially false narrative about the world and thus deceive the British people'. In support of his thesis, Lloyd points to the aggressive interviewing techniques which assume politicians are dissembling liars.

Tony Wright, MP, chair of the Public Administration Select Committee, argued (*Guardian*, 10 October 2005) that the media should accept some responsibility for the 'culture of contempt', which had contributed to a collapse of trust in politics and politicians. The late Anthony Sampson, reviewing a number of other contributors on Lloyd's argument, concluded that most felt he was right and that many distinguished people 'felt genuine anguish ... at being misrepresented by the media'.

Finally, David Leigh, for the 'hacks', chipped in with his own experience, that most politicians, when asked difficult questions, constantly evade or tell 'downright lies'. In addition, they utilise skilled public relations firms or intimidating lawyers: 'They conceal what they can conceal and what they can't they distort'. If left unchallenged, he argues, the powerful will invariably act in this way and in a democracy it is necessary for civil society to be 'truculent and unfettered'. His idea is that the media provide an essential counterbalance to power, even if it is democratically elected power.

---

her message over properly rather than the few minutes she was allowed. For voters, the problem is that such control of the media would mean the government would be able to channel out only information favourable to it and to suppress any criticism. This, of course, is what tyrants and dictators of every stripe have done for centuries, and especially since the advent of mass communications: Hitler, Stalin and Saddam come to mind, but experience suggests that democratic politicians, too, will seek to control the media, unless they are checked and watched closely (see Box 16.3).

Do the media reinforce existing power distributions?

Marxists assert that, given that a privately owned capitalist economy gives so much power to governments and institutions in their societies, they inevitably include the media in their orbit of influence and use them as part of their own armoury of societal control. This powerful argument is associated with Theodor Adorno and others in the Frankfurt School. However, when applied to conditions in Britain a number of objections can be adduced:

- Media organisations in Britain are jealous of their independence and strongly resist attempts by government to bend them to their will. The BBC, frequently a target of government attempts to exert control, has regularly fought its corner, whether the government has been headed by Thatcher or by Blair. Moreover, 'Death on the Rock', a *This Week* investigation of SAS killings of IRA terrorists on Gibraltar, was eventually shown in 1988, despite the Conservative government's attempts to put pressure on the Independent Broadcasting Authority.
- Even if the media tend to favour 'consensus values' (and the point is arguable), radical views do frequently manage to gain an airing, especially when they concern news items – for example, the riots over the poll tax in 1990 – and radical subjects are often featured in drama offerings across all the television channels. One example of this concerns satirical takes on current politics, which can be savage – *Spitting Image* during the 1980s and *Bremner, Bird and Fortune* more recently, and not forgetting that wicked send-up of New Labour spin, *The Thick Of It*.
- Persistent investigative reporting can also shame the establishment into ordering investigations or retrials, as the freeing of the Guildford Four and the Birmingham Six demonstrated.
- While print journalism is openly partisan, television journalism has by law to be even handed and the consequent airing of alternative views in news broadcasts and discussion programmes must apply some influence and check the dominance of 'consensus values'.
- No government or social group is immune to that most toxic of events for politicians: scandals. Revelations of financial misdoings or sexual peccadilloes regularly intrude into the news and, for a while, hold the nation fascinated in their thrall. As celebrity culture comes to dominate the media, this operates as a kind of Achilles' heel for the political system: anyone and everyone is vulnerable and – as John Major found to his cost when Edwina Currie published her memoirs – few politicians have absolutely no skeletons in their cupboards.

How important is language in political communication?

Obviously, words and pictures are the commodities used by the media and language, with its infinite sensitivity to nuance, plays a crucial role, as the following examples illustrate:

- In Northern Ireland, where deep historical conflicts created dangerous sensitivities, certain words acquired symbolic status. The nationalists hated the idea that they should give up their arms and so 'decommissioning' became a euphemism for it. Even then, Sinn Fein shied away from the 'permanent' giving up of arms. As important as words was the tone employed. Northern Ireland ministers tended to cultivate a studiedly calm style of talking, as if keen not to arouse any negative feelings.

- In the House of Commons, the style is rather antique; for example, speakers have to address one another through the Speaker of the House (hence 'Through you, Mr Speaker') and to refer to their 'honourable friends' if they are in the same party and 'honourable members' if not. Certain kinds of words are forbidden, such as common insults and 'liar'. On 15 April 2007, Des Browne expressed his 'regret' at not vetoing permission given to the returned Iran hostages to sell their stories to the press. The opposition insisted he say 'sorry' and in response the Defence Secretary finally complied.
- In journalism, new words and phrases constantly enter the political discourse. For example, in 2006 the term 'eye watering' came in, somewhat

---

Box 16.4 Media coverage:
do the British media overdo sensationalist child stories?

Simon Jenkins, in the *Guardian* on 18 May 2007, felt the coverage of the Madeleine McCann story, after she had disappeared from a Portuguese holiday resort, was excessive but still came down in favour of a media unafraid to investigate any cranny of national life.

> I have found the coverage of the McCann story prurient and tedious beyond belief. That the BBC should regard it as more important than Brown's ascension to national leadership crumbles my faith in that great organisation. Tabloid values have come to British public service broadcasting with a vengeance and without even the commercial pressure of the private sector.
>
> In this spirit I must constantly remind myself that the British media does not do responsibility. It does stories.... It kicks down doors and exposes the hidden corners of the human condition. It fights competition, plays dirty and disobeys the rules. There is nothing it finds too vulgar or too prurient for its wandering, penetrating lens.
>
> Journalists may have cooked the McCann story to a burnt crisp. But they cook many other stories that way and I say, thank goodness. There are plenty in power who feel too much was written and said on the Royal Navy hostages, on cash-for-honours, on BAE sleaze and on David Kelly. Tough luck on them.... Sometimes there is no better way to alert the nation to street violence, racism or even the dangers faced by families abroad than through the tragedy visited on an individual victim.
>
> The British press plays hard cop to the soft cop of the British constitution. It goes where politics dares not tread, certainly the present pusillanimous parliament that still cannot find a way of holding the government to account for Iraq, as Congress is finally doing in America. The press does not operate with any sense of proportion, judgment or self-restraint because it is selling stories, not running the country. The unshackled and irresponsible press sometimes gets it wrong. But I still prefer it, warts and all, to a shackled and responsible one.

mysteriously, to describe hefty increases. Interestingly, in the very different political context of Iraq during April 2007, the supporters of Moqtada al Sadr withdrew their ministers from the government; a senior spokesman employed a term borrowed from soccer to explain: it was a 'yellow card' for making 'a bad foul' in not stating a withdrawal date for the occupying forces.

- Quite a few new words enter the language after traversing the Atlantic. After '9–11', certain suspects were flown by the CIA to countries where there were fewer scruples regarding the use of torture in interrogation. This practice was called 'extraordinary rendition' and in his statement in February 2006 Jack Straw happily used the word 'render' in denying British involvement in such transportation.

New media: has the internet 'revolutionised' political communication?

The major innovation resulting from the internet has been the phenomenon of 'blogging'. Free software is available for users to create their own websites whereby they can offer their thoughts on whatever topics they choose. Over 50 million 'blogs' now exist and more are being started every minute.

However, it would be a mistake to see this as a 'revolution' in political communication, for the following reasons:

- Some 10–15% of blogs do not survive beyond a few months, as their authors become bored by the need to keep it updated.
- In the UK, as of early 2007, over 40% of households were not connected to the internet and those that were were disproportionately in middle-class areas of the south-east of the country.
- Only a small proportion of blogs are concerned with politics (the others will address a wide range of topics, from allotments to vintage cars, or may be online personal diaries).
- Many blogs provide platforms for their authors to express their opinions and the interactive comment facility enables readers to engage in debate (blogging is not for the thin skinned, as some people leaving comments ignore the conventions of polite debate), but often the topics chosen are those being discussed in the mainstream media with, for example, electronic links provided to press articles or even videos on other sites. So, despite the fact that newspaper sales have been in decline for many years, they still set the agenda for this brash new medium.
- Connected to the above point, people tend to visit blogs which more or less match their own political outlook, which is not so very different from the way we read newspapers.

At the time of writing, there seem to be more popular blogs on the right (e.g. Guido Fawkes, Iain Dale's Diary) than on the left (e.g. Bloggers 4 Labour) but maybe this is a function of there having been a left-of-centre government in power for over a decade.

In the United States, where political blogs are ubiquitous, they have been able to have a direct effect on political events. But it is significant that their influence has been reserved to peddling gossip, which has in some cases brought down certain political careers. Similarly, in Britain political blogs have become popular largely through disseminating gossip. Significantly also, when documents are leaked they are still leaked to newspaper journalists rather than bloggers, though this may change. Blogs are not unimportant and could well become more so. Peter Riddell, political editor of *The Times* and doyen of political commentators, told the author in September 2006 that he spends at least half an hour each day surfing the major political blogs as yet another way of taking the country's political temperature. But it has to be said that, at present, blogs fulfil only a supporting role and not a major one. However, time and technology may elevate their role into one of more influence and power.

Recommended reading

Jones, B., *et al.* (2007) *Politics UK* (6th edition), Pearson: chapter 10.
Kavanagh, D., *et al.* (2006) *British Politics* (5th edition), Oxford University Press: chapter 25.
Kingdom, J. (2003) *Government and Politics in Britain: An Introduction* (3rd edition), Polity: chapter 8.
Leach, R., *et al.* (2006) *British Politics*, Palgrave: chapter 9.
Moran, M. (2005) *Politics and Governance in the UK*, Palgrave: chapter 16.

Other texts

See reading for previous chapter and in addition:

Lloyd, J. (2004) *What the Media Are Doing to Our Politics*, Constable.
Ornstein, N. and Mann, T. (2000) *The Permanent Campaign and Its Future*, AET.
Whale, J. (1977) *The Politics of the Media*, Fontana.
Zakaria, F. (2004) *The Future of Freedom*, Norton.

Websites

Guido Fawkes' blog, www.order-order.com.
Normblog (Norman Geras), http://normblog.typepad.com.
Skipper blog (Bill Jones), http://skipper59.blogspot.com.

17

Voting behaviour in Britain

How the electorate votes is a key element in the politics of any democracy and comprises, along with polls, a major part of media coverage of political matters. Voting behaviour is closely connected to many aspects of society, as this chapter explains.

Who votes and who stands?

Most British subjects aged eighteen years or over are entitled to vote in local, parliamentary and European elections. To do so, they have to be a citizen of the UK, a Commonwealth country or the Republic of Ireland, and to be resident in a constituency and on the electoral register, and voters in Northern Ireland must have lived in the constituency for the previous three months. In addition, British citizens who have lived abroad for up to twenty years may vote. There are also some exclusion criteria, and the following may not vote: members of the House of Lords (though they can vote in local and European elections); people convicted of a crime and in prison (remand prisoners are allowed to vote); some categories of people who are mentally ill (e.g. those detained in psychiatric hospital); and people convicted of election malpractice within the previous five years.

Candidates had to be over twenty-one until the Electoral Administration Act 2006, but now have to be only eighteen or over. Civil servants, members of the armed forces and ordained members of the Church of England are not eligible to stand for Parliament.

Electoral system(s)

Traditionally, the British electoral system has been perceived as simple 'first past the post'. However, even though the 'against' camp has been seen to have the upper hand for most of the time, several electoral aspects of Britain's democratic system have been reformed:

Supplementary vote

As described in Chapter 12, this is used to select the London Mayor and entails voters indicating a first and second choice. If no candidate wins 50% of the vote, second preferences are distributed, adding to the first preferences, until one candidate exceeds the halfway mark.

Single transferable vote

This is most commonly associated with Ireland but, given its ability to produce very representative legislatures, it has been used for all elections in Northern Ireland. Voters register their preferences right down the list of candidates in large multi-member constituencies. A quota is set based on the number of voters divided by the number of candidates plus one. Candidates who make it first time are elected outright and subsequent ones come through on the basis of second, third and, if necessary, other preferences until the quotas are filled (see Figure 17.1 for an example of an Irish voting paper).

Additional-member system

Based on the German system, this entails voters having two votes. The first is cast for candidates in a geographical constituency, elected via first past the post; the second is cast for candidates in a 'top-up pool' and is for a party. The percentages won by each party – as long as they are over 5% – determine how many members of each 'party list' are judged elected. This system is used for the Scottish Parliament, the Welsh Assembly and the Greater London Assembly.

Regional party list

Voters choose from party lists in multi-member constituencies, with the percentages gained by each party determining their share of the available seats. This is the system used for the Euro-elections. Those at the top of the lists are the candidates likely to be elected.

First past the post (sometimes called the 'simple plurality' system)

This is still the one used at general elections for seats in the Westminster Parliament. While this system tends to large majorities likely to provide stable and decisive government, it has been found lacking from the democratic viewpoint:

Marcáil ord do rogha sna spáis seo síos
Mark order of preferences in spaces below.

Marc Oifigiúl
Official Mark

	BARLOW COMMUNITY (Hannah Barlow – Community, of 67, Shantalla, Beaumont, Dublin. Alderman, Housewife, Midwife)
	BELTON – FINE GAEL (Paddy Belton, of Ballivor, Howth, Co. Dublin. Director of Family Business)
	BIRMINGHAM – FINE GAEL (George Birmingham, of 'Denville', 498 Howth Road, Raheny, Dublin 5. City Councillor and Barrister-at-Law)
2	**BRADY – FIANNA FÁIL** (Vincent Brady, of 138, Kincora Road, Dublin 3. Company Director)
	BROWNE – SOCIALIST LABOUR PARTY (Noel Browne, of Stepaside, Church Road, Malahide, Dublin. Medical Doctor)
	BYRNE – FINE GAEL (Mary Byrne, of 177, Seafield Road, Clontarf, Dublin 3, City Councillor)
5	**CURLEY – THE COMMUNIST PARTY OF IRELAND** (John Curley, of 44, Greencastle Road, Coolack, Dublin 5. Storeman)
	DILLON (Andrew Dillon, of Drumnigh, Portmarnock, Co. Dublin. Solicitor)
4	**DOHERTY** (Vincent Doherty, of 76, Pembroke Road, Dublin. H Blocks Campaigner)
1	**HAUGHEY – FIANNA FÁIL** (Charles J. Haughey, of Abbeville, Kinsealy, Malahide, Co. Dublin. Taoiseach)
	MARTIN – THE LABOUR PARTY (Michael Martin, of 28, Seafield Road. Insurance Agent)
	O'HALLORAN – THE LABOUR PARTY (Michael O'Halloran, of 141, Ardlea Road, Artane. Public Representative and Trade Union Official)
3	**TIMMONS – FIANNA FÁIL** (Eugene Timmons, of 42, Copeland Avenue, Dublin 3. Public Representative)

TREORACHA
I. Féach chuige go bhfuil an marc oifigiúil ar an bpáipéar.
II. Scríobh an figiúr 1 le hais ainm an chéad iarrthóra is rogha leat, an figiúr 2 le hais do dhara rogha agus mar ain de.
III. Fill an páipéar ionas nach bhfeicfear do vóta. Taspeáin *cúl an pháipéir* don oifigeach ceannais, agus cuir sa bhosca ballóide é.

INSTRUCTIONS
I. See that the official mark is on the paper.
II. Write 1 beside the name of the candidate of your first choice, 2 beside your second choice, and so on.
III. Fold the paper to conceal your vote. Show *the back of the paper* to the presiding officer and put it in the ballot box.

Figure 17.1 *Example of an Irish ballot paper, with voter's preferences filled on left*

- Candidates can be elected on a minority of the vote; for example, with four candidates standing, all with similar levels of support, someone with 26% of the vote could win, with all the other votes cast effectively 'wasted'. Reformers argue that the preferences used in other systems help to make every vote count.
- The system favours the bigger parties, as any party with wide but shallow support will not win many individual contests. For example, in 2005 Labour won only 35% of the vote but 55% of the seats; in 1983, the Alliance won 26% of the vote yet under 4% of the seats.
- This bias to towards the big parties tends to perpetuate two-party dominance, regardless of the range of political preferences 'on the ground'.

The system as practised in Britain also tends to encourage parties which seek to maximise their appeal by offering policies in the centre of the political spectrum. With systems of proportional representation, parties can afford to appeal to more specific groups in society; this tends to produce multi-party systems. Nonetheless, most proportional systems specify that parties have to achieve a minimum percentage of the vote – often 5% – before they are entitled to any seats in the legislature. Moreover, British MPs do not have 'substitutes' as in many proportional systems and if someone dies or resigns their seat, a by-election takes place. Finally, because the deposit required to stand is only £500, a variety of candidates tend to stand, either for the fun or for the fleeting publicity; virtually all of these 'joke' candidates lose their deposits, but succeed in adding some eccentric colour.

Mandate

This is the authority governments feel they have once their manifesto has been endorsed by electoral victory. Inevitably, there are questions surrounding this idea. Is every item to be fulfilled? Does it cover the whole nation or just those sections which voted for it? Experience can be found to support several interpretations but it would seem that, in the wake of a landslide victory, governments assume broad authority to interpret their 'mandate' as they think fit.

The diminishing influence of class on voting

As the country which first experienced the Industrial Revolution, Britain, by the early twentieth century, had a well defined and clearly stratified class system, with working-class people (for the most part, those working with their hands) living in older parts of the big cities and the middle classes (mostly white-collar workers) settled in the suburbs and the shires. In 1911, three-quarters of the population were working class; by 1951 this proportion had reduced to two-thirds. People tended to vote for the social group to which they felt they belonged. Working people felt Labour was 'their' party, just as the middle classes felt the Conservatives represented their interests best. In the 1960s, an Oxford University scholar, Peter Pulzer, produced a lapidary sentence which has since appeared on countless examination papers followed by the word 'discuss': 'Class is the basis of British party politics; all else is embellishment and detail.' For the most widely used system of defining class, see Box 4.1 (p. 26).

Socialisation

The way votes are cast will reflect upbringing, which will give people certain loyalties and ways of interpreting the world. Those brought up in lower-income homes might easily identify with Labour, the party which has traditionally championed the disadvantaged; however, they might just as easily reject Labour's prescriptions for one, like the Conservatives', which levies less tax and allows more economic freedom. The role of parents is crucial, in that families have a huge influence in moulding those who are nurtured within them. Consequently, despite the fact that there are many rebels, the strong tendency is for children to share the same political outlook as their parents.

Partisan dealignment

The predictability of class allegiances was a feature of the 1950s and 1960s; two-thirds of the working class voted Labour and four-fifths of the middle class voted Conservative. The fact that, in addition, 90% voted for one or other of the big parties made voting behaviour very stable. The country was also homogenous; swings from one party to another tended to be reflected throughout the country, so that after only a few results in a general election it was often possible to predict the result with some accuracy.

However, over the next few decades a number of factors began to reduce this stability. This has been termed 'partisan dealignment'. Voters used to identify strongly with one or other of the big parties – in 1964, 45% identified 'very strongly' with a party, but by 2001 that figure had declined to 13%: a major weakening in the moorings of voter loyalties, which had all kinds of implications. Why did this occur? Several possible reasons are listed below (see Denver, 2006, ch. 4).

- *Changes in occupational structure.* During the last half of the twentieth century, traditional industries declined (manufacturing workers declined from about half of the workforce in the early 1960s to less than a fifth thirty years later), to be replaced by new, mostly service industries (70% of the workforce by 1991), mostly staffed by non-manual workers. This meant that a fair proportion of middle-class jobs were filled by people deriving from the working class. The new industries were not so intensively unionised and their workers did not live in such close proximity as in the days when rows of terraced houses characterised inner cities. Traditional social bonds, which had helped to maintain stable voting patterns, were thereby weakened. Tables 17.1 and 17.2 illustrate how class allegiances have changed strikingly since the 1980s.

- *Changing mix of class characteristics.* As the economy changed, so did society, and with rising prosperity millions more people were able to buy their own homes – previously seen as a middle-class aspiration – instead of renting or living in those traditional repositories of Labour voters, council estates. By the end of the century, over half of non-manual workers owned their own houses – assisted by Margaret Thatcher's policy of 'right to buy' for council tenants. Furthermore, working-class trade union members were in steep decline, while white-collar union membership was on the increase.

- *Employment/consumption distinctions.* The utility of the old, simple class division was largely superseded by two new divisions: between public and private sector employment – with the former's middle-class cohorts favouring Labour; and between council-house-dwelling consumers of state-financed services and the home-owning consumers of private medicine and education, who favoured the Conservatives.

- *Changing working-class interests.* Denver cites Crewe's analysis of how the interests of the working classes had tended to fragment, so that home-owners differed from renters, and better-paid workers had more interest in tax cuts than the poorer paid. Despite their possible class allegiances, working-class voters could thus be persuaded to support the Conservatives.

- *Educational advances.* The proportion of people receiving post-secondary education increased immensely after the 1960s – about 5% attended university in that decade, compared with over 40% in the 1990s – and

Table 17.1 *How Britain voted in general elections, 1983–2005 (%)*

	2005	2001	1997	1992	1987	1983
Conservative	32.4	31.7	30.7	41.9	42.2	42.3
Labour	35.2	40.7	43.2	34.4	30.8	27.6
Alliance/Liberal Democrat	22.0	18.3	16.8	17.8	22.6	25.4
Others	11.0	9.3	9.3	5.8	3.4	4.7

Source: Robert Leach *et al.* (2006), *British Politics*, Palgrave, table 9.2. Reproduced with permission.

Table 17.2 *Decline of class voting, 1992–2005 (%)*

	A, B (middle class)	C1 (lower middle class)	C2 (skilled workers)	D, E (unskilled workers)
Conservative				
1992	56	52	39	32
1997	41	37	27	21
2001	39	36	29	24
2005	37	37	33	25
Change, 1992–2005	−19	−15	−6	−7
Labour				
1992	19	25	40	49
1997	31	37	50	59
2001	30	38	49	55
2005	28	32	40	48
Change, 1992–2005	+9	+7	0	−1
Liberal Democrat				
1992	22	19	17	16
1997	22	18	16	13
2001	25	20	15	13
2005	29	23	19	18
Change, 1992–2005	+7	+4	+2	+2

Source: J. Curtice (2005) 'Historic triumph or rebuff?', *Politics Review*, vol. 15, no. 1, September. Reproduced by permission of Philip Allan Updates.

this tended to encourage a more sceptical, discriminating appreciation of political issues, programmes and politicians, rather than the automatically accepted class affiliation which those students might otherwise have inherited from their parents.

- *Experience of parties in power.* Few would claim that Labour enjoyed a period of outstanding success in the 1960s, nor that the beleaguered Conservative Prime Minister Edward Heath did all that much better in the 1970s; nor did Labour Prime Minister Jim Callaghan's 'winter of discontent' impress the voter, or the massive unemployment caused by Thatcherism and the sleaze associated with John Major's Tory government. In other words, voters had come to realise that both parties were flawed and had only limited competence in solving the nation's problems.
- *Ideological polarisation.* During this period, gaps opened up between party leaderships, activists and their rank and file; activists tended to be more

ideological than the bulk of both the party leadership and rank-and-file party supporters.

• *Television coverage*. Television began to take a role in elections after the late 1950s and its intense coverage, together with probing, in-depth interviews, helped to inculcate a keener understanding of what was on offer politically. Moreover, television coverage was not partisan like the print media (which was thus likely merely to reinforce traditional loyalties) but was legally obliged not to take sides.

Voter volatility

The above factors collectively served to weaken the emotional class link between parties and voters, with the result that voters were freer to use their own perceptions and powers of reason in deciding on which party to bestow their support. Apart from the smaller numbers which now gave more or less automatic support, voters' allegiance was 'up for grabs'. Denver points out that even the apparent stability of Conservative successes during the 1980s was not based on an unchanging, solid block of voters but on 'A temporary coalition of voters which then dissolved in the inter-election periods'.

So it seems voters had emerged from the chrysalis of class loyalty as a butterfly which fluttered from party to party, depending on perceptions of their competence and the attractiveness of their policies. While party managers might complain at how their jobs of winning support has become so much harder, all these changes have, in fact, devolved more power to the individual voter, making the system, in theory at least, more democratic. However, voters did not necessarily view themselves as empowered by all these changes.

Low turn-out in recent elections

During the 1950s, turn-out in general elections averaged well over 75%, but thereafter it began to decline, especially as the new millennium approached: 71% in 1997, 59% in 2001 and 61% in 2005 (see Figure 17.2). Other elections registered even lower figures: 49% for the Scottish Parliament in 2003, 38% for the Welsh Assembly in 2003, 38% for the Euro-elections in 2004 and even lower percentages for council elections.

Does this matter? Some suggest that the 41% who did not bother to vote in the 2001 general election might have been basically happy or content with life and saw no reason to vote. However, the abstainers were, overall, less well educated and less well paid than the voters, which might suggest that contentment as a cause would be unlikely. Another worrying aspect of abstention was the high proportion of younger people not voting, which suggests that they were turned off by politics. Others point to the United States,

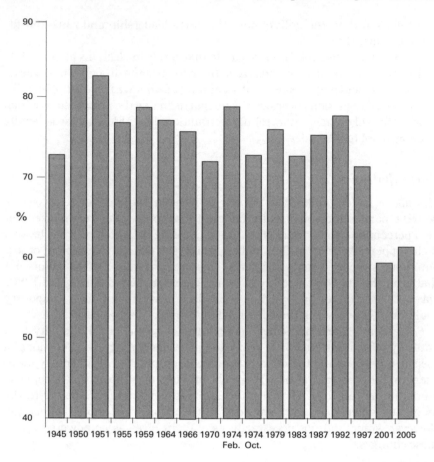

Figure 17.2 *Turn-out in general elections, 1945–2005*
Source: *Daily Telegraph*, 20 September 1997. © Copyright of Telegraph Group Limited 1997, reproduced with permission.

where hugely noisy and media-dominating presidential campaigns fail to attract much more than half the electorate into the voting booths. Election turn-out has also been in decline in most European countries, too (with the Nordic countries notable exceptions).

But as political scientist Paul Whiteley commented in 2001: 'If this [the low election turn-out] is not a crisis of democratic politics, then it is hard to see what is.' Representative democracy depends on people having some engagement with the system – if they fail to vote, it suggests they do not trust it or cannot see any reason to support it. In such circumstances there is a danger that extremist parties might move in to fill the vacuum or that democratic politics itself might atrophy. Some reformers have urged that voting be made easier, but this is not the cause of the problem. Some have sought cultural explanations; Robert Putnam, for example, suggested that people have retreated from any 'public space' into their own homes, where they watch too much television. Others, like David Denver (2006) and Anthony King, think that all that is needed is 'a close fought election at which a great deal is at stake, and, make no mistake, they will again turn out in droves' (King, *Daily Telegraph*, 17 May 2001). However, the 2005 election had achieved yet another term for the by then widely discredited Blair, with continuing involvement in the Iraq War a central issue, yet this added little to the turnout, which improved by only 2% over that in 2001.

Other factors influencing voting behaviour

Religion

Britain has moved a huge distance from the sixteenth and seventeenth centuries, when religion dominated the political life of the nation. By the nineteenth century, the Church of England was said to be 'the Conservative Party at prayer', while the Liberals attracted support from Methodists and other Nonconformists. In the next century, Labour inherited the latter legacy, so that it was possible to say that Labour owed more to Methodism than to Marxism. But, apart from Northern Ireland – which arguably existed in a kind of time warp – the UK disengaged from religion and became much more secular, reducing the role of religion in politics to such factors as the personal Christianity of Tony Blair, when Prime Minister, or Gordon's Brown's upbringing as the son of a minister of the Church of Scotland.

Age

This factor tends to favour the Conservatives, in that voters tend to move this way as they grow older and, a key factor in apathetic times, they are much more likely to vote than younger citizens. In 2005, 35% of the population were over fifty-five years of age, yet they constituted 42% of those who voted. Why do older people tend to vote Conservative? Some say that, as people age, they become less willing to change, and acquire a bigger stake in property, making them tack to the right. Others argue that it has more to do with the era in which voting preferences were established: people coming to maturity in the 1950s, for example, would be influenced by that Conservative-dominated decade.

Gender

Women used to support the Conservative Party disproportionately: 44% in 1987 compared with 31% of women supporting Labour, with men divided

44% and 33%, respectively. However, by 2005 these figures had changed substantially in Labour's favour: for men, to 33% Tories and 38% Labour; for women, 32% Conservatives, 38% Labour.

North–south divide

In the 1980s, Labour held only a smattering of seats below a line from the Wash to the Bristol Channel. Since then, the three Labour victories from 1997 changed the picture, but the more middle-class south is still very much Conservative territory and the more working-class north, Labour.

Ethnicity

Ethnic minorities number some 4–5 million out of the total population, so are now an important voter group to be wooed and won over. This is especially true in areas where they are concentrated, like Southall in the south and Blackburn in the north. Traditionally, Labour has won some three-quarters of the ethnic vote and also has more ethnic minority MPs than the Conservatives, though the latter are striving hard to improve this situation.

The general election of 7 May 2005

Voting behaviour is essentially about elections and as the most important are the general elections, what follows is a brief analysis of the 2005 one (the most recent at the time of writing).

The battleground

Blair wanted to win a third term for Labour and, despite his promise that he would go before the end of that term, it was generally expected he would not wait that long. For the Tories, under the experienced and professional Michael Howard (though tainted by association with Thatcher), this was a chance to revive their brand and, if not defeat Labour, then at least to make serious inroads into its majority. Blair entered the contest with a healthy majority of over 100 seats. Could he win another workable majority?

Labour's record

The economy

While the Conservatives had managed an annual growth rate of 1.7% per annum over the period 1979–97, Labour had easily exceeded that with a figure of 2.7%. Most people had grown more prosperous since 1997 and the economy was a strong platform on which Labour's campaign could be built.

The Tories claimed they had set the economy on its winning ways before Labour acceded to power and that Brown had wasted many opportunities to increase British economic competitiveness.

Social justice

Labour could boast of its introduction of the minimum wage, taking a million children out of poverty, a reduction of pensioner poverty from 40% to 17% and huge refunding of the health and education services, with resultant reductions in waiting times and improvements in staffing. The Tories challenged how these billions had been spent on public services, citing examples of waste and incompetent government. Polls showed that perceptions of public services tended to be closer to the sceptical Conservative view than to the more positive Labour one, and claims on child poverty could not remove the fact that 23% of children remained in poverty, even after eight years of Labour in power.

Crime

The Labour Party claimed a reduction in crime of over 40% since it came to power but the Tories challenged this, reflecting public doubts that crime rates had in fact gone down.

The campaign

The Conservatives, under the guidance of their Australian election guru Lynton Crosby, sought to make immigration the dominant issue of the campaign – polls had shown it to be something which elicited concern across the political spectrum. During the campaign, a numbers battle ensued, with statistics shuttling backwards and forwards; this left the electorate confused rather than illuminated. As polling day approached, evidence emerged that some reluctant Labour voters were being energised to turn out by their perceptions of the Conservative tactic.

Labour fought a lacklustre campaign for the first two weeks, burdened, as it was, by 'Forward Not Back', surely the most drearily anodyne slogan ever coined by a spin doctor. Gordon Brown, who had taken a back seat to Blair, was encouraged to end his 'sulking' and step up to the front line. Once he did, the campaign seemed to gain energy; it seemed the public appreciated the unity the two men symbolised when working together. But Blair was a master at dominating the middle ground, where most elections are won or lost (Figure 7.1, p. 67, shows him perfectly placed just to the right of centre in the view of voters, unlike Howard, who was seen as being fifty-two points to the right). Evidence of the potency of Blair's political positioning was given on election day (Table 17.3).

Blair had won his unprecedented third successive victory for Labour; the Conservatives, even against an unpopular government, had not done

Table 17.3 *Results of the 2005 general election*

Party	Percentage of votes	Change on 2001	Seats	Change on 2001
Labour	35.2	−5.5	356	−47
Conservative	32.3	+0.5	198	+33
Liberal Democrats	22.0	+3.7	62	+11

anywhere near well enough and the 2% swing to them had won them only a score of extra seats. The Liberal Democrats, too, must have felt they had missed a chance to stage a breakthrough, given their opposition to the much hated war in the Middle East, but they managed only modest gains.

Bias in the voting system

Over the past few decades, the first-past-the-post voting system has developed a bias in favour of Labour. This comes about largely because fewer Labour votes are needed to elect MPs than are to elect Conservative MPs, whose votes are both more thinly spread over the country and tend to stack up in safe constituencies in the south-east. Further, Labour managed to do well out of the Boundary Commission's review of constituency boundaries in the 1990s.

According to the Electoral Reform Society, even if both main parties had polled the same number of votes in 1997, Labour would have won 336 seats and Conservatives only 220. Further, at the next election, due in 2010, the Conservatives will need to poll a 7.5% lead over Labour even to draw level in terms of seats.

Voting and groups

Table 17.4 shows how the different social classes and categories voted. Women voted for Blair by some margin, rather than for Howard, suggesting Labour's child-care provision was thus paying a dividend. But class-based voting was by no means negligible: A, B and C1 voters heavily supported the Conservatives, while C2, D and E voters went for Labour by a significant margin.

Labour still polled well among younger groups, while the Conservatives had the edge really only in the over-sixty-five category.

Turn-out

Only 37% of those aged eighteen to twenty-four years voted but 75% of the over-fifty-fives did, comprising over 40% of all those who voted on the day.

Box 17.1 Apathy and ignorance in the British political system

Polly Toynbee in the *Guardian* (8 March 2008) addressed the topic of political apathy. The Hansard Society conducts annual audits of the electorate regarding their willingness to participate in politics and 2008's results included the following:

- only 53% of voters say they are certain to vote;
- only 4% have ever made a political donation;
- 55% say they know nothing much about politics, and are indifferent to a bill of rights or a written constitution;
- only 23% of the eighteen to twenty-four age group say they will vote, in contrast to the 78% of the over-sixty-fives.

Toynbee said 'Newspaper reading is falling, BBC news and current affairs struggle for audiences. People are good at grumbling about everything, yet they won't lift a finger to change anything.'

The fact that young people are the most apathetic suggests the problem is not going to get better any time soon. If we continue down this road, where are we likely to end up? With political parties which are mere shells, lacking membership but winning the votes the constitution says are needed to win office, with a huge wilderness of voters who are ignorant, disaffected and not a little angry at why they have somehow brought about this state of affairs. These are the perfect conditions for parties on the extreme to wade in with their seductively easy simplicities; as de Tocqueville wrote, the public then 'assents to the clamour of the mountebank who knows the secret of stimulating its taste'.

These would be dangerously uncharted waters for our political leaders to navigate and who knows whether they would succeed, assailed, as they will be, by an ever-growing intensity of problems to solve (for example those originating in the exhaustion of the world's natural resources). Some experts – Professor Anthony King, for example, as we have seen (p. 191) – believe all is basically okay and that all we need is a 'closely fought election at which a great deal is at stake' for voters to turn out again 'in their droves'.

Polly Toynbee opts for constitutional change. Jack Straw has ruled out making voting compulsory, as is the case in parts of Europe and in Australia, and proportional representation seems still to scare Labour's loyalists. Instead, Toynbee goes for the small but useful: introduce the alternative vote system, which will stop minority vote victories and give more space to smaller parties, which can then play a role in tactical voting.

This would be a useful beginning and some progress towards the voting reform some say Britain has needed for a long time. It is odd, they say, that we have introduced proportional representation for devolved assemblies, Scottish and Ulster local government and the London Assembly but not for the most important elections in the country.

Table 17.4 *Voting by social group in 2005 (and 2001 in parentheses) (%)*

	Conservative	Labour	Liberal Democrat
Men	33 (28)	38 (47)	21 (17)
Women	32 (35)	38 (43)	23 (17)
A, B (middle class)	37 (43)	32 (30)	24 (21)
C1 (lower middle class)	34 (35)	35 (37)	24 (21)
C2 (skilled workers)	32 (28)	43 (52)	18 (13)
D, E (unskilled workers)	28 (21)	45 (58)	19 (15)
Age 18–24	24 (25)	42 (50)	26 (17)
Age 25–34	24 (27)	42 (50)	26 (17)
Age 35–64	33 (31)	38 (43)	22 (18)
Age 65+	42 (38)	35 (42)	18 (15)
Home-owners with mortgage	30 (32)	39 (41)	23 (19)
Home-owners owning outright	43 (42)	30 (36)	20 (16)
Council tenants	16 (15)	56 (65)	19 (13)
All voters	33 (31)	36 (43)	23 (17)

Source: IBM. All campaign polls (sample 13,730 in 2005, 10,000 in 1997) weighted for outcome; Britain only.

Some 70% of those in social class A and B voted but only 54% of those in class D and E, suggesting that a worrying class gap has opened up in terms of voter participation. Box 17.1 looks at some reasons for voter apathy.

Election in 2010

At the time of writing Gordon Brown is Prime Minister but must hold an election before June 2010. His period in office since 2007 has been disappointing for him, with his political judgement frequently called into question and the chronic economic crisis caused by bank failures in 2008 overwhelming public finances by 2009. Poll leads for David Cameron of up to 20 points in 2009 suggest Labour's period in power may well be limited.

Reference

Denver, D. (2006) *Elections and Voting in Britain*, Palgrave.

Recommended reading

Jones, B., *et al.* (2007) *Politics UK* (6th edition), Pearson: chapter 9.

Kavanagh, D., *et al.* (2006) *British Politics* (5th edition), Oxford University Press: chapter 20.

Kingdom, J. (2003) *Government and Politics in Britain: An Introduction* (3rd edition), Polity: chapter 9.

Leach, R., *et al.* (2006) *British Politics*, Palgrave: chapter 5.

Moran, M. (2005) *Politics and Governance in the UK*, Palgrave: chapter 17.

Other texts

Butler, D. and Kavanagh, D. (2002) *The British General Election of 2001*, Palgrave.

Butler, D. and King, A. (eds) (2005) *Britain at the Polls*, CQ Press.

Butler, D. and Stokes, D. (1970) *Political Change in Britain*, Macmillan.

Geddes, A. and Tonge, J. (1997) *Labour's Landslide*, Manchester University Press.

Kavanagh, D. and Butler, D. (2005) *The British General Election of 2005*, Palgrave.

Norris, P. (1997) *Electoral Change Since 1945*, Blackwell.

Sarlvik, B. and Crewe, I. (1983) *Decade of Dealignment*, Cambridge University Press.

Websites

Richard Kimber's Political Science Resources, University of Keele: British governments and elections since 1945, www.psr.keele.ac.uk/arca/uk/uktable.htm.

David Boothroyd's UK election results page, www.election.demon.co.uk.

18

Local government I: provenance and decline

The importance of local government seems obvious, in that what matters most to people are the things which affect them and their families on a daily basis: their environment, street hygiene, safety and so forth. Yet in the twenty-first century, local government in Britain can sometimes seem less than relevant, with few people aware of its existence and caring even less. Given such indifference, it is hard for this lowest tier of democratic government to assert itself. However, it still disposes of billions of pounds every year, employs over 2 million people and affects every citizen; furthermore, most people are required to pay local taxes. This chapter explores the provenance of local government and its coming to maturity in the twentieth century, followed by a worrying decline.

Historical development of local government

Early history

There has always been some kind of local government but before the nineteenth century it was seldom well staffed or efficient and in some areas was pretty thin. The three administrative levels of 'county', 'borough' and 'parish' date back to Norman times and functioned during the Middle Ages, when justice was dispensed via the county assizes, which also raised militias or defensive forces. 'Improvement commissioners' were appointed from the late seventeenth century to take care of paving and lighting, financed by a local rate. From 1600, the Poor Law obliged parishes to make provision for the poor and indigent with an 'overseer for the poor' given responsibility. After 1723, workhouses were established to accommodate those unable to care for themselves, though the 'care' provided was scarcely worth the name by modern standards.

Nineteenth century

The reason why local government burgeoned during the nineteenth century was the rapid progress of the Industrial Revolution, which imposed huge changes on localities in respect of health, sanitation, poverty, law and order, transport and the environment. Hundreds of thousands now lived in localities where before only a few hundred had; the skeletal local government agencies were quickly overwhelmed and it was evident they were in dire need of a major overhaul. This, then, became the century of local government innovation and expansion. Because Parliament, since 1688, had been the axis of political power, it was central government in London which took the initiative and used its powers to set up new, devolved localised centres of authority to solve this new range of problems.

In 1834 the Poor Law Amendment Act set up boards of guardians to run a new kind of workhouse. In 1835 the Municipal Corporations Act required members of town councils – many of which had become self-perpetuating oligarchies – to be elected by ratepayers and for annual accounts to be published. A third of councillors came up for election each year and aldermen were elected from within the council to serve a six-year term. Later in the century, a series of ad hoc boards were set up to organise functions like health, highways and education.

However, the vast increase in urban populations and the overlapping of boundaries of various authorities made thorough-going reform inevitable. In 1888 the Local Government Act set up sixty-two new elected councils plus sixty-one county boroughs, administering all functions in England and Wales. Further subdivisions arrived after 1894, when 535 urban district, 472 rural district councils and 270 non-county borough councils (with fewer powers) were established.

Twentieth century

Interestingly, apart from a 1929 Act which transferred the functions of the Poor Law guardian to local government, the next four decades were free of structural change, allowing local government bodies freedom to develop their functions and acquire new powers and responsibilities, for example over gas, electricity and telephones. This is often referred to as local government's 'golden age'. But this expansion only proceeded up to a certain point; by the 1960s, the patchwork of 1,400 separate local authorities was too complex and baffling, and a major reform was required. This took place with Redcliffe-Maud's royal commission report in 1969. The report recommended a nationwide pattern of unitary authorities but the Conservative government feared this would play into the hands of Labour, which tended to control urban areas. Instead, Edward Heath introduced a 'two-tier' pattern, with different functions being performed at the 'shire county' (the Conservative heartlands) and the 'district' level.

Local Government Act 1972
This was a huge rationalisation of the patchwork pattern of local government. The number of county councils was reduced to forty-seven, with 334 constituent district councils. In addition, a new urban kind of authority was created in the place of urban and rural district councils: six metropolitan counties were set up, along with their thirty-six districts.

The idea behind the reform was to create bigger units, to improve efficiency and to make the system clearer for voters, who tended to ignore local government and not bother to vote in its elections. However, many voters ended up even more bewildered as: their old familiarities had been swept away; town halls were mostly even further away than before; and different functions were now performed by different tiers of government. Waiting in the wings was a politician determined to continue reform in local government but only according to her own particular political beliefs. However, the process of decline had already started regarding funding and loss of function.

The decline of local government before Thatcher
Moran (2005, pp. 250–3) reflects on how innovations in the dynamic local government sphere in many ways anticipated the formation of the welfare state after 1945 – schools, policing, public health, hospital care, road provision and maintenance, water and sewage disposal, child health, gas, electricity and public libraries. Some of this 'municipal socialism' was provided by councils dominated by business people who would have been horrified to describe anything they authorised as 'socialism'. But from the middle of the century onwards, a clear decline can be discerned:

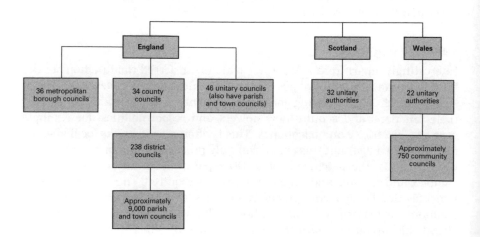

Figure 18.1 *The structure of local government in England, Scotland and Wales*
Source: Jones, B., *et al.*, *Politics UK*, 5th edition (Pearson, 2004), fig. 22.2.

Table 18.1 *Functions of local authorities*

Function	County	District	Unitary
Education	*		*
Housing		*	*
Social services	*		*
Highways	*	*	*
Transport	*		
Museums and art galleries	*	*	*
Libraries	*		*
Planning		*	*
Strategic planning	*		*
Economic development	*	*	*
Recreation, parks, sports facilities	*	*	*
Weights and measures	*		*
Food and health inspection	*		*
Cemeteries		*	*
Markets		*	*

Funding

As the range of services expanded and standards increased, local government was forced to look to central government for the extra cash. By the end of the twentieth century, funding which originated at the centre – including business rates set in Whitehall – was over three-quarters of the whole. Council taxes now provide only around 20% of the whole, leaving local government very much in the supplicant role regarding its dealings with the centre.

Functions

Local government has seen a wide raft of its functions stripped away, especially since 1945. Provision of gas and electricity disappeared at that time, as well as hospitals, as the National Health Service came into being. Then senior criminal courts were lost (1973), water and sewage (1974), ambulances (1974) and elements of education, such as the polytechnics (1989) and colleges of further education (1993), not to mention police and fire services (1986) and airports (1987), as well as over a million council houses, sold to tenants during the 1980s. Local government retains responsibility for education but its control is limited; for example, the national curriculum now determines what has to be taught in schools and school budgets have been handed over, in many cases, to the schools themselves.

Fragmentation

As central government became impatient with local government, it began to intervene. Agencies were set up that were more independent of the existing structures; examples include the urban development corporations, which aim to stimulate urban renewal, or the variety of government-appointed quangos (quasi non-governmental organisations) to take care of functions that in many cases were once performed by local government, such as local training.

'Contracting out'

This process began with the Conservative government in the 1980s, which, as ever, was convinced private provision was more efficient than public. Councils were forced to put a growing range of functions out to tender, the best-known of which has probably been rubbish collection services. Instead of local authorities running their own operation, they 'contracted out' the job to private companies, often saving money, though many would dispute that efficiency was invariably improved. This approach to local authority work marked a demotion of importance for the council and a shift away from direct provision; it rather turned councils into 'enabling' authorities, which delegated work to private agencies and then monitored the quality of service provided.

Thatcherism and her 'war' with local government

It could almost be argued that Margaret Thatcher waged unrelenting war on local government after she came to power in 1979. She tended to perceive local government as overstaffed, inefficient and too dominated by Labour councillors. So she decided to restrict its activities by a series of new statutes:

Local Government Planning and Land Act 1980
This established:

- *compulsory competitive tendering*, which required local authorities to offer certain functions – initially building projects and the like, but later extended to white-collar services (e.g. legal services) and sport and leisure and so on – to public tender so that private enterprise could compete with public on efficiency and price;
- *urban development corporations*, the function of which was to provide dynamic redevelopment for run-down areas, free of the restrictions of local government bureaucracy.

Local Government Finance Act 1982
This set up the influential and effective Audit Commission in 1983, tasked with checking the expenditure of a range of public agencies, including local government, as well as reviewing efficiency and performance.

Rates Act 1984
This Act introduced the mechanism of rate-capping. Over half of local authorities' income originated from central government and some, faced with

a reduction in grant, sought to increase revenue by increasing rates raised on property within their areas. This piece of legislation allowed the London government to 'cap' rates at a level according with a Whitehall view of what was required. Local government supporters argued that this represented far too much central control.

Local Government Act 1985

With this Act Thatcher abolished the Labour-dominated six metropolitan counties, plus the Greater London Council. This caused outrage within local government circles and on the left but the government was able to do this as there are no extra 'entrenched' defences within the British constitution. Perhaps surprisingly, the demise of the metropolitan counties was not mourned for long; their functions were devolved to districts or joint boards and life proceeded pretty much as before. The Greater London Council, however, was a different matter and a powerful consensus emerged that London required a new form of regional government, which eventually came to be installed after 1997, by Tony Blair's Labour government (see Chapter 12).

Local Government Finance Act 1988

This Act introduced the 'community charge', or 'poll tax' as it became notoriously known. Thatcher had long hated the way the property-based 'rates' were paid disproportionately by the better-off, while poorer people received discounts or exemptions. Politically, this meant that Conservative voters – who favoured low rates – tended also to be the biggest payers of them, while Labour – which advocated high rates to fund high levels of service – was supported by people who did not pay any rates at all. This was 'power without responsibility' argued the Tories and the community charge was designed to distribute responsibility to every voter in the country. It was a flat charge payable by all, though discounts were available to students and others. The theory was that once voters realised they had responsibility for charge levels, they would vote to keep it low, and that all parties would compete to keep it low as well.

Theory was one thing, practice another. The tax was expensive to collect, many avoided registering for it in the first place and some (well publicised) rebels refused to pay altogether. The basic problem was the regressive nature of the charge; it required the cleaning lady to pay as much as the Duke of Westminster and this was seen as plain unfair. In the spring of 1990, demonstrations against the tax spilled over into riots and this further weakened a premier whose imperious style had thoroughly tested the patience of her party. While the politics of British membership of the European Union was the immediate cause of her departure, few failed to recognise the major role played by her stubborn insistence that the poll tax was both a fair and a potentially efficient means of raising local revenue.

Local Government Finance Act 1992

This measure, conceived by Thatcher's partial nemesis, Michael Heseltine, shifted the basis of local government taxation back to property. Houses were categorised and payments made basically according to house values. As richer people tended to live in bigger houses, this seemed much fairer and instantly removed a huge public animus against the government of the day.

Local Government Act 1992

The two-tier system of allocating functions had proved confusing and less efficient than the 'unitary' (all-purpose) county authorities. Labour had always favoured Redcliffe-Maud's unitary authorities, as the party's strength lay in urban centres. The Conservatives, with strength in the shires, went for the two-tier approach, with the top tier controlling the bigger spending functions. However, this preference was reversed by the mid-1990s, with the Major government coming around to the view that unitary authorities were the clearer, more efficient and accountable option. A Local Government Commission, chaired by Sir John Banham, was tasked with reviewing local government structures. However, Banham refused to impose the unitary solution uniformly, preferring retention of the two-tier approach in some localities. His successor proved more compliant but by 1998 only forty-six unitary authorities had been formed, some way short of uniformity.

Reforms in the Celtic fringe

Reforms in Scotland and Wales emphatically adopted the unitary model. County and district authorities in Wales were replaced in 1994 by twenty-two unitary authorities, while Scotland's regional and district councils gave way to thirty-two unitaries. The Local Government Act (Northern Ireland), back in 1972, had set up twenty-six district councils, replacing the tiered system bestowed upon the whole of Ireland back in 1898. Naturally, local government in these areas comes under the control of the relevant elected assembly and not the central, Westminster government in London.

Parish councils

There are about 8,700 of these, the smallest units of local government; they are related to original church parishes but are civil, not religious. They are more common in rural than urban areas but since 1997 150 new councils have been appointed. (See also 'New initiative on town and parish councils' in the next chapter, p. 214.) These councils are run by some 70,000 councillors, and 80% of them serve populations of less than 2,500. Their funding is often only a few thousand pounds, gathered via a precept on the council tax, although collectively they employ some 25,000 people and spend £400 million per annum. Their functions include things like youth activities, transport for the elderly, maintenance of cemeteries, play schemes, footpaths and litter collection. Often these small units group together to provide services – like transport – over a wider area; often they also share the services of the same parish council clerk.

Local Government Association

Constant discussions and negotiations take place between Westminster and representatives of local government. Dating back to the nineteenth century, each unit of local government administration used to have a separate body to represent its interests. However, in 1997 a single group, the Local Government Association (LGA), was set up to spearhead the interests of all councils above the parish stratum. Like local government as a whole, it is subject to partisan control; by 1997 its general council was Labour controlled, but after a decade the pendulum had swung to the Conservatives.

The LGA has a permanent staff and sub-committees to deal with the detailed work of representing the complex web of local government activities to the central departments in Whitehall and, more often in recent years, Brussels.

In addition to the LGA, a number of other representative bodies exert influence, including: the Society of Chief Executives and Managers, the Society of Personnel Officers in Local Government, the Society of Procurement Officers in Local Government and Local Government Employers (an organisation set up by the LGA to coordinate pay and conditions of employment).

Politics and local government

In the early days of local government, control was exercised more by local property owners than by 'politicians'. This is not to say that political parties had no role to play in local politics, merely that it was occasional and of varying intensity; for example, Joseph Chamberlain, used his position as a Birmingham city councillor (in 1869), then Mayor (in 1873), to apply radical Liberal ideas and create a model city. His highly efficient organisation of the Liberal Party in Birmingham ensured his party dominated it for decades to come. He himself became a Liberal MP at a by-election in 1876. By the end of the century, the Liberals and Conservatives became dominant in local politics but still many candidates disguised their party affiliations so as not to dilute their apparent local concerns.

During the next century, Labour entered the picture and, for the most part, made the big cities its own. Its activities in London encouraged emulation by the other parties and by the middle of the twentieth century local parties were heavily involved in areas hitherto unaffected by party

Box 18.1 Local government: election and function

Eligibility to vote
Anyone aged over eighteen can vote if they: are citizens of Britain, Ireland or the Commonwealth; live in the locality; and are registered to vote.

Eligibility to stand as a candidate
Anyone over eighteen years can stand in a local election if they live locally and have the support of ten local people.

Electoral system
Local elections in England and Wales are via first past the post, but in Northern Ireland and Scotland the single transferable vote system is used, which produces more coalition councils.

Timing of elections and terms of office
Local elections take place virtually every year, usually on the first Thursday in May.

County councils are elected in their entirety every four years but district councils have a choice of having elections for the whole council every four years – at the mid-term point for the counties – or via one-third of councillors standing for re-election in each non-county year.

Numbers of councillors
In 2006 some 22,000 councillors were elected: 8,181 Conservative, 6,514 Labour and 4,754 Liberal Democrat. In addition, the Scottish National Party had 186 elected councillors, Palid Cymru 182 and 2,206 were independent of political parties.

Functions of local authorities
In metropolitan counties it was the district tier which exercised the most expensive functions like education, housing and social services, while the county level had more regional functions, like transport and planning – functions which disappeared when these councils were abolished in 1986 (districts now perform most of these functions, apart from joint boards for county-level functions).

In shire counties, it is the county councils which have the major functions while the districts are limited to housing, planning and environmental health.

campaigning. After the 1974 reforms this intensified, so that some 90% of local councils were 'politicised' either by a single party or by coalitions of them. It used to be the case that discussions of policy took place in the open council but party hegemony has caused the ruling party group to discuss future policy in private. Once agreed, the party line has to be followed by its related group of councillors on pain of disciplinary action or even expulsion.

Some regret this invasion by 'external' political forces but, given the large resources they distribute, it was perhaps inevitable that local party members, already existing to select, campaign for and support local MPs, would seek to establish locally elected beach-heads of power. To some extent, local government provides a training ground for future political leaders: John Major started his politics as a councillor; so did Ken Livingstone; and David Blunkett was leader of Sheffield council before he entered the Commons.

One consequence of this party politicisation of local politics which has been criticised is that the fortunes of the national parties influence the local level. So the party in power at Westminster usually finds that the vicissitudes of politics causes its support to wane at the local level, as voters express their discontent by voting for other parties, or, all too often, not voting at all. Local election results, every spring, moreover, have become 'mini-general elections', with local government psephologists Rallings and Thrasher poring over them to extrapolate local trends to the national picture (see list of websites at the end of the chapter).

Westminster responsibility for local government

Naturally, major issues concerning local government will be considered in Cabinet, with the lead taken by that minister tasked with looking after local government. Cabinet committees will undertake the groundwork for new ventures – Thatcher set up committee MISC 79 to consider alternatives to the

---

Box 18.2 Compulsory competitive tendering (CCT)

The 1980 Local Government and Land Act made it compulsory for local authorities to put out to tender the functions of highway repair, building construction and maintenance work. 'In-house' provision had to compete for the 'business' with outside bidders, the work usually going to the lowest offer. In 1988, a raft of new functions were added, including school meals, refuse collection and street cleaning. A White Paper in 1991 proposed further extensions, even into the heart of administration itself: finance, personnel, central administration and legal work. These developments caused great controversy, as they affected the jobs and promotion prospects of thousands of people.

How successful was CCT? There is no clear answer. Some claim savings and useful innovations have resulted but others claim quality has plummeted as 'work on the cheap' has become the effective watchword. The controversy about school dinners ignited by television chef Jamie Oliver in 2005 directed attention to CCT. The fact was that contracting out school meals had allowed in some very cheap operators, who fulfilled the brief, saved money, but fed children with harmful, non-nutritious food.

rates and the abolition of the metropolitan counties. Labour's Deputy Prime Minister John Prescott went on to chair this committee after 1997.

The department dealing with local government has varied over the years, from Housing and Local Government in the 1960s, to Environment during the 1970s, then Transport, Local Government and the Regions, and then the Office of the Deputy Prime Minister; at the time of writing, local government was the responsibility of the Department of Community and Local Government (from 2006). The department has nine regional offices to assist its work throughout the country.

Reference

Moran, M. (2005) *Politics and Governance in the UK*, Palgrave.

Recommended reading

Jones, B., *et al.* (2007) *Politics UK* (6th edition), Pearson: chapter 22.
Kavanagh, D., *et al.* (2006) *British Politics* (5th edition), Oxford University Press: chapter 15.
Kingdom, J. (2003) *Government and Politics in Britain: An Introduction* (3rd edition), Polity: chapter 19.
Leach, R., *et al.* (2006) *British Politics*, Palgrave: chapter 17.
Moran, M. (2005) *Politics and Governance in the UK*, Palgrave: chapter 12.

Other texts

Chandler, J. A. (2008) *Local Government Today*, Manchester University Press.
Copus, C. (2004) *Party Politics and Local Government*, Manchester University Press.
Rallings, C. and Thrasher, M. (1997) *Local Elections in Britain*, Routledge.
Wilson, D. and Game, C. (2002) *Local Government in the United Kingdom*, Palgrave.

Websites

Local Government Association, www.lga.gov.uk.
Local Government Chronicle Elections Centre at the University of Plymouth (Directors Colin Rallings and Professor Michael Thrasher), www.plymouth.ac.uk/pages/view.asp?page=16182.
Local Government Information Unit, www.lgiu.gov.uk.
Standard Boards for England, www.standardsboard.gov.uk.

19

Local government II: revival?

The previous chapter examined the emergence of local government, together with its reform and workings. While the dominant theme was one of decline, this chapter considers whether more recent developments have suggested it might be possible to discern some kind of revival.

Writing in the *Guardian* on 3 September 1997, Tony Blair declared: 'Local government is the lifeblood of our democracy'. While more cynical observers might dismiss this as anodyne political rhetoric, there have been a number of signs, both from the earlier 1990s and since the Labour victory in 1997, which suggest local government has begun to reverse the slow decline which characterised it in the latter half of the twentieth century.

Best Value

In 1999, Labour passed a new Local Government Act, which introduced 'Best Value' in place of compulsory competitive tendering. Essentially, this is a system whereby targets are set for efficient delivery of services; if public agencies or contractors fail to meet these targets, then they lose the right to do the work. The agencies or contractors may be public bodies like schools, or private companies to which work has been contracted out or, indeed, charities supporting children or the elderly. Local councils will set many of the targets, while others will be set by central government; note is taken of what similar authorities set as targets when such calculations are made. Frequently, a competitive element is introduced, to provide incentives for improvement. The Audit Commission, the local government watchdog, monitors levels of performance.

Simple reliance on the lowest bid has thereby been replaced by considerations of quality, trustworthiness and other criteria. Consultation with the local community has also been built into the system to some degree. The elected council, then, has undergone a major change, one which has added new vitality. It is still not a general provider of services, as it was in the past, but it has become an 'enabler', a 'commissioner' of services from external sources, signing contracts and monitoring progress to ensure targets are regularly hit.

Ethical framework

In the 1970s, the architect John Poulson built a business empire through bribing elected members to secure contracts, including the leader of the council in Newcastle upon Tyne, T. Dan Smith. In the late 1980s, Shirley Porter, leader of the Conservative-controlled Westminster Council, instigated a policy of selling council housing to maximise votes for her own party. However, such examples are rare and very much the exception: corrupt practices are not widespread in Britain, as they are in parts of Europe and in the United States.

In 2000, Labour introduced yet another Local Government Act, to provide a cohesive ethical code for the guidance of councillors. This code was devised by the Department of Local Government, Transport and the Regions, but allowed for adaptation to local conditions. Each councillor is obliged to sign the code. Where a councillor has a personal interest in a matter and attends a meeting in which the matter is discussed, the member must declare the interest before proceedings begin. Local authorities have to form a standards committee comprising two councillors and a co-opted member, who is not an elected councillor. The Local Government Association was active in helping to devise the code. All activities of councils, moreover, must be open to public scrutiny, apart from the Cabinet meetings of local authorities. Under that Act, the National Standards Board (now the Standards Board for England) was formed to ensure the ethical probity of elected members. Its 'ethical standards officers' (ESOs) investigate complaints from the public. If action is deemed necessary, cases will be heard by an adjudication panel for England and a variety of sanctions are available to punish transgressors of the code. In 2004, a total of 3,752 complaints were made to the Board, of which only sixty-six required no further action.

Ombudsman

Should citizens wish to seek redress against a council, they can take a case to court, for example in the event of injury or loss of income. Or they can refer their case to the Commissioner for Local Government or 'Ombudsman'. The ethical code is not meant to replace this officer, who exists to investigate cases of bad judgement or inefficiency.

Economic development

The Local Government Act 2000 gave local authorities the power to promote the social and economic well-being of their residents, as well as the environmental quality of the area. Even before this Act, some local authorities had been highly proactive in stimulating economic development; Manchester, for example, threw itself into developing, or rather transforming, its run-down areas like Salford Docks, preparing for the Commonwealth Games in 2002 and renovating the city after the hugely destructive IRA bomb in 1996. Many of these projects involved public–private financial collaboration. A good example is the Manchester Metrolink tram network: the network itself is owned by Greater Manchester Transport Executive, while operations are run by a collection of private consortia.

The city of Bath is very proactive in promoting tourism and the managers responsible are required to submit monthly figures on turnover and profit. In the London Borough of Brent, all services have been downsized from their bureaucratic past and are now required to 'sell' their services to other parts of the authority. This business model serves to highlight costs and to keep them under tight control. Moran (2005) cites the case of Cleethorpes, a seaside resort which has sought to improve tourism by seeking grants from the European Union (EU) and the regional development agency to regenerate seafront facilities.

The EU connection

As the reach of the European Commission and other institutions has extended, so pressure groups and other bodies, including local authorities, have sought to strike up close relationships. A comparison might be made to US experience, where state governments seek to extract federal funding by negotiating with and lobbying federal agencies. In a similar way, local government lobbies Westminster and the EU, seeking funding and further influence. Many authorities have now set up offices in Brussels so that their lobbyists have constant opportunity to intervene and establish networks.

Political innovation

Local government has always been willing to innovate to solve problems – witness the record over welfare and economic development – and this continues to be the case. One innovation involved new forms of voting in an attempt to improve turn-out. Turn-out has never been good for local elections – Britain has the lowest local government turn-out figures in Europe, at an average of 40%. In 2001, the Electoral Commission experimented at the local level with both text message voting and voting using the web, via PCs and special voting booths.

Elected mayors

One major new political form introduced in local government over the past decade has been the directly elected mayor. The idea originated most obviously in the United States, where it is common for an elected mayor to be granted substantial powers to run a town or city efficiently and peacefully. The New York mayoralty is probably the best-known example to British people and it offered a striking contrast to the largely ceremonial role the office of mayor has had in the past on this side of the Atlantic. It was first taken up by the Conservative Michael Heseltine when he was at Minister of the Environment; the idea appealed to him as someone who believed a strong leader could transform a situation if given the authority to do so. New Labour took up the idea, with Tony Blair possibly being of the same mind and personality as the Conservative Cabinet minister.

The fact was that executive structures in local government were not especially effective. Functions used to be run by large committees, with the chairperson wielding a great deal of power. A report by Sir John Bains in 1972 urged a reduction in the number of council committees and recommended that a central committee be formed to coordinate activities which would include committee chairs. This was not unlike a Cabinet for local government and many councils adopted the model during succeeding decades.

The Local Government Act 2000 sought to change decision-making structures in local government by obliging all councils with over 85,000 population to choose from three alternatives:

- a directly elected mayor;
- a mayor and a council manager;
- an indirectly elected leader and Cabinet.

It may seem surprising that the third option proved the most popular but the fact is that it came closest to existing structures, influenced by Bains several decades earlier. The idea here was for the ruling group in a council to elect its leader as leader of the council, who thereupon would select up to nine colleagues to form a Cabinet (in the event of the council being under 'no overall control', the make-up of the Cabinet would change). This was more or less what had happened before, so many councillors felt comfortable with this arrangement and they tended to distrust the notion of a directly elected mayor, whose provenance seemed to bestow an over-mighty legitimacy and, by comparison, reduced their own importance. Copus (2007, p. 577) questions the rationality of this attitude, as the powers of the elected mayor and the indirectly elected leader are nearly identical.

The elected mayor was to be chosen via the supplementary vote used to elect the London Mayor, to ensure that the winner received a majority of votes cast. The cause of the councillors' caution at such a proposal can be appreciated by the role such a publicly elected official would perform. As the highly visible 'first citizen', the elected mayor would have a mandate to lead, to form a policy framework, to prepare the budget and to drive ideas through the council. Moreover, the directly elected mayor would have a legal status as the head of the executive, with councillors relegated to a 'legislative' checking role.

The 2000 Act required councils to consult with voters via referendums and it transpired that voters have not been especially excited by the idea. Of the thirty referendums so far held, only twelve have endorsed the option of a directly elected mayor: in Watford, Doncaster, Hartlepool, Lewisham, North Tyneside, Middlesbrough, Newham, Bedford, Hackney, Mansfield, Stoke-on-Trent and Torbay. Elections took place in May and October 2002 and produced some surprising results in that, of the twelve mayors elected, four were independents, the Mayor of Hartlepool, Stuart Drummond, being the local football team's monkey suit mascot (he has proved to be a committed and, by all accounts, competent official who was re-elected in June 2009). After the subsequent elections for mayors, Labour ended up, by 2008 with seven out of the twelve (including London), suggesting that old party patterns are beginning to re-emerge. Following an Act in 2007, however, Stoke-on-Trent abolished its elected mayor. The 2008 London contest, featuring Ken Livingstone, ex-policeman Brian Paddick and the eccentric blond-haired old Etonian Boris Johnson sparked much interest, with David Cameron championing his old school chum Boris, the eventual winner with 53% of the vote to 47% (see also Chapter 12 on the London Mayor).

Only time will tell if this new seedling form of local government will take root and grow into a strong and vigorous plant. It should also be noted that the government was forced to accept, as an amendment in the Lords, the provision that councils with under 85,000 population were not obliged to introduce a political executive but had an 'alternative' of a slimmed down committee system, comprising five 'policy committees'; over two-thirds of councils chose to pursue such an alternative.

The professional in local government

At Westminster, the tradition has been for elected ministers to be advised by civil servants who are 'generalist' in their talents and outlook: the theory is that someone educated to a high level, whether it be in classics or history, is as well able to advise a Chancellor, say, as any economist (see Chapter 14). In local government, such an approach has never been dominant. Councils are concerned with sewers and roads and buildings and have never had any doubts about employing architects, lawyers, engineers or town planners. Councillors are advised not by 'Sir Humphrey' types but by hard-bitten professionals with long years of experience in local government. This means that management of local government tends to be conducted by elites, comprising senior elected members in close alliance with their professionalised chief officers.

Consulting the public

The 1998 White Paper *Local Democracy and Community Leadership* encouraged local authorities to engage with the public and involve them in policy formation. Previously, many local authorities tended to regard the public as a nuisance, to be ignored if possible or as a reason for pushing measures through with minimal consultation, to avoid the time and demanding diplomacy which consultation entails. The White Paper urged the following methods for involving citizens:

- citizen juries;
- focus groups;
- 'visioning' conferences;
- deliberative opinion polls;
- citizen panels;
- community forums;
- interest and user group forums;
- referendums on specific issues.

Some local authorities have long used such devices but others still find the public an uncomfortable source of advice and minimise the kind of involvement the White Paper envisaged. Studies show that most people know very little about this sector of government, much less than they do about the central tier (and seem care to about the same degree – hence the worryingly low turn-out figures in local elections).

New initiative on town and parish councils

On 15 February 2008, the government announced that from that day local councils would be able to create town and parish councils without seeking permission from the government. Town and parish councils vary in size and function considerably, serving populations from 100 right up to 70,000. A 'town council' is a council representing a parish but which chooses to call itself a town council. The idea of the initiative is to give councils the chance to create smaller units, closer to the public, which can operate more quickly and efficiently than normal councils. Consultation must precede any such creations. The number of people who can be represented by *parish meetings* rather than a full council has been increased from 200 to 999 electors. According to local government minister John Healey, councils will be able to make 'some local bye-laws' without having 'to seek Government's approval'.

New Labour and local government assessed

In his book *Transforming Local Governance* (2003), Professor Gerry Stoker analysed the degree of success Labour had achieved with its attempts to revive local government. He saw 'some very real gains'. Roughly half of all councils had been placed in the 'excellent' or 'good' categories by the Audit Commission, suggesting that 'New Labour's commitment to inspection, peer review, Best Value and better service delivery has had a positive impact' (Stoker, 2003, p. 216). Moreover, the new executive structures had been quickly adopted and made operational; a 'myriad' of new partnerships had been set up; consultation and participation had been enhanced. He concluded that 'on much of the modernization agenda set out by New Labour there has been progress'.

Box 19.1 Local elections, May 2008

Local election results massive blow for Labour

Given the poor public reception of the March budget and the schoolboy howler which caused the Treasury to overlook the 5 million losers from the abolition of the 10p tax band, Labour supporters could hardly have expected the local elections on 1 May 2008 to go their way. But few could have predicted the sheer scale of the defeat which awaited them. At stake were 4,000 council seats in England and Wales, involving the political control of scores of councils. In the event, the Conservatives won 44% of the vote, 256 seats and twelve more councils, bringing their total to sixty-five; the Liberal Democrats won 25% of the vote, thirty-four seats and one more council, taking their tally up to twelve; while Labour came last of the mainstream parties, polling only 24% of the vote, losing 331 seats and nine councils (including the symbolically important Reading and Hartlepool plus the bell-weather Bury), reducing its total to eighteen. Councils with no overall control ended up numbering sixty-four. In Wales, where all seats were up for election, Labour did especially badly, losing several heartland councils. These were the worst local election results for Labour since 1968 and ranked with the disastrous Conservative performance in 1995, which presaged their rout two years later.

Trailing in third place, twenty percentage points behind the Tories, was bad enough, but the worst blow by far was the loss of the London mayoralty to old Etonian Boris Johnson, who gained 53% of the votes to Ken Livingstone's 47% after second preferences had been allocated.

On Sunday 3 May the press reflected that if the local result were to be replicated nationally, David Cameron would have a Westminster majority of over 100. Clearly, these local elections had shown that the Conservatives, under their old Etonian leader, had removed the stigma once attached to their party and made the thought of a Conservative government seem possible in 2010, and for many even a desirable outcome.

Box 19.2 The need for a new spirit in local politics

Writing on 27 February 2008, Simon Jenkins used his *Guardian* column to argue that much was wrong with British local government. At times, he complained, it seemed only the police stood between the citizen and the state:

> A tier of social control has been lobotomised from British public life. There is nothing between the individual or family unit on one hand and the central state on the other. Britain has fallen into De Tocqueville's trap of an atomised society, where 'every man is a stranger to the destiny of others. He is beside his fellow citizens but does not see them ... while above them rises an immense and tutelary power, that of the state'. We have lost the habit of association. The nearest any British community has to local government these days is the police force. Local leadership is a 999 call.

Part of the problem is the sheer size of the British units of administration and the small number of representatives:

> In France there is an elected official for every 120 people, which is why French micro-democracy is alive and kicking. In Germany the ratio is 1:250; in Britain it is 1:2,600. In France the smallest unit of discretionary local government (raising some money and running some services) is the commune, with an average population of 1,500. In Germany that size is 5,000 people. In Britain the average district population is 120,000, and even that body can pass the blame for any service deficiency to central government.

He concludes that local leadership 'abroad' is superior to that in Britain:

> [It] appears to yield communities more able to discipline themselves and their young, and more satisfied at the delivery of their public services. They do not throw nearly so many people in jail. Local newspapers are not, as in Britain, filled with impotent whinges against central government. Local leadership is considered a duty by citizens permitted to exercise it.
>
> Attempts by Labour to renew and engage with local politics have been 'top down' paternalism.
>
> Democracy bites only when it votes, taxes and delivers. Only then do its participants have the legitimacy to enforce social responsibility and communal discipline. We can moan as much as we like, but all else is for the birds.

However, Stoker also pointed out that three-quarters of voters were still ignorant, uncaring about and unengaged with local government. There is still a gaping chasm of distrust; central government has been happy to ignore elected councils when appointed quangos appear preferable; there has been no great move to enable councils to raise their own funding; and the mayoral issue has been ducked, with only one major city, London, plumping for the option. In his analysis of local government, Chandler (2009) judges the Labour government 'lifted some restraints imposed by Conservative governments on revenue and capital spending and restraints on local authorities' capacity to benefit their communities'. He also noted that Best Value 'restored ... some discretion' to local government. But he qualified this by noting the retention of many central controls, enabling Westminster to intervene more or less at will and to deny any right of local authorities to criticise central government (Chandler, 2009, pp. 80–1).

References

Bains, J. (1972) *The New Local Authorities – Management and Structure*, HMSO.
Chandler, J. A. (2009) *Local Government Today*, Manchester University Press.
Copus, C. (2007) 'Local government', in B. Jones, *et al.* (eds), *Politics UK* (6th edition), Pearson: pp. 536–88.
Moran, M. (2005) *Politics and Governance in the UK*, Palgrave.
Stoker, G. (2003) *Transforming Local Governance: From Thatcherism to New Labour*, Palgrave Macmillan.

Recommended reading

Jones, B., *et al.* (2007) *Politics UK* (6th edition), Pearson: chapter 22.
Kavanagh, D., *et al.* (2006) *British Politics* (5th edition), Oxford University Press: chapter 15.
Kingdom, J. (2003) *Government and Politics in Britain: An Introduction* (3rd edition), Polity: chapter 19.
Leach, R., *et al.* (2006) *British Politics*, Palgrave: chapter 17.
Moran, M. (2005) *Politics and Governance in the UK*, Palgrave: chapter 12.

Other texts

Chandler, J. A. (2009) *Local Government Today*, Manchester University Press.
Copus, C. (2004) *Party Politics and Local Government*, Manchester University Press.
Rallings, C. and Thrasher, M. (1997) *Local Elections in Britain*, Routledge.
Wilson, D. and Game, C. (2002) *Local Government in the United Kingdom*, Palgrave.

Websites

Audit Commission, www.audit-commission.gov.uk/localgovernment/index.asp.
Electoral Commission, www.electoralcommission.org.uk.
Local Government Ombudsman, www.lgo.org.uk.
Standards Board for England, www.standardsboard.co.uk.

20

The judiciary and politics

Overlooked?

Technically the term 'judiciary' refers to the body of judges in any country but it is usually interpreted to embrace the law courts and legal system as well. The judiciary tends to be overlooked in studies of British government as:

- it is a branch 'subordinate' to Parliament, in consequence of the doctrine of 'parliamentary sovereignty' (i.e. the elected part of it – the legislature – decides the law unchallenged);
- it has been perceived as 'autonomous' and detached from the political system, in that it interprets rules made elsewhere.

Hence the judiciary has been seen as somewhat peripheral, irrelevant even. However, this is no longer the case, as explained in this chapter.

Subordinate?

As the first point suggests, the judiciary cannot strike down a statute law as being in violation of the constitution – because Britain has no single, written constitution and Parliament is the supreme body. But this was not always the case, as once the common law was held to be superior and monarchs could always over-ride statute law using their own judicial machinery. The Glorious Revolution (1688–89) put an end to this route, as royal power was curtailed; from then on, statute law become superior to any other form of law.

However, 'judicial activism' has worked in such a way as to make the judiciary less subordinate. Courts can:

- interpret the precise wording of the law in practice (sometimes interpretations can change over time and judges exercise influence through their ability to apply the law in different ways);

- review the actions of ministers to judge whether they are within the law and not beyond it (or 'ultra vires').

Governments are reluctant to change the law if they have been over-ruled in this way as it looks like they are changing the rules of the game.

Autonomous?

Judges have virtual security of tenure, except in extremis, and it takes both Houses of Parliament to sack one. Also, they get their salaries on a permanent basis, as their contracts are not renewed every year. The Commons tries hard not to mention any case appearing before the courts and hence 'sub judice'; ministers and civil servants do the same. Judges avoid partisan activity or indeed any kind of comment, following the Kilmuir guidelines of 1955 which forbade it. These guidelines were relaxed in the 1970s but renewed in the 1980s by Lord Hailsham when he served as Lord Chancellor (1979–86).

Nonetheless, the dividing line between the spheres of government are tenuous. This is in large part because membership of the legislature, executive and judiciary is not mutually exclusive in Britain (Figure 20.1):

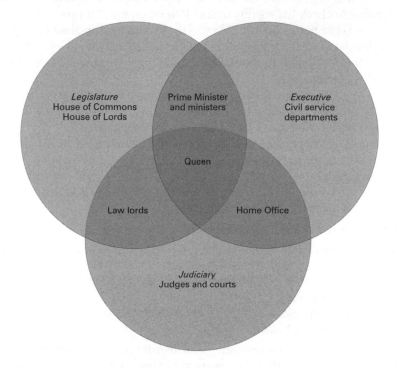

Legislature
House of Commons
House of Lords

Prime Minister
and ministers

Executive
Civil service
departments

Queen

Law lords

Home Office

Judiciary
Judges and courts

Figure 20.1 *The three spheres of government*

- *The Lord Chancellor* was a member of all three: legislature (presiding in the Lords), judiciary (appointing judges) and executive (sitting in Cabinet). Often the Lord Chancellor is a prominent party politician like Hailsham, Irvine and Falconer. The last named used to be head of the judiciary until the Constitutional Reform Act 2005 transferred his functions to the Lord Chief Justice. The Lords fought to retain the title of Lord Chancellor and it still exists as complementary to the Secretary of State for Justice (Jack Straw in 2009), but the office is now much reduced in function and power. For example, under the terms of the Act the incumbent no longer has to be a qualified lawyer. Possibly this is an office, like Chancellor of the Duchy of Lancaster or Lord Privy Seal, which will come to have only vestigial duties and which will become, like the last mentioned, an office given to people whom the Prime Minister wants to perform specific tasks such as chairing Cabinet committees.
- *The Attorney General (AG) and Solicitor General (the AG's deputy)*. Both these posts also have a judicial and executive role. The AG represents the government in the courts and gives advice on the legality of government actions (a prominent example was the AG's ruling on the legality of Britain going to war in Iraq). Writing in the *Guardian* (27 February 2008), Professor Jeffrey Jowell argued that the AG should be non-political and hence 'have more time to check the legality of decisions emerging from government'.
- *The Lords* is the highest court of law in the land. The Appellate Committee of the Lords sits as the highest court of appeal (see section below on recent reforms). (The Commons cannot be entered by a judge – the two spheres are held to be separate.)
- *Judges* say controversial things but can be rebuked by the head of the judiciary (the Lord Chief Justice) (for example, the judge who excused a man for raping a twelve-year-old because his wife was pregnant).
- *The Home Secretary* has quasi-judicial powers (including the ability to refer cases to the Lords until the Criminal Cases Review Commission took over this responsibility in 1997). The Home Secretary could also influence terms of imprisonment for prisoners and David Blunkett had furious arguments with judges over this issue in 2003.

Other 'crossings of the line' include:

- the AG can intervene in the public interest to stop a case, and can also initiate cases under the Official Secrets Act;
- judges often chair public inquiries (e.g. those chaired by Scott, Nolan, Hutton and Bingham);
- judges have been more willing to enter public debate since Lord Woolf served as Lord Chief Justice.

So, many members of the executive and legislature have judicial roles; it cannot be said therefore that the courts are either truly subordinate or truly autonomous.

The courts and their personnel

The court system (Figure 20.2) has two branches, one dealing with criminal law, the other with civil law (although magistrates' courts, at the lowest level, can deal with either type).

Criminal law

This is the body of law associated with offences against *society*: motoring, speeding, robbery, violence.

The Crown Prosecution Service (CPS)
This office is headed by the Director of Public Prosecutions. The police used to decide whether to prosecute but this was deemed unfair and in 1986 the new structure was set up. It has forty-two areas, each headed by a chief crown prosecutor; it is staffed by trained lawyers.

Magistrates' courts
Overall, 98% of criminal cases are tried in magistrates' courts, which amounts to about 2 million cases a year. Many fines are now 'fixed penalty', which has reduced the burden on magistrates as these cases do not have to go to court. Magistrates can levy fines and imprison those convicted, but only for up to six months. Mostly they deal with motoring offences but can also deal with cruelty to children and animals on the highway. It takes about 100 days from an offence taking place for it to be tried in a magistrates' court. Often the business only takes seconds where there is a guilty plea.

Professional magistrates are now called 'district judges' and are full-time; they tend to sit in cities. 'Lay' magistrates mostly operate in rural areas; often they are white, middle aged and middle class, and this uniformity of background has been criticised.

People who disagree with their conviction can appeal; appeals go up from magistrates' courts up to crown courts (see below).

Crown courts
Crown courts are presided over by a judge who can impose longer sentences than or quash the judgement of a magistrates' court. Appeals to crown courts are rare and most of their time is taken up by 'indictable' (more serious) offences. These are subject to a jury and can involve lengthy sentences. Around 100,000 cases are heard in crown courts every year.

The crown court is divided into six 'circuits'. A High Court judge presides over the most serious cases; a circuit judge or recorder hears the rest. The latter are often part-time but are trained lawyers (solicitors as well as barristers).

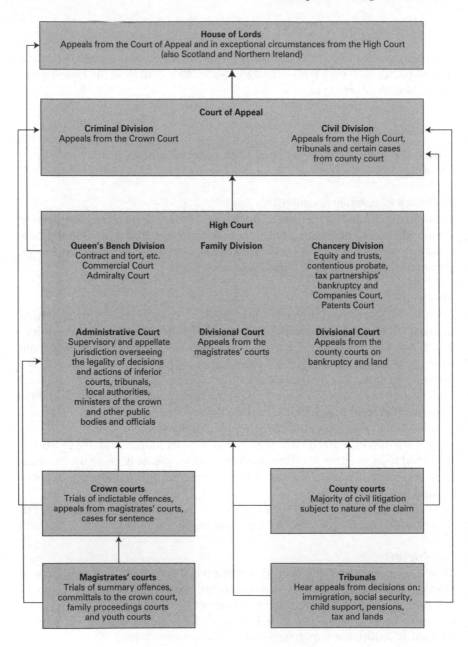

Figure 20.2 *Simplified diagram of the English court system*

Around 10% of those convicted in a crown court appeal against their sentence. The Court of Appeal (see below) may quash the conviction, uphold it or vary the sentence imposed. Sentences may be appealed against with the permission of the Appeal Court. The Attorney General may intervene if he or she thinks a sentence is too lenient. The sentence may be increased in these cases.

Court of Appeal

This comprises twelve law lords ('lords of appeal in ordinary', appointed to do judicial work) plus five ex officio judges: the Lord Chancellor, Lord Chief Justice, Master of the Rolls, President of the Family Division of the High Court and the Vice Chancellor of the Chancery Division. Appeals are usually heard by three judges. Further appeal is possible to the House of Lords if a point of law of public significance is involved. The Lord Chancellor organises this work, which is carried out in committees of five and sometimes seven. The Lord Chief Justice is head of the Criminal Division of the Court of Appeal and, since the Constitutional Reform Act 2005, is the head of the judiciary.

Judicial Committee of the Privy Council

This is a legacy of Britain's colonial history: it acts a final court of appeal for a number of former colonies, comprising law lords plus several ex officio members. It also hears legal challenges to the devolved assemblies, acting as a kind of 'constitutional court' at this level of government.

Civil law

This kind of law is connected with disputes between people (e.g. landlord–tenant, or seller–buyer, or parties to a contract). Some cases are heard in magistrates' courts but most are heard on one of the following.

County courts

County courts are presided over by circuit judges. They hear most civil cases.

High Court

The High Court hears the more important civil cases. It is divided into three divisions:

- *Queen's Bench Division*. This used to be headed by the Lord Chief Justice but, since the Constitutional Reform Act 2005, the President of the Queen's Bench now fulfils this role. The court deals with commercial, contract law and negligence cases and has an important supervisory role in relation to lower courts. Admiralty cases may involve collisions or sinking of ships at sea. It also hears appeals from magistrates' courts on points of law.
- *Chancery Division*. This deals with business – trusts, probate and land law for the most part.

- *Family Division.* This deals with divorce, children and medical treatment (for example, the case where the court gave authority to a hospital to separate conjoined twins).

Master of the Rolls

Originally, this was the officer charged with care of the Lord Chancellor's parchment scrolls. In time he became a judge and in 1881 a member of the Court of Appeal. The Master of the Rolls presides over the Civil Division of the High Court and has responsibility for solicitors. Given the high status of the Master of the Rolls, the office-holder is a very influential judge and can help determine the legal climate of the times on a wide range of issues.

Tribunals

Tribunals cover: unfair dismissal, rents, social security, benefits, immigration, mental health and compensation for compulsory purchase. Those appearing can call witnesses and cross-examine on most occasions. A tribunal usually comprises three people, often a mix of legal professionals and lay persons. Industrial tribunals have an independent chairperson plus two representatives of both sides of industry.

Tribunals are cheap and quick and less formal than court proceedings. In 1996, an employment tribunal told the Labour Party that all-women short-lists were in breach of sex discrimination law. Labour withdrew such regulations but later changed the law when in power.

Judges

Judges come below the Lord Chancellor and the law lords; they are professional full-timers (see Table 20.1):

- *Lords of Appeal in Ordinary.* There are twelve of these and to be appointed they must have held high judicial office for two years. They are members of the House of Lords and remain so even when they have given up the law.
- *Lord Chief Justice (LCJ).* This judge heads criminal appeals and, since 2005, is the overall head of the judiciary (rather than the Lord Chancellor, as previously).
- *Master of Rolls.* This officer heads civil appeals.
- *President of the Family Division and Lords Justices of Appeal.* This official is drawn from High Court judges or barristers of ten years' standing.
- *High Court, circuit judges and recorders.* These judges are drawn from barristers – though the High Court can appoint solicitors and circuit judges.
- *Magistrates.* Magistrates are appointed by the Lord Chancellor.
- Judges are paid from £80,000 a year, rising to £180,000 for the LCJ.

Table 20.1 *Judges*

Called	Court	Referred to as[a]	Title[a]	Addressed in court as	Retiring age	Salary
Lord of Appeal in Ordinary or law lord	House of Lords	Lord Wise	Peerage – Lord Wise	My Lord	70	£152,072
Lord Justice of Appeal (Appeal Court judge)	Court of Appeal	Lord Justice Wise	Knighthood – Sir John (or Dame Jean) Wise	My Lord (or My Lady)	70	£144,549
High Court judge	High Court	Mr (or Mrs) Justice Wise	Knighthood – Sir John (or Dame Jean) Wise	My Lord (or My Lady)	70	£127,872
Circuit judge	Crown court or county court	His (or Her) Honour Judge Wise QC (if a QC)	None	Your honour[b]	70	£95,873–£103,516
Recorder	Crown court	Mr (or Mrs) Recorder Wise	None	Your honour	70	£436 per day

Notes: [a]For a judge named John/Jean Wise. [b]Judges of the Old Bailey, although strictly ordinary circuit judges, are addressed as 'My Lord' (or 'My Lady').

J. A. G. Griffiths' critique

Griffiths (1997), a professor at the London School of Economics, accused judges of being exclusive: white, elderly, middle-class males.

- They do not have to retire until they are over seventy.
- Critics point out that only 5% of judges are female and there is only one woman law lord.
- 80% went to public school and most went to Oxbridge universities.
- Senior judgeships go to former barristers, although solicitors can now qualify in certain conditions (13% circuit judges are so selected).

Critics claim that judges are out of touch with the majority of society and cannot understand women in rape cases, for example. Also, they tend to have a bias towards the government of the day and to the Conservatives, a tough version of law and order and the interests of the state. The judiciary's greater activism, and hence importance, has focused more attention on the exclusivity issue.

'Judicial activism'

This is the term, as we saw above, used to describe the power judges have to strike down acts by government for which they had no legal authority or which were in violation of natural justice (i.e. were deemd to be ultra vires). The power was not much used before the 1960s, as courts were deferential towards the government. This changed at end of that decade, when judges began to worry that civil liberties were being encroached upon; consequently, they began to use their powers of judicial review. A famous example was the abolition of grammar schools in Tameside in 1976, when government action was overturned. Several Conservative actions in the 1980s went the same way.

At the beginning of the 1980s there were about 500 applications for review each year but by 1985 it had risen 1,000; the figure had increased to 1,500 in 1987 and up to 2,000 in 1990. In 1994, it was higher still, at 3,208; since 2000 there have been some 4,000–5,000 a year.

In July 1993, the law lords declared that the Home Secretary had acted beyond the law over an asylum case; *The Times* commented the ruling was 'historic' and 'hailed a key defence against the possible rise of a ruthless government in the future' (28 July 1993).

Michael Howard as Home Secretary was overturned several times in the 1990s in relation to: the criminal injuries compensation scheme; the referral of parole applications by 'lifers'; and a petition demanding a minimum sentence to be served by the two young killers of the Liverpool toddler Jamie Bulger. Jack Straw, when Home Secretary (1997–2001), was similarly found wanting in the case of journalists interviewing prisoners regarding miscarriages of justice in 1999.

Other cases, too, have made the judiciary more newsworthy and thus more prominent. In addition, judges have to interpret laws and sometimes lack of clarity enables them to change the law quite significantly. Lord Denning in particular was able to insert his 'own policy judgments into the loopholes left in legislation' (Oliver and Drewry, 1998).

But the judiciary's leeway is circumscribed and most applications concern local authorities and not ministers. Also, most applications fail: only 10% win against the government. Moreover, only a quarter or so are allowed in first place. But lost cases attract negative publicity, because when ministerial decisions are overturned it reflects badly on the government's competence.

European law

The UK became a member of the European Community on 1 January 1972 and on that day all Community law became 'UK law'; all future Community law became our law in addition. Parliamentary assent is not required for such legislation: it is automatic. Questions of law are decided by the European Court of Justice (ECJ). Lower courts in the UK may ask the ECJ for a ruling on questions of law relating to the EU treaties. Domestic law is *always subordinate* to EU law, a point which infuriates the Euro-sceptics, who resent Parliament losing its historic, exclusive powers.

Two cases will serve to illustrate the domestic influence of Community law:

- *Factortame case 1990*. This demonstrated the superiority of Community law. The case concerned Spanish trawler owners, who challenged a ruling against them made under the UK Merchant Shipping Act 1988; the ECJ eventually found for their plea and over-ruled British domestic law.
- *Ex parte Equal Opportunities Commission 1999*. This concerned a dispute over part-time workers, who were not allowed to claim under a 1978 Act for unfair dismissal or redundancy; it was claimed this was unlawful in terms of Community law and this was indeed judged to be the case. Philip Norton (2007, p. 611) comments that 'Although the Factortame case attracted considerable publicity, it was the EOC [Equal Opportunities Commission] case that was the more fundamental in its implications. The courts were invalidating the provisions of an Act of Parliament.'

All this has placed a big burden on the ECJ, so much so that in 1989 the EU created a new court, the Court of First Instance, an independent court attached to the ECJ that, as the name suggests, gives an initial hearing to cases involving European treaties or institutions. The greater the integration of nations within the EU, then the greater the significance of the courts has tended to be in applying European law. Maastricht also gave the ECJ the power to fine nations which do not obey European law. The body of case law built up is now huge.

'Parliamentary sovereignty' is believed to remain intact, in that Britain could always simply leave the EU, but some say this is a fiction and that the power of the EU has intruded too deeply inside the political system. British courts now therefore have a precautionary role in interpreting law to see if it is congruent with European law, thus strengthening their role.

Enforcing the European Convention on Human Rights

This further strengthens judges, as it adds a new dimension to domestic law: human rights. British judges now can decide whether human rights have been violated. This role used to be performed only in the Strasbourg court, which heard cases until 1998, when the Human Rights Act was passed. Some of those earlier cases were controversial: in relation to three IRA members killed in Gibraltar, Britain was ruled to have violated the right to life. The Human Rights Act makes it illegal for local authorities to act in a way inconsistent with Convention rights. If a law is inconsistent, then courts can leave it up to Parliament to do something about it. This role makes the judges much more political and increases the tension between the executive and the judiciary. Already the Convention, via the Human Rights Act 1998, has had a major effect on many cases (see Box 20.1).

Box 20.1 The European Convention on Human Rights (ECHR)

The Human Rights Act 1998 came into force on 2 October 2000. For the first time, individuals have a range of civil rights, as embodied in the ECHR, which are enforceable in British courts:

Article 2   Right to life
Article 3   Prohibition of torture
Article 6   Right to a fair trial
Article 8   Right to respect for private and family life
Article 9   Freedom of thought, conscience and religion
Article 10   Freedom of expression
Article 11   Freedom of assembly and association
Article 12   Right to marry
Article 14   Prohibition of discrimination

In addition, under article 1 of the sixth protocol to the Convention, the death penalty is prohibited.

Impact of devolution

The Acts creating the devolved assemblies allow for their powers to be challenged, via the Judicial Committee of the Privy Council. Devolution issues can also be referred to higher courts and via them to the Judicial Committee. An Assembly may have exceeded its powers and its measures can be suspended or struck down. The Judicial Committee of the Privy Council has been described as a 'judge on the shoulder' of the Scottish Parliament.

Criticisms of the system

An entrenched Bill of Rights

Some have argued that Britain needs a Bill of Rights. Such rights are described as 'entrenched' if special procedures are needed to remove them. The arguments made in favour have included:

- interpretation would be in the hands of independent judges;
- it would help educate the public on rights;
- it would increase confidence in the political system.

Arguments against include:

- vague terms would have to be interpreted by courts, putting wide powers in the hands of unelected judges, and public officials could still get round its provisions;
- the rights of one generation are not necessarily those of another and the special procedures needed for the removal of rights would insert immobilism into the system. (David Blunkett, when Home Secretary, even raised the possibility of 'suspending' the European Convention on Human Rights.)

Criticism of appeal courts

The cases involving the Birmingham Six, the Guildford Four and the Bridgewater Four all showed Britain's legal machinery in a bad light. Lord Denning even went so far as to suggest the criticism should stop, as it was undermining public confidence in the law.

Rape cases

- One judge called a nine-year-old girl victim of sexual abuse 'no angel'.
- A rape victim was awarded £500 to go on holiday and forget all about it.
- Around 40% of convicted rapists have been sentenced to four years or less, despite recommendations that five years should be the starting point.

Public confidence

One poll in 2004 revealed that 60% of respondents were satisfied or very sat-isfied with judges but this percentage was less than that satisfied with doctors or teachers. On the other hand, only 15% of respondents were dissatisfied.

Cost

Critics point out that court action favours the rich, as it is so costly; at the same time, legal aid for the less well-off is held to be grossly inadequate.

Reforms to the judiciary

Few have denied that the senior levels of the British judiciary were in dire need of reform but the way in which Tony Blair approached the matter in 2003 caused huge perturbations in legal circles. After an unhappy start, the reform process got under way after a landmark Act in 2005 and changes since then have done much to bring an archaic system into the twenty-first century.

Lord Chancellor

For a Cabinet reshuffle in 2003, it was announced that the historic office of Lord Chancellor was to be abolished and the attendant department merged into a new one called Constitutional Affairs. This unleashed a storm of protest in legal circles and the House of Lords, and it took a while to research, draft, debate and pass the Constitutional Reform Act 2005. This stripped away from the office the function of presiding over the Lords, this role passing to the new Lords Speaker. At the same time, the role of heading the judiciary was passed to the Lord Chief Justice. The Department of Constitutional Affairs was merged into the new Department of Justice in 2007, with Jack Straw put in charge and also holding the residual title of Lord Chancellor.

The Judicial Appointments Commission

This is an independent body set up in 2006 as part of the Constitutional Reform Act. Previously, judges were appointed by the Lord Chancellor on the basis of a complex process of information feedback, which, despite Lord Irvine's assurances (when Lord Chancellor) to the contrary, was perceived as a glorified part of the 'old boys' network'.

In October 2006, the new Commission set about looking for candidates to fill ten High Court judgeship vacancies and fifteen for a reserve list. Candidates were to submit an application form and short-listed candidates were then interviewed. All candidates were evaluated according to core criteria such as intellectual capacity, fairness, and ability to communicate and to work efficiently.

Ministry of Justice

The Ministry of Justice is a department formed from the reorganised former Department of Constitutional Affairs. It took over responsibility for sentencing policy, probation and prevention of reoffending from the Home Office in May 2007.

Supreme Court of the United Kingdom

This was formed by Part 3 of the Constitutional Reform Act and came into operation in 2009, when its allocated premises became ready. Effectively it replaces the judicial functions of the House of Lords and some of those belonging to the Judicial Committee of the Privy Council. It is the final court of appeal relating to English and Welsh law but in Scotland the High Court of Judiciary will continue to hear criminal cases.

The UK Supreme Court will also determine 'devolution' issues. These are legal proceedings relating to the three devolved 'Celtic' administrations. The Appellate Committee of the House of Lords came to an end after October 2009. The Judicial Committee of the Privy Council will continue, however, located within the new Supreme Court building, as it is the final court of appeal for several states in the Commonwealth and British overseas territories.

Juries

These comprise groups of twelve citizens gathered to decide whether, on the evidence provided in a trial, an accused person is guilty or innocent. Juries date back to Norman times and are mostly found in English-speaking countries where the right to be tried before a jury is usually regarded as a basic civil right. They are used only in the case of serious offences and mostly in criminal, not civil cases. Unanimous verdicts were required at one time, but a majority of ten to two is now accepted.

In the 1990s, suggestions were made to reduce or remove the right to a jury trial in certain cases, for example complex fraud trials. So far the jury system – defended by a powerful lobby of lawyers and civil rights activists – has survived most efforts to minimise its role in British law.

References

Griffiths, J. A. G. (1997) *The Politics of the Judiciary*, Fontana.

Norton, P. (2007) 'The judiciary', in B. Jones, *et al.*, *Politics UK* (6th edition), Pearson: p. 611.
Oliver, D. and Drewry, G. (1998) *The Law and Parliament*, Macmillan.

Recommended reading

Jones, B., *et al.* (2007) *Politics UK* (6th edition), Pearson: chapter 23.
Kavanagh, D., *et al.* (2006) *British Politics* (5th edition), Oxford University Press: chapter 24.
Kingdom, J. (2003) *Government and Politics in Britain: An Introduction* (3rd edition), Polity: chapter 20.
Leach, R., *et al.* (2006) *British Politics*, Palgrave: chapter 14.
Moran, M. (2005) *Politics and Governance in the UK*, Palgrave: chapters 5, 22.

Other texts

Adler, J. (2005) *Constitutional and Administrative Law*, Palgrave.
Banner, C. and Deane, A. (2003) *Off With Their Heads: Judicial Revolution in Modern Britain*, Imprint Academic.
Bradley, A. W. and Ewing, K. D. (1997) *Constitutional and Administrative Law*, Longman.
Griffiths, J. A. G. (1997) *The Politics of the Judiciary*, Fontana.
Nolan, Lord and Sedley, Sir S. (1997) *The Making and Remaking of the British Constitution*, Blackstone.
Windlesham, Lord (2006) 'The Constitutional Reform Act 2005: ministers, judges and constitutional change', *Public Law*, winter.

Websites

European Court of Human Rights, www.echr.coe.int.
European Court of Justice, http://curia.europa.eu/en.
Magistrates' Association, www.magistrates-association.org.uk.
Ministry of Justice, www.justice.gov.uk.

21

The European Union and British politics

It is no secret that the British have not taken too warmly to Europe, since we joined the European Community in 1972. The referendum in 1975 gave a two-to-one majority in favour of staying in but since then Euro-scepticism has grown if anything. As the arguments are so complex, dealing with an organisation with twenty-seven members and twice as many people as the United States, many people switch off the subject of the European Union (EU), while maintaining what seems to be a fundamentally hostile or at minimum unsympathetic attitude. This chapter seeks to sketch the major changes membership has had for Britain and for its politics.

Background and context: historical, geographical and cultural factors

Island geography

The English Channel has been crucial in determining aspects of Britain's cultural outlook: separation from Europe; an outward-looking attitude to sea and Empire; a focus on the navy and not the army; a romantic attitude, maybe, towards islands in our culture – *Treasure Island*, *Robinson Crusoe* and the like; and a sense of being different, and maybe superior to 'foreigners'.

Empire

Britain had accumulated a vast Empire by the end of the nineteenth century and prided itself on its moral superiority to others, especially Europeans, as the following quotations (and further below), drawn from Jeremy Paxman's book *The English* (2007), suggest:

> Cecil Rhodes: 'We happen to be the best people in the world, with the highest ideals of decency and justice and liberty and peace.'

Lord Rosebery: '[the Empire is] the greatest secular agency for good the world has seen.'

Disraeli, at the height of Empire: '[Britain is more of an] Asian power than a European one.'

Attitudes towards foreigners

This has always tended to be condescending, superior and a little vain.

- The Duke of Württemberg in 1592 wrote of the English that 'they are extremely proud and overbearing ... they care little for foreigners but scoff and laugh at them.'
- Mrs Frances Trollope overheard a stranger saying, upon reaching Calais: 'What a dreadful smell!' His companion answered 'That Sir, is the smell of the continent.'
- We have tended to abuse the French and this has left marks upon the language in phrases such as 'French leave', 'French kisses', 'French letters', 'excuse my French' (when swearing).
- Nelson's advice to a midshipman: 'You must hate the French as you do the devil.'
- Robert Walpole: 'Paris a dirty town with a dirtier ditch calling itself the Seine.'
- We like to condemn the Vichy regime yet who could deny we would probably have had one ourselves if the Nazis had invaded?
- George Orwell gave the British stereotypes of foreigners: the Frenchman 'wears beard, gesticulates wildly' while the Chinese is 'sinister, treacherous, wears pigtail'.

Preference for the United States

It has possibly been the case since the nineteenth century that the British have not really seen the United States as 'foreign', as Americans mostly speak the same language, and share the same culture of literature, films and television; also, the two countries exchange plentiful tourism. Harold Macmillan, Conservative Prime Minister, saw us as the 'Greeks' to the US 'Romans': cleverer, wiser, less corrupt and able to control them. The United States, for its own part, while possibly bridling at Macmillan's vision, saw its destiny as shared with Britain's in the two World Wars.

Perspective on the role of the state

The British perspective on this topic after World War II differed from those of Germany, France, Belgium, Luxembourg and Holland, in that we had not been invaded and occupied, either by the Allies or by Germany. After the war,

British statesmen like Ernest Bevin and Winston Churchill supported the idea of European unity, Bevin (Foreign Secretary after 1945) once looking forward to the time when he could buy a ticket at Victoria station to travel anywhere in Europe without a passport. However, this vision did not necessarily include Britain, the political elite of which still saw the country as one of the 'Great Powers'. As far as they were concerned, life would be easier if those warring Europeans could cooperate and live together peacefully.

The idea of a united Europe and the emergence of the European Communities

For the continental European countries the war had been catastrophic and faith in the nation state had been undermined. They faced the need to recover economically, and to contain both the threat of Germany and the threat of the Soviet Union in the east. Supranational cooperation seemed the answer to certain key politicians. The 'Marshall Plan' required such cooperation, as did the North Atlantic Treaty Organisation, set up in 1949; from these starting points a new approach was born to international integration in Europe.

Marshall Plan

After World War II, US Secretary of State George Marshall floated the idea of building up western Europe as a bulwark against the threat of the Soviet Union by channelling in economic assistance. The idea was born at a meeting of European states in July 1947. Bevin leapt at the chance and sought to turn it into reality. The Organisation for European Economic Development was established as the body whereby the recipient nations would administer the Marshall Plan. Over the next four years, some $13 billion was invested in Europe's recovery and by then all the nations concerned had achieved output in excess of their prewar levels. Such success provided a vital fillip for the movement for European unity.

European Coal and Steel Community (1952)

This was the product of the 1950 Schuman Plan, designed to entrench Franco-German cooperation by uniting major basic industries. Its institutions proved to be an anticipation of the future European Economic Community and its later manifestation as the EU.

European Economic Community (1957/58)

This alliance of nations was set up by the Treaty of Rome together with the European Atomic Energy Community.

European Community (1967) and European Union (1993)

The Coal and Steel Community merged with the Economic and Atomic Energy Communities in 1967 to become the European Community (EC). In 1993 it became the European Union (EU), after the 1992 Maastricht Treaty came into force.

British applications

Britain applied to join when Suez revealed the limits of the 'special relationship' with the United States and the British economy began to decline relative to the rest of Europe. The 1959 and 1967 applications were vetoed by French President General Charles de Gaulle, who feared Britain would threaten the leadership of Europe and be a 'Trojan horse' for US influence. (Anticipating future Euro-sceptics, he had insisted on member governments having such a veto, to ensure the organisation could not over-rule sovereign nations.)

The difficult General eventually died and Britain joined in 1973, along with Ireland and Denmark. But there was opposition in Conservative ranks and Prime Minister Edward Heath needed the help of Labour MPs to endorse the treaty of accession. The central point of contention was the loss of 'sovereignty': Britain's right to rule its own affairs.

Integration and enlargement

The 1979, the European Monetary System (EMS) – a means of coordinating exchange rates – was established as the embryo of economic integration. The movement to unify currencies developed at the end of the 1980s, with Economic and Monetary Union.

Enlargement
In 1981 Greece joined the European Community and in 1986 Spain and Portugal did so, taking the membership to twelve countries.

Deepening
The 1987 Single European Act set up a single market in the European Community and strengthened the powers of its institutions. It sought free trade and free movement of workers within the area.

Maastricht Treaty, 1992
- The 'Social Chapter' attempted to strengthen social policy and workers' rights. It was much opposed by the ruling Conservative Party in Britain.
- The institutions of the supranational body were strengthened and the term 'European Union' was introduced.

- The EU embodied the European Community (tariff and economic matters) as one 'pillar'; defence and foreign policy as another; and justice and home affairs as the third.

Further enlargement

In 1995, Finland, Sweden and Austria joined now that the Soviet Union was no longer a controlling influence, so now there were fifteen member states – though Norway refused to join after a referendum.

In 2004, another ten nations joined, bringing the total to twenty-five, with two more shortly afterwards to make twenty-seven by 2008.

EU institutions

The European Commission

This is the 'civil service' of the EU but it can initiate policy as well as play a role as the 'conscience of Europe'. It has a staff of 16,000 (including 2,000 translators). The Commission is led by its President (currently José Manuel Barosso) and twenty-seven commissioners, who serve for terms of five years. Romano Prodi, the Italian politician, was made President in 1999, when all the commissioners resigned over poor management and sleaze accusations. Neil Kinnock and Chris Patten were the two British commissioners until Peter Mandelson took over in 2004 as the sole British official at that level. In October 2008 Mandelson was replaced by Baroness Ashton.

The Council of Ministers

This comprises ministers from each member state, but its composition varies with topic: for example, if agricultural matters are being discussed, the Council will comprise the ministers for agriculture from all the EU countries and similarly for energy, health, finance and so on. In 1998, there were twenty-one different formations of the Council. High policy is decided by this body and is assisted by:

- *COREPOR*, a body of permanent representatives, in which civil servants often substitute for their ministers;
- *the EU Presidency*, which circulates every six months and carries with it an obligation to take the political initiative in solving current pressing problems;
- *the Secretariat of the Council*, which has 2,000 staff to support its work.

Qualified ('weighted') majority voting (QMV)

This allows the Council to make majority decisions according to size of country; for example, France, Germany, Italy and Britain have twenty-nine

British politics today: the essentials

votes each, while Luxembourg has only four (see Table 21.1). A QMV majority requires 255 out of the available 345 votes (74%). Britain, therefore, could be over-ruled on a decision on an issue covered by QMV but still have to implement it. Significant sovereignty, it can be argued, has been lost; in practice, however, unanimity is always sought.

Table 21.1 *Qualified majority voting: numbers of votes in the Council of Ministers*

Member states	Number of votes
France, Germany, Italy and Britain	29
Poland and Spain	27
Romania	14
Netherlands	13
Belgium, Czech Republic, Greece, Hungary and Portugal	12
Austria, Bulgaria and Sweden	10
Denmark, Finland, Ireland, Lithuania and Slovakia	7
Cyprus, Estonia, Latvia, Luxembourg and Slovenia	4
Malta	3
Total	345

Note: Decisions in the Council arc taken by vote. The bigger the country, the more votes it has, but the numbers are weighted in favour of the less populous countries.

European Council

This was set up in 1974 as a gathering of chief executives and foreign ministers of the member countries. It meets twice a year and has set the ball rolling on, among other things, European Economic and Monetary Union, the Single European Act and the single currency in 1999.

European Parliament (EP)

There are 786 Members of the European Parliament (MEPs) (see Table 21.2), who sit in groups according to ideology, for example socialists, liberals and the like. It used to be dominated by socialists but since 1999 the centre-right has had a small majority. The UK has seventy-eight MEPs, elected by proportional representation. The Parliament used to suffer from lack of powers and was little more than a talking shop but it has been strengthened by the implementation of a 'cooperation' procedure (after the Single European Act of 1986) which enables it to influence the Council during the legislative process and the 'co-decision' procedure (after the Maastricht Treaty of 1992), which gives it the power to reject items completely. The Amsterdam Treaty (1997)

Table 21.2 *European Parliament: number of seats per country*

	1999–2004	2004–7	2007–9
Belgium	25	24	24
Bulgaria	–	–	18
Cyprus	–	6	6
Czech Republic	–	24	24
Denmark	16	14	14
Germany	99	99	99
Greece	25	24	24
Spain	64	54	54
Estonia	–	6	6
France	87	78	78
Hungary	–	24	24
Ireland	15	13	13
Italy	87	78	78
Latvia	–	9	9
Lithuania	–	13	13
Luxembourg	6	6	6
Malta	–	5	5
Netherlands	31	27	27
Austria	21	18	18
Poland	–	54	54
Portugal	25	24	24
Romania	–	–	36
Slovakia	–	14	14
Slovenia	–	7	7
Finland	16	14	14
Sweden	22	19	19
United Kingdom	87	78	78
Total	626	732	786

extended this power to cover a wide range of EU legislation plus the power of veto over new accessions.

But the European Parliament's profile is still weak: it rarely produces memorable speeches and suffers from the fact that its plenary sessions are held in Strasbourg while its committees sit in Brussels. The Parliament offers 'rival' legitimacy to national parliaments; however, there really is not much of a contest, as turn-out in elections is low: 49% on average (a shaming 24% in Britain in 1998). In 2009, the British National Party won two seats for the first time at Euro-elections. Affected by the MPs' expenses scandal of that year, Labour polled only 16% of the vote, third behind the UK Independence Party overall, and fifth behind the Greens in the south, the east and south-west.

Table 21.3 *European Parliament election turn-out by country, 1979–2004 (%)*

	1979	1984	1989	1994	1999	2004
Germany	65.7	56.8	62.3	60	45.2	43.0
France	60.7	56.7	48.7	52.7	46.8	42.7
Belgium	91.4	92.2	90.7	90.7	91.0	90.8
Italy	84.9	83.4	81.5	74.8	70.8	73.1
Luxembourg	88.9	88.8	87.4	88.5	87.3	90
Netherlands	57.8	50.6	47.2	35.6	30.0	39.3
United Kingdom	**32.2**	**32.6**	**36.2**	**36.4**	**24.0**	**38.4**
Ireland	63.6	47.6	68.3	44	50.2	59.7
Denmark	47.8	52.4	46.2	52.9	50.5	47.9
Greece		77.2	79.9	71.2	75.3	63.4
Spain			54.6	59.1	63.0	45.1
Portugal			51.2	35.5	40.0	38.8
Sweden					38.8	37.8
Austria					49.4	42.4
Finland					31.4	41.1
Czech Republic						28.3
Estonia						26.9
Cyprus						71.2
Latvia						41.3
Lithuania						48.4
Hungary						38.5
Malta						82.4
Poland						20.9
Slovenia						28.3
Slovakia						17.0
Average EU turn-out	63	61	58.5	56.8	49.8	45.6

Note: Turn-out in the UK in 2009 was 35%.
Source: www.europarl.europa.eu.

European Court of Justice

- A process of 'constitutionalisation' is taking place as a result of the Court's interpretations of the founding treaties.
- Community law takes precedence over domestic law (e.g. the famous Factortame case in 1990 when the Court over-ruled British courts applying British law – see above).
- The fifteen judges of the Court interpret and effectively make law as well.

Other bodies

The Court of Auditors checks EU spending and the Economic and Social Committee (ECOSOC) is consulted on legislation as a 'parliament of interests'.

There is, in addition, a Committee of the Regions, set up after the Maastricht Treaty. The European Central Bank in Frankfurt sets interest rates for 'Euroland' countries (i.e. those sixteen that have adopted the euro); it would take over the role of the Bank of England if Britain ever joined the single currency.

Interest groups

There are around 500 interest groups actively engaging with the EU, most of which coordinate groups from member countries. The Committee of Agricultural Organisations represents farming bodies like the British National Farmers' Union. The EU will only deal with 'umbrella' organisations representing EU-wide interests. Local governments seek representation in Brussels because of the Structural Funds and other sources of finance which have become important, especially to declining areas.

EU decision-making

Under the Community 'pillar' (see below on the pillars), initiatives usually begin in the Commission after consultation with interests; they are then sent to the Council of Ministers. COREPOR helps during the consideration process. At same time, proposals are sent to ECOSOC, which submits an opinion on the proposal; and the Parliament, which uses one of four procedures (consultation, cooperation, co-decision or assent), depending on the type of issue involved. Lobbying occurs during this second consultation stage. The Council then reaches a decision, often via working parties.

EU decision-making and British politics

The above EU procedures are unfamiliar to British practice and are often portrayed as 'interference', even when a minister has approved the decision.

The EU's main impact is on economic policy: it acts as a 'regulator', by setting frameworks for competition and various rules affecting agriculture, telecommunications, the environment, energy and equal opportunities. This is akin to technical bargaining between the government and EU bodies.

'Europeanisation' of British policy-making

- Draft legislation is often reviewed by government officials to gauge its likely impact on Britain.
- The government defines a position and presents it to the Council of Ministers and officials from the EU; representatives may need to speak different languages for this. Thousands of such working groups take place each year.

- Most ministries set up coordinating agencies involving: the Foreign Office, the Department of Trade and Industry, the Cabinet Office (the staff of which act as the Prime Minister's advisers) and the Treasury.
- The Prime Minister and other ministers are involved via the Council of Ministers: nearly 100 ministerial meetings of the Council take place every year.
- The same ministries have to ensure that EU legislation is implemented, otherwise Britain may face referral to the ECJ.
- MPs and members of the devolved assemblies have to learn how to affect the policy-making processes of the EU.
- Local government has also had to learn the same processes.
- Political parties have to learn to cooperate with like-minded party groupings in the European Parliament. For example, Blair was keen to establish links with German socialists, as joint action is always better than appealing to individual members.
- Interest groups also have to learn the multi-level system: regional, national and supranational. British Conservatives, influenced by their Euro-sceptic wing, left the European People's Party in March 2009, claiming it was too 'federalist'. It announced it would instead form a new grouping of Euro-sceptic MEPs after the June Euro- elections in that year.
- Public opinion is a factor. For example, a referendum on the euro is promised in Britain, should the government ever decide it would be right to join; voters have been very dubious so far on this, according to opinion polls, and this would influence the decision itself.

Key policy areas: the three pillars

The economic policy (common market) 'pillar' is the 'supranational' one – where weighted majorities are often used – while other two 'pillars' – foreign and security policy, and justice and home affairs (Figure 21.1) – are settled via inter-governmental negotiation; decisions are not binding in the same way that law is for the latter two pillars.

Community pillar

This provides for:

- the removal of tariffs on trade;
- the free movement of goods, services, people and capital;
- the harmonisation of legislation affecting the way the common market works.

In the event, the first of the above had largely been achieved by 1968, but the second and third took much longer: 1992. Margaret Thatcher was generally

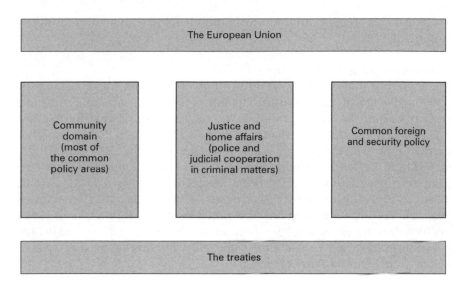

Figure 21.1 *Pillars of the European Union. The EU is founded on its treaties. The three 'pillars' represent different policy areas, with different decision-making systems*

sceptical regarding the European Community but was supportive of the single market idea, as it was part of free market philosophy, although she later claimed she had not meant to endorse the Single European Act, which was ratified in 1986, when she was Prime Minister.

Common Agricultural Policy (CAP)
This sets guaranteed prices for farmers. The CAP has tended both to protect inefficient farmers and to result in the EU producing food surpluses ('butter mountains' and 'wine lakes'); moreover, in the past it took up to 70% of the EU budget. Joining the Community increased food prices in Britain. Because British agriculture was efficient, it did not receive much benefit from the CAP, which led Thatcher to demand 'our money' back in the early 1980s. Reforms have been introduced since then, reducing the percentage of the budget spent on the CAP to under 50%. British agricultural policy has been heavily de-pendent on agreement with Brussels, as the BSE outbreak in the late 1980s and the episodes of foot and mouth in 2007 proved.

Common Commercial Policy
The common external tariff is set by the whole of the EU, with majority-weighted voting by the member states, and so Britain has very little immediate

say in this area of policy; ministers essentially bargain with EU over the application of the rules.

Economic and Monetary Union (EMU)
The Exchange Rate Mechanism (ERM), to which Britain had signed up in 1990, and which preceded the introduction of the European single currency, entailed keeping the exchange value of the pound in a set relationship to other major currencies, especially the Deutschmark. However, in September 1992 there was a run on the pound and Britain came out of the ERM, delivering a fatal blow to the Conservative government. John Major negotiated an 'opt-out' from the single currency and the Social Chapter provisions of the Maastricht Treaty in 1991. Labour joined the latter but has maintained the Conservative 'wait and see' line on joining the euro. Sixteen of the twenty-seven EU states are already in the euro, which has been in circulation since 2002. The British government promised a referendum before entry but this has been postponed and may not occur for years, if ever.

Other policy areas
The Regional Development Fund was set up in 1975 to help poorer areas and the Social Fund to help really deprived ones. 'Cohesion' policy aims to reduce differences between different regions. The Social Chapter aimed to protect working conditions. The Conservatives kept out but Labour joined in 1997. In the 1990s, the Home Office became 'Europeanised' like the rest of

---

Box 21.1 Europe: a controversial issue

- Divisions existed in both main political parties from the start and ratification of entry required Labour votes in the House of Commons to add to Heath's Conservative ones. Wilson used a referendum to side-step his own problems once he was in government after 1974.
- The defection of the Social Democrat MPs from Labour in 1981 was partly in response to Labour's then left-wing policy of withdrawal.
- There were three senior Conservative casualties of the European issue: Lawson in 1989; Ridley in 1990; and Howe in 1990.
- Even Margaret Thatcher was finally brought low partly as a result of her hostility to European integration; it was this that finally prompted Sir Geoffrey Howe to make his move against her.
- John Major found the behaviour of his 'sceptics' frustrated his government embarrassingly until he was forced to suspend the party whip from them.
- In 1996/97 Major obstructed EU dealings to assuage the sceptics.
- The BSE outbreak caused a major row with the EU and Major blocked its decision-making for a month in protest against what he saw as unfair treatment.

Whitehall when the Maastricht agreement on justice and home affairs was implemented. Foreign policy is still not coordinated at EU level, as the initially chaotic response to the Kosovo crisis revealed.

EU budget

In 1999, this was £67 billion or 1.11% of the EU's total gross national product (GNP), so the whole organisation is not especially costly; the main public expenditure remains with national governments, despite the protestations of the Euro-sceptics.

Labour in power

Generally, Labour has pursued a more united approach to the EU; while dissenters exist in Labour ranks, they are not as numerous as in the Conservative Party. However, despite a desire by Tony Blair to assert a leading role in the organisation, he was forced by his Chancellor, Gordon Brown, to hang fire on joining the euro. Blair also took the lead in seeking agreed foreign policy positions on key questions like Bosnia and Kosovo and was keen to coordinate defence and foreign policy more closely. However, he was later strictly restrained in this by his perceived closeness to President George Bush and his support for the invasion of Iraq in 2003.

For all the efforts of the Labour government, the British public has not really responded; turn-out in Euro-elections has remained relatively low. William Hague (Conservative leader 1997–2001) decided this was a sign that British voters are basically sceptical and – following success in those 1999 Euro-elections – he gambled heavily, and wrongly, on this in the 2001 general election.

Lisbon Treaty

Jack Straw, when Foreign Secretary, led attempts to reform EU institutions and make them more democratic. An EU constitution to make the EU more able to cope with its expanded membership was drafted by former French President Giscard d'Estaing but surprise defeats of the document in France and Holland in 2005 caused a hiatus. The resultant redraft of the constitution, now called a constitutional treaty, agreed at Lisbon in 2007, was not offered to British voters as such because Gordon Brown (Prime Minister after June 2007) did not want to enter the risky area of a referendum involving the generally unpopular EU. The excuse given was that the new treaty was completely different from the old draft constitution, but other heads of government claimed the treaty retained up to 90% of the original provisions.

Box 21.2 Key terms in EU politics

- *Supranationalism*. The European Parliament, the Commission, the Council of Ministers and the European Court of Justice operate in a way which places constraints on national sovereignty.
- *Inter-governmentalism*. The primacy of governments in decision-making (i.e. decisions are between governments and not over them).
- *Sovereignty*. The (old-fashioned) idea that each state is able to do whatever it likes, without constraint.
- *Subsidiarity*. The idea that decisions should be made at the lowest practicable level.

The Lisbon Treaty was designed to build on the failed draft constitution by incorporating much of its thinking in seeking to streamline the decision-making processes of the EU. Accordingly, it aimed:

- to increase the number of issues subject to majority decisions;
- to reduce the number of commissioners from twenty-seven to eighteen;
- to strengthen the power of the European Parliament to influence decisions;
- to create a permanent President of the EU, able to speak for the organisation as a whole.

Gordon Brown signed the treaty on behalf of Britain shortly after taking power but, perhaps to avoid provoking opposition, did so separately from

---

Box 21.3 Joining the euro

The euro was launched in 1999 and in 2002 euro notes and coins were circulated. Advocates of Britain joining maintain that this would: bring Britain into the centre of decision-making; reduce the costs of currency exchange; and provide direct access to the biggest market in the world outside China. Opponents maintained: a 'one size fits all' interest rate for such a huge area is bound to prove troublesome; obedience to the European Central Bank would be a surrender of sovereignty; and the whole single-currency policy is part of a 'European super-state' design, which Britain should totally resist.

Five tests
Gordon Brown was notoriously sceptical over the currency, while Tony Blair was warmly in favour. Brown encouraged the Treasury to draw up a list of 'five conditions' to be met before Britain could consider entry: essentially these insisted that entry would not damage Britain's economic prospects – perhaps more of a subjective than an objective list of criteria.

Box 21.4 Growth of Euro-scepticism in Britain

A poll for *The Economist* on 30 May 2009 revealed that British enthusiasm for the EU had been declining for a number of years. Over the previous quarter of a century:

- the percentage of people thinking the EU is a good thing had declined from 43% to 31%;
- those thinking it a bad thing had risen from 30% to 37%;
- support for more integration had fallen from 33% in 1995 to 20% in May 2009;
- over the same period, those favouring a fully fledged EU government had declined from 10% to 5%;
- support for loosening ties had increased from 36% to 51%;
- those wanting withdrawal had increased from 12% to 21%.

The poll showed, surprisingly, that Liberal Democrat supporters were slightly less keen on the EU than Labour supporters and that scepticism tended to increase with age.

---

the rest of the EU heads. Eventually, twenty-four of the members ratified the treaty but a huge problem arose when Ireland rejected it 53.4% to 46.6% in a referendum in June 2008. If even one member fails to ratify the treaty, it cannot be implemented. Since then, the reform of the EU has been on hold but EU supporters hope Ireland can be persuaded to vote again and this time produce a collective 'yes'.

Multi-level government

Regional and devolved government will deal separately with the EU on agriculture and other areas. More institutional reform regarding the enlargement and deepening of the EU is likely to be carried forward as countries continue to queue up to join. Some commentators now argue that the EU is already too large to run successfully. But in its fifty years of existence the EU has transformed the politics of its member countries; hugely improved their economies; and established itself as an agency which penetrates not only to the heart of their governments but also to their regional and local levels as well.

Reference

Paxman, J. (2007) *The English: A Portrait of a People*, Penguin.

Recommended reading

Jones, B., *et al.* (2007) *Politics UK* (6th edition), Pearson: chapter 13.
Kavanagh, D., *et al.* (2006) *British Politics* (5th edition), Oxford University Press: chapter 8.
Kingdom, J. (2003) *Government and Politics in Britain: An Introduction* (3rd edition), Polity: chapter 4.
Leach, R., *et al.* (2006) *British Politics*, Palgrave: chapter 26.
Moran, M. (2005) *Politics and Governance in the UK*, Palgrave: chapter 6.

Other texts

Bache, I. and Jordan, A. (2006) *The Europeanization of British Politics*, Palgrave.
Bainbridge, T. and Teasdale, A. (2004) *The Penguin Companion to the European Union*, Penguin.
Dinan, D. (2004) *Europe Roast*, Palgrave.
Geddes, A. (2003) *The European Union and British Politics*, Palgrave.
Magnette, P. (2005) *What Is European Union? Nature and Prospects*, Palgrave.
Nugent, N. (2006) *The Government and Politics of European Union*, Palgrave.
Young, H. (1998) *This Blessed Plot: Britain and Europe from Churchill to Blair*, Macmillan.

Websites

Council of the European Union, http://ue.eu.int/en.
European Commission, http://ec.europa.eu.
European Parliament, www.europarl.europa.eu.
Foreign and Commonwealth Office, www.fco.gov.uk.
UK Office of the European Parliament, www.europarl.org.uk.

22

Policy-making in British government

In a sense, the making of policy is the focus of most political science activity. Policy is the end product, the 'output' of political systems; it is what affects us all in our day-to-day lives. During the 1980s, Margaret Thatcher pursued a very clear set of policies – implement privatisation, reduce union power, increase productivity, reduce taxation – which had a huge impact on the country, for good or ill. By studying how a political system finally focuses on what it wishes to do, we find out something central and basic about its character. Throughout these chapters so far we have examined how the various 'players' – be they in the legislature, executive, pressure groups, media or judiciary – affect the making of decisions. In this chapter we sharpen the focus a little and examine the machinery at closer range.

Policy-making as a 'system'

Writing in 1979, Martin Burch suggested the process of government decision-making could be seen in terms of 'inputs', in the form of demands on the system, and 'outputs', in the form of consultation and White Papers, guidance notes, statutes, delegated legislation, public services, benefit payments, ratified treaties and so forth (Figure 22.1). The government machine, comprising legislative, executive and judicial elements, can be seen the 'processing' mechanism whereby these inputs are converted into the outputs. Implementation of the outputs will also require the mobilisation of resources like land, capital, taxation revenue, skilled labour and technology. Precisely how this conversion takes place is the subject of much study and academic 'model-making', key elements of which are examined below.

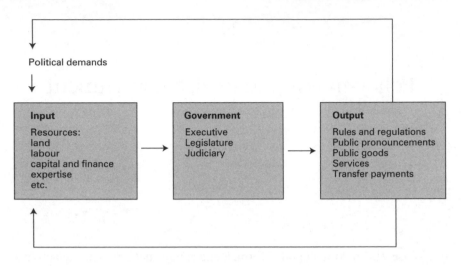

Figure 22.1 *The process (inputs and outputs) of policy-making*

Models of policy-making

The Westminster model

This is the 'official' or conventional interpretation of how policy is made. According to this view, MPs form a government out of the biggest party returned after an election on the grounds that this represents an expression of the country's will. The leader of that party becomes Prime Minister and appoints a team of ministers, both in Cabinet and at the junior levels. Armed with the 'mandate' to enact its manifesto, these ministers set about doing so, utilising the government machine, staffed by civil servants. Ministers, armed with their legitimacy bestowed upon them by their election victory, tell their staffs what they want to do, which is thereupon brought into being.

The ruling-class model

This model is built around a Marxist analysis. Those who own the means of wealth production also dominate the institutions of a society, and so can determine its values and fundamental ideas. It follows that the personnel of all influential centres of power in society will be drawn from this elite and that the bulk of the population will have been persuaded (brainwashed?) to accept the values underpinning the power of the property-owning 'bourgeoisie' – to use the Marxist term. It also follows, according to this view, that the machinery of democracy in such countries will always be a sham, mere window-dressing disguising the real sources of power and influence.

Pluralism

Associated with US political scientist Robert Dahl, this approach sees various centres of power, represented by associations of interests or groups, all competing for influence. The government in this situation acts as a 'referee', holding the ring to ensure everyone has a say. Critics observe that stronger groups will be able to speak 'louder' than the weaker ones; for example, the business lobby is likely to be stronger than that representing, say, asylum seekers. Indeed, Marxists would say the former is more powerful than all other groups and is almost never bested.

Corporatism

Phillipe C. Schmitter is associated with this analysis, which suggests ministers, civil servants and leaders of pressure groups come together in a kind of 'unholy alliance' to 'fix' what should be done, with those pressure groups becoming a virtual extension of government, or a kind of 'proto-government'. So, the argument runs, trade union leaders made deals with ministers during the 1970s which did not necessarily reflect the views or the wishes of the mass of the people, let alone union members.

Party government model

This view accepts the idea that parties formulate policies in opposition which they implement in government. In other words, the mainspring of policy is the political party and it follows that the party's leadership, publications and conferences provide the clues as to how government policies evolve and change. This view maybe neglects the roles of groups and bureaucracies.

Whitehall model

This argues that it is the well informed and staffed departments which really sweep ministers along and decide the main outlines of policy. Ministers are drawn from a variety of backgrounds: some are well educated and others less so; they remain in the same job on average less than two years; and they are often appointed for reasons other than ability. Civil servants, on the other hand, at the senior level, have benefited from excellent education; have served a lifetime dealing with the problems of their departments; and have made their way to the top strictly on merit. Ministers therefore, according to this point of view, find it hard to resist the advice of their official advisers.

Rational decision-making

This line of argument sees decision-makers acting rationally, considering options presented by their civil servants and then opting for the best one.

Critics question whether external factors do not distort this process, for example whether politicians' emotional attractions to an idea might not pre-dispose them to adopt it; for example, Tony Blair seemed not to question the idea of supporting Bush's Iraq policy, so keen was he to write a 'blank cheque' of support for the US President.

Incrementalism

Charles Lindblom is the guru behind this approach, which doubts the rationality of decision-makers but sees them as 'muddling through', using precedent and a range of less rational strategies. This approach conforms to the 'cock-up' theory of history: that events usually happen through blunders and miscalculations rather than design.

Policy communities and networks

Some political scientists – Jordan and Richardson, Rhodes – perceive the exist-ence of policy 'communities', comprising a range of inter-communicating groups and individuals. Membership of the community will depend upon conformity to the accepted 'rules of the game', as well as a measured confiden-tiality regarding the progress of consultations. Rhodes additionally discerned a less organised community of networks, outside the inner core and subject to frequent change of membership.

Political marketing

Another approach is to conceive of parties as 'marketing' themselves, rather like businesses. Jennifer Lees-Marshment reckons parties design their mess-ages for their 'markets' and refashion them when they prove inappropriate. She sees Labour as being 'product based' in the early 1980s – offering up something no one wanted and failing in 1983 as a result. The party then tried a 'sales-oriented' approach, improving its campaigning and advertising; but the message was still so off-centre it failed again in 1987 and yet again in 1992. Once the party began to listen to what the 'market' really wanted, under the name of New Labour, there was voter response and, finally, success, ultimately three times over. Whether parties can so cynically abandon any genuine idealism and merely pursue power through public relations and marketing is both controversial and dubious. Blair's career suggests that, in the end, voters see through such strategies and are turned off by them. Voters still hope that their elected leaders subscribe to some worthwhile set of ideas.

The policy cycle

The many writers on policy studies disagree on most things but most accept the three-stage policy cycle of *initiation, formulation* and *implementation*, with the *consequences* of the measure then feeding back to influence future inputs.

Policy initiation

How a policy starts is fascinating, in that sources are so diverse, from a single person's bright idea or a letter to *The Times* to a think-tank bursting with brilliant intellectuals or a major government department's decades of experience dealing with the problem under discussion. As important as coming up with the idea is the means whereby it is pushed up the political agenda high enough for it to be thought worth dealing with. Using the metaphor of 'distance' from the inner core of Number 10, we can identify a range of possible 'initiators' (Figure 22.2).

General public
The government is often very assiduous in listening to what the public thinks: polls, focus groups and pressure group activity can all serve to advance policy ideas or, equally important, to negate them. Sometimes, government fails to heed the public but then there is often a price to pay. Blair failed to listen to public opposition to the Iraq war and, arguably, this served to cut short his period in power.

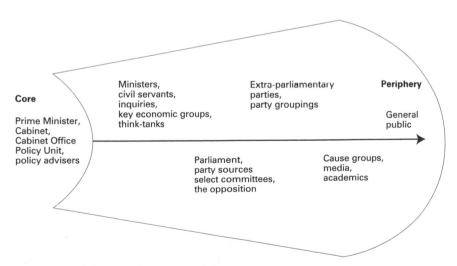

Figure 22.2 *Policy-making initiators*

Cause groups, media, academics

Certain groups pummel away at government for years and then, because the political situation can suddenly become receptive, their ideas are adopted. Charter 88, a group advocating constitutional reform, trod water for much of the 1980s but then found many of its ideas were taken up wholesale by the Labour Party in the late 1990s. Media campaigns can also push issues up the agenda, while academics may find that a new book suddenly captures the *Zeitgeist* and substantially influences policy in a big party. Perhaps the best example of this in the twentieth century was Maynard Keynes' ideas on macro-economic management of the economy.

Extra-parliamentary parties and party groupings

These are at their most influential when their party is in government. Then, ministers turn up to their meetings and the various party committees can exert direct influence.

Parliament

Groups of MPs constantly seek to impose their views on their leaderships, occasionally with success (e.g. Labour MPs urging more funding for public services during the late 1990s) and on other occasions without (e.g. MPs from the same party seeking to persuade their leaders to support the unilateral abolition of nuclear weapons). On still other occasions an active group can succeed in merely blocking progress on a range of issues, like John Major's EU rebels during the 1990s.

Ministers, civil servants, inquiries and think-tanks

Ministers will seek to push through their favourite policy ideas in order to attract praise and recognition. For example, Labour's Michael Foot as Employment Secretary in the 1970s felt that his health and safety legislation represented his most worthwhile achievement. Departments also devise policies of their own, every week of the political year, but there will always be politicians waiting to walk away with the credit for themselves.

Think-tanks tend to be more a feature of US policy-making but Thatcher, frustrated by a civil service she felt was still immersed in the consensus views of the 1960s, reached out to right-wing think-tanks like the Adam Smith Institute for ideas which chimed in more closely with her own instinctive beliefs. This is how the 'community charge' or 'poll tax' idea came into being, though perhaps this is not the best advertisement for think-tanks (see Dorey, 2006, pp. 19–25).

Core executive

This is the term now commonly used to describe the phalanx of people who take the major decisions in British politics. It comprises the Prime Minister, of course, plus Cabinet colleagues, principal aides like the press secretary, members of the Policy Unit and other close advisers on foreign affairs, the EU and so forth, the Cabinet Secretary, the permanent secretaries of the departments of state and members of Cabinet committees. These people, it should be noted, are not all elected but in the mix of policy-making such distinctions do not necessarily apply when knowledge and force of argument are just as important as rank or status.

Policy formulation

This occurs once the initiative has been absorbed by the government machine and enters a period of consultation and refinement. This stage can take hours, days or months, depending on its complexity and the time available; with international crises there may be only minutes in which to formulate a policy and take the consequent decisions.

Emergencies
Prime Ministers inevitably have all the most intractable problems ending up on their desk. On many of them, they have precedents to guide them and an able staff to advise. But on some issues – a hijack, or a kidnapping, a plane crash or a terrorist outrage – there may be no files in the cupboard to guide responses: decisions, upon which life and death may depend, may have to be made in a very short timescale.

Consultation, evolution and amendment
Some ideas are mulled over and refined, while others are rejected once their down sides are fully realised. David Evans, MP for Luton, for example, suggested an identity card system for football supporters to Margaret Thatcher which was initially welcomed by his Prime Minister, but after a long period of silence it was assumed, correctly, that Number 10 had looked at the idea and thought it best not to pursue it.

Policies almost always produce winners and losers, and deciding which to pursue involves weighing the advantages against the disadvantages, as Table 22.1 illustrates in relation to economic policy.

Legislative hurdles
In addition to the above bureaucratic obstacles to acceptance of policy, there are of course the not necessarily easy passages through the Houses of Commons and Lords (Figure 22.3). Mostly the Commons majority, which supports the government of the day, will ensure measures get voted through, but sometimes they fail. The Sunday Opening Bill in 1986, for example, was voted down through an accumulation of dissident pressure group activity. Other measures can be extensively amended, like the initiative to introduce university top-up fees for students in 2004. Opposition to this Bill succeeded in passing several amendments substantially changing the detail of the final

Table 22.1 *Guide to economic policy-making*

Area of policy	Policy direction	Advantages	Disadvantages
Exchange rate	Increase	Reduces inflation	Makes exports more expensive
	Decrease	Makes exports cheaper	Increases inflation
Interest rates	Increase	Makes borrowing money more expensive so reduces amount of money in the economy and so reduces inflation	Makes survival for some companies harder, resulting in bankruptcies and unemployment
	Decrease	Makes it cheaper for businesses to borrow and thus improves investment	Can cause inflation
Taxation	Increase	More revenue into Treasury; anti-inflationary: selective use can discourage undesirable spending (e.g. smoking)	Upsets voters
	Decrease	Pleases voters	Reduces revenue, can be inflationary and increases consumer spending
Public spending	Increase	Increases employment, improves public services, pleases voters	Increases taxation, which displeases voters, and worries overseas investors
	Decrease	Reduces taxation which pleases voters	Increases unemployment and public services suffer, which displease voters
Employment laws	Favouring workers	Unions happy	Business costs increase, loss of competitiveness
	Favouring business	Business happy, costs decrease, competitiveness improves	Unions unhappy

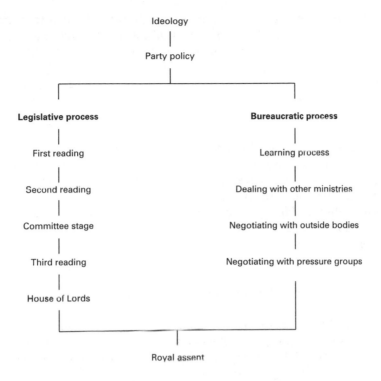

Figure 22.3 *Policy-making: bureaucratic and legislative hurdles*
Source: Tyne Tees TV/Jones (1986).

Act. The Lords, too, seldom manage to end the life of something the government seriously wants to pass into law but, as in the case of the Hunting Act 2004, hugely contentious to Conservative MPs and supporters in the country, it was delayed for quite some time and it took the invoking of the 1949 Parliament Act to put it onto the statute books.

Policy implementation

Jordan and Richardson (1987) observe that implementation can never be taken for granted and, to be successful, requires a number of conditions to be fulfilled:

- there must be no conflict of authority to weaken control;
- uniform norms and rules in the control system are required;
- there must be perfect obedience or perfect control;
- there must be perfect information, communication and coordination;
- and sufficient time is required for the necessary resources to be mobilised.

Merely passing an Act does not change reality unless all of these requirements are met to some degree. The two students of policy in practice might also have added that another idea/requirement is 'perfect acceptance' by the voters.

For example, the legislation creating the poll tax in 1988 (a uniform per capita local tax replacing the historical 'rates' levied on property) was passed and the Act was implemented for a while but there was much popular dissent: many people refused to pay a levy which taxed the poor as much as the rich; many had refused to register their vote, disenfranchising themselves to disguise their liability for payment; and still others took to the streets and there were serious riots on 31 March 1990 in Trafalgar Square. This failure of acceptance was a decisive element in the fall of Thatcher in the autumn of that year, and one of the first actions of John Major's successor government was to abolish the hated tax and to replace it with the council tax.

See Table 22.1 for an illustration of how certain policy 'levers' can produce desired results.

Constraints upon policy-makers

Clearly, as the poll tax example demonstrates, the democratic system imposes more constraints upon policy-makers than an autocratic one might. However, there are many other factors which are common to all, whatever the system.

Finance

Governments must have the means to fulfil their policy objectives. Harold Wilson's Labour government in the 1960s was stronger on stating objectives than achieving them, simply because the economy was in decline, with balance-of-payments deficits and devaluation of the pound arising from a manufacturing base which was atrophied and uncompetitive. Similarly, Gordon Brown was lauded as a brilliant Chancellor but as Prime Minister, after 2007, found his policies had contributed to a worldwide banking crisis that forced him to borrow huge sums of money to bail banks out in 2008–9. With such a mountain of debt, his spending options became severely curtailed in consequence.

Time

Passing new measures can take many months and legislative time is always severely limited, so much so that MPs who win ballots to float private members' bills are often assailed by government departments seeking to persuade them to adopt one of their bills. New measures also often need time to settle in and some are 'piloted' in different parts of the country before being rolled out nationwide.

Political support

This is required for a measure to be initiated, naturally, but is also necessary for it to pass through what may be a tortuous process of sniping and lobbyists seeking to amend it in certain ways or even out of existence. The identity card project, for example, has attracted varying degrees of support throughout its history. The Conservatives considered it and rejected it in the 1990s but when Labour brought it back after terrorist outrages, support was seldom unanimous, with the Conservatives and Liberal Democrats opposing it and, by the spring of 2008, large sections of the Labour Party had become sceptical. At the time of writing, even Gordon Brown, while less enthusiastic than his predecessor, was trying to 'tough it out' but economic pressures may prove hard to resist.

Competence of key personnel

The crucial person in this equation is the minister. An able, ambitious minister is likely to have the energy to push plans through to completion, while a weak 'time-server' will be happy to let an issue lie if civil servants are less than enthusiastic about it. A measure's chances of being passed can also depend on a minister staying in the ministry. By the same token, key civil servants who have absorbed expertise in a complex area might be 'poached' by the private sector. This happened during privatisations in the 1980s, when newly privatised businesses looked to those who had helped create them to help run them.

Coordination

Some measures straddle a variety of departmental responsibilities – poverty, crime, infrastructure projects – and coordinating them can prove difficult. New Labour came to power offering 'joined up government' to remedy such problems but few would claim the problem has been solved or anything near. One approach by Blair was to set up units in the Cabinet Office, such as the Exclusion Unit, which seeks to provide a more comprehensive and coordinated attack on the problems caused by poverty.

Personality factors

Most large departments have a team of ministers and sometimes their personalities clash. Some evidence of this was provided in May 1997, when Ann Widdecombe (former Home Office Minister of State) criticised her former boss, Michael Howard, as having 'something of the night about him'. The comment is thought to have done much to torpedo the former Home Secretary's then current bid for his party's leadership. The most notorious clash of personalities, however, is provided by the Labour Party, in the form of Tony Blair and Gordon Brown. These two former firm friends in opposition feuded when Prime Minister and Chancellor respectively over whether Blair had promised Brown he would step down and allow his Chancellor to contest the leadership after a given period of time. The constant warring between the party's two major figures had major implications for several policy areas, including possible euro membership, the reform of public services and top-up fees for universities.

Influence of the EU

Membership of the EU remains a contentious matter within both major parties, mostly on the grounds that it reduces British national sovereignty and threatens the encroachment of a 'federal' Europe into all spheres of policy. While such claims are probably highly exaggerated, it is true that the scope of EU concerns have spread from the narrowly economic into social affairs as well as defence and foreign policy. Any minister now has to consider the implications of EU membership whenever a policy initiative is raised.

International events

One of the most famous quotations regarding the work of a Prime Minister was made by Harold Macmillan when he responded to a question on what, as Prime Minister, kept him awake at night with a shaking of the head and 'Events, dear boy, events'.

Hijackings, revolutions, natural disasters or terrorist atrocities can steamroll their way into the best-laid agenda for ordered progress, and demand instant action. So '9-11' precipitated major losses on the stock exchanges and catalysed security policies the world over. In January 2008 another run on the stock exchanges – this time the result of foolish lending related to financially non-viable 'sub-prime' mortgages in the United States – caused the loss of several trillions of dollars and posed questions which, at the time of writing, western finance ministers are still trying to answer.

Managing the economy

As Chapter 4 on the social and economic context emphasised, much of politics is about the economy. This should not be surprising in a democracy, as most people's primary concern is with material things like their job, income and housing: Bill Clinton's slogan in his successful 1992 US presidential campaign was 'It's the economy, stupid', designed to exploit the fact that opponent George Bush Senior's stewardship of the economy had produced a recession. Ensuring that the people are delivered prosperity is the *sine qua non* of democratic government, so this area of policy is the most important. Policy has to overcome the disadvantages Britain suffers economically.

Geography

As a small island, Britain lacks good land communications with Europe and any substantial natural resources, apart from coal.

History

As the first industrial power, Britain was able to establish a position of hegemony in the nineteenth century, which was reinforced by its imperial role. But competitors soon caught up and were able to utilise modern equipment to narrow the gap with the 'workshop of the world'. During two World Wars, Britain had to sell many of its assets to survive and ended up in 1945 virtually bankrupt. Moreover, once most of the former colonies gained independence after World War II, a valuable cushion for the economy was removed.

Culture

Britain's dominant class, even when its wealth has been founded in manufacturing or trade, has tended to disdain such activity and to value the arts as a profession or the countryside as a place to live.

Politics

Labour, after World War II, produced a massive public sector, which disadvantaged private enterprise. Successive governments, furthermore, kept changing the national approach to economic management.

Economics

After World War II, Britain suffered from poor industrial relations, poor productivity and poor design compared with competitors like Germany, Japan, Sweden and Italy. There was also a tendency for investment in future industrial activity to be inadequate.

Two approaches to managing the economy

Since 1945, there have been two major approaches to managing the economy.

Keynesianism
In his book *The General Theory of Employment, Interest, and Money* (1936), John Maynard Keynes argued that the best way to deal with recessions was, counter-intuitively, to spend and not save. He argued that the government could stimulate economic activity in this way, thereby creating demand and employment. He also argued that skilful use of interest rates (monetary policy)

and taxation (fiscal policy) should be used to manage the economy, controlling demand and staving off the slumps which had traditionally followed booms. This approach was initially regarded as heresy by traditional economists and Treasury mandarins but the war seemed to legitimise it and by 1945 it had become the orthodoxy followed by both major parties. However, when growth began to slow in an economy failing to stand up to the competition, government spending seemed to coincide with galloping inflation rather than the desired growth. This presaged the emergence of a new approach.

Monetarism

This analysis, formulated most famously by the Chicago economist Milton Friedman, argued that inflation was the product of too much money circulating in the economy. The theory is that if business people and workers know the money is there, the former will push up prices for their products while the latter will demand more for their labour. The antidote to inflation, therefore, is to increase interest rates, to make money more expensive to borrow and thus less prevalent in the economy. Reducing money supply is held to reduce inflation. After the run-away inflation of the mid-1970s, Labour Chancellor Dennis Healey came to accept this equation but less enthusiastically than Conservative converts like Enoch Powell, Sir Keith Joseph and Margaret Thatcher.

When the Conservatives came to power in 1979, this approach was applied more full-bloodedly than under Healey. Monetarism, combined with cutting back or restricting public spending, caused widespread bankruptcies and unemployment but it did eventually make the British economy more efficient and, by the early 1990s, Labour dropped its vehement opposition and came to accept the Thatcherite approach to the economy, while still rejecting totally its concomitant attitudes towards public spending. So important was the control of interest rates in curbing inflation for Chancellor Gordon Brown that, immediately on coming into power in 1997, he gave this responsibility to the newly independent Bank of England, advised by an expert committee called the Monetary Policy Committee.

The instruments of economic management

Governments do their best to control the economy to make it perform more effectively. Available to them are a number of instruments:

- *Fiscal measures.* They can adjust direct or indirect taxation to achieve objectives such as raising revenue or discouraging certain activities like those causing pollution.
- *Monetary measures.* Controlling interest rates is the key instrument, as it controls the amount of money available through lending, the major means whereby business is financed and sustained.

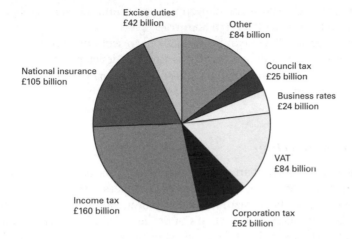

Excise duties
£42 billion

Other
£84 billion

National insurance
£105 billion

Council tax
£25 billion

Business rates
£24 billion

VAT
£84 billion

Income tax
£160 billion

Corporation tax
£52 billion

Total receipts £575 billion

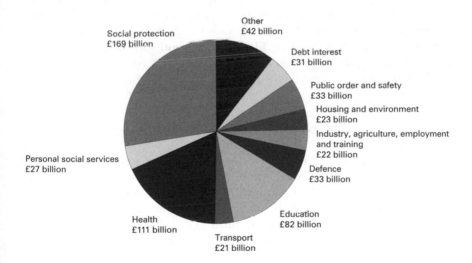

Social protection
£169 billion

Other
£42 billion

Debt interest
£31 billion

Public order and safety
£33 billion

Housing and environment
£23 billion

Industry, agriculture, employment
and training
£22 billion

Defence
£33 billion

Personal social services
£27 billion

Education
£82 billion

Health
£111 billion

Transport
£21 billion

Total expenditure £618 billion

Figure 22.4 *Projected government receipts and expenditure, 2008–9*
Source: HM Treasury, 2008–9 projections, published in *Comprehensive Spending Review* (2008).

- *Stimulating trade.* Governments can encourage economic activity by en-couraging trade deals with foreign countries.
- *Support and subsidies.* These can be handed out to sections of the economy which either are in trouble or require assistance to develop.
- *National infrastructure.* Improving transport or information technology capacity, for example, can stimulate economic activity and produce efficiency savings.

Who makes economic policy?

Clearly, as the most important area of policy-making, this 'policy community' will include the Prime Minister, the Chancellor, members of the core executive like the top officials in the Treasury, close economic advisers (Brown relied much on Ed Balls for such advice when Chancellor) and the Governor of the Bank of England. Inputs will also be received from connections with the EU, Washington and other international bodies, like the World Bank.

Relations between Prime Minister and Chancellor are always crucial. Thatcher treated Geoffrey Howe disrespectfully, for example, and paid for it by alienating him in November 1990 when her sources of support had begun to ebb. Blair endured ten years of constant tension with Brown, who was intent on taking his place in Number 10. As part of this tension they disagreed over joining the euro; Blair was in favour but Brown so opposed he defined five tests to be met before joining could be contemplated (see Box 21.3, p. 246).

Government income and expenditure

Figure 22.4 shows how revenue is raised and also how spending is allocated across the various sectors. Spending in 2007 was calculated at £589 billion, with a figure of £618 billion planned for 2008–9, £647 billion in 2009–10 and £678 billion 2010–11. Following the economic crisis of 2008–9, both taxation and spending plans were destined to be adjusted as economic con-traction reduced revenue and applied severe downward pressure on spending.

References

Burch, M. (1979) Chapter 14, in B. Jones and D. Kavanagh (eds), *British Politics Today*, Manchester University Press: pp. 127–37.
Dorey, P. (2006) *Policy Making in Britain*, Sage.

Recommended reading

Jones, B., *et al.* (2007) *Politics UK* (6th edition), Pearson: chapter 25.

Kavanagh, D., *et al.* (2006) *British Politics* (5th edition), Oxford University Press: chapter 13.

Kingdom, J. (2003) *Government and Politics in Britain: An Introduction* (3rd edition), Polity: chapters 14, 15.

Leach, R., *et al.* (2006) *British Politics*, Palgrave: chapter 27.

Moran, M. (2005) *Politics and Governance in the UK*, Palgrave: chapter 20.

Other texts

Burch, M. and Wood, B. (1990) *Public Policy in Britain*, Martin Robertson.

Castles, F. (1982) *The Impact of Parties*, Sage.

Dorey, P. (2006) *Policy Making in Britain*, Sage.

Downs, A. (1957) *An Economic Theory of Democracy*, Harper and Row.

Easton, D. (1965) *A Framework for Political Analysis*, Prentice Hall.

Ham, C. and Hill, M. (1998) *The Policy Process of a Modern Capitalist State*, Harvester Wheatsheaf.

Hogwood, B. (1992) *Trends in British Public Policy*, Open University Press.

Jordan, G. and Richardson, J. J. (1987) *Governing Under Pressure*, Martin Robertson.

Lees-Marshment, J. (2001) *Political Marketing and British Political Parties*, Manchester University Press.

Parsons, W. (1995) *Public Policy*, Edward Elgar.

Smith, M. (1993) *Pressure, Power and Policy*, Harvester Wheatsheaf.

Wildavsky, A. (1979) *Speaking the Truth to Power*, Little Brown.

Websites

Demos think-tank, www.demos.co.uk.

No 2 ID anti-identity card campaign, www.no2id.net.

Prime Minister's Office, www.number10.gov.uk.

23

British and US government
and politics compared

British and US government is often compared and such exercises can be illuminating, so much so that some examination boards focus specifically on this comparative aspect. This chapter offers a brief survey of the similarities and differences to point up how different systems can be while appearing so similar on the surface. We begin, after check-listing overall similarities, by looking at the political and economic base upon which politics in both countries is founded. Governments and their political cultures are rooted in their own particular societies, so it follows that some understanding of the latter is a useful requirement for understanding the former.

Similarities

At first sight these seem obvious and substantial.

- *Economy.* Both countries have free enterprise systems and are engaged in worldwide trade.
- *Society.* Both societies are characterised by: inequalities of wealth; high levels of crime, Christianity, English language, multi-ethnic populations, similar leisure habits (for example popular music, television/film watching), heavy use of modern technology like cars, computers and so forth.
- *Democratic constitution.* In both countries ultimate sovereignty is placed with voters.
- *Legislatures.* Both have bicameral systems.
- *Executives.* Both executives are answerable to their legislatures and are headed by a chief executive (Prime Minister in Britain and President in the United States).
- *Pressure groups.* In both countries such groups seek to influence policy.
- *Political parties.* Both have an essentially two-party system.

- *Open elections.* Both use first past the post – and have similar problems with non-participation.
- *Bureaucracy.* Bureaucracies serve government at central and local level.
- *Judicial systems.* Both have courts and penal systems plus procedures for appeal.

Key areas of difference

'American exceptionalism'

This is the belief – held by commentators and (often proudly) public alike – that there are profound differences between Europe, Asia and America arising from the unique experience and provenance of the United States, which developed, in one sense, in reaction to (or even as a rejection of) Europe. The first person to use the term was the famous writer Alexis de Tocqueville in 1831; in practice it often is used by Americans to denote a sense of superiority, especially religious ('chosen by God') and moral, to other nations.

Historical experience

The United States, of course, since 1607 when Jamestown was founded in Virginia, was peopled by immigrants, initially from Europe and latterly from Africa (via the slave trade), Hispanic countries and Asia. Now it numbers 265 million people, with 12% African-American and 8% other races. Currently, a large number of illegal immigrants enter the country from Mexico and other Hispanic countries in Latin America. Forming a unified country from an amalgam of different immigrant groups is a remarkable achievement and explains some of the emphasis one encounters in the United States on patriotism and 'Americanism'. This can jar with Europeans, who tend to have centuries of history to reinforce their sense of who they are.

Britain, in contrast, is an ancient country dating back over a 1,000 years. It has a history as a unitary state for the past three centuries with a monarchical and then parliamentary system of government. It also has relative ethnic homogeneity – of its 60 million people in 2001, only 7.9% were ethnic minorities (half of Asian origin). However, immigration in the early years of the twenty-first century has increased the numbers of eastern Europeans – entering often to work via common membership of the European Union – and refugees from war-torn areas like Bosnia, Somalia, Afghanistan and Iraq.

Economies

The United States is a huge country, of 3.6 million square miles, containing almost all the things needed to provide for the nation – Texas alone is larger than Germany and Italy combined. The US economy generates around $27,000 of gross domestic product per person (2005 figure) and is the biggest manufacturing country in the world – though China is fast catching up. The US regions are vastly different in nature, size and prosperity, providing lines of division politically: California is the sixth largest economy in the world; the mid-west is more agricultural; the north-east is an industrial powerhouse, now in decline; the south is very important politically, as long-serving southern Congressmen and women control many committees in Congress.

Britain has an area of only 94,202 square miles – more than thirty times smaller than the United States – and lacks most natural resources except coal; gross domestic product per head was about $19,000 in 2005. Even so, Britain until the 2009 economic crisis, was the fifth largest economy in the world after the United States, Japan, China and Germany. Regions differ but not as much as in the United States; the south-east is richest region, with the north the poorest, giving rise to a 'north–south divide', economically and politically.

Social comparisons

Social comparisons produce a mixed picture of differences but also important sameness as any examination of wealth and poverty will reveal.

Inequality

Both societies are based on a free market economic system in which it is inevitable that some will earn much more than others. But the differences in United States are substantially greater than in Britain.

Wealth

In the United States, the richest 1% own 38% of all wealth; the richest 5% own 59% of all wealth; and the richest 20% own 80% of all wealth. Meanwhile, the poorest 20% own virtually nothing. If house values are removed from the calculation, it is a very small group, 10%, which owns 85% of the stocks and shares in the big companies. Black Americans own less wealth than white Americans, Hispanics even less.

In Britain, the richest 1% own 23% of all wealth; the richest 5% own 43% of all wealth; and the richest 25% own 74% of all wealth.

Wealth is therefore unequally distributed in both countries but more so in the United States than in Britain. The comparison used to be closer, but since the 1970s inequality has rocketed in the United States, especially during the 1980s Reagan era. However, the most recent figures show inequality has been increasing in Britain – where liberal tax laws attract the 'globalised' mega-rich – even under a Labour government after 1997.

Income

In the United States, the richest 20% earn 50% of all income; the poorest 20% receive 3.7%. Race skews income significantly: a white male earns on average $29,000; a black male $21,000; an Asian male $30,000; a Hispanic male $19,000.

In Britain, income differences declined after the World War II but took off again in the 1970s, as in the United States. The richest 20% now earn 45% of all income, with the poorest 20% earning less than 8%.

Super-rich

In the United States, globalisation and tax breaks have created a new breed of super-rich, comprising a small but significant portion of the population. They usually have degrees and high-status occupations, provide the best education for their children and earn executive salaries upwards of $500,000 p.a.; some rich Wall Street dealers can earn up to several billion dollars a year. However, since the worldwide banking crisis in October 2008, such salaries are not so easy to earn and 'conspicuous consumption' by the super-rich has been toned down.

In Britain, there has been a similar surge in the super-rich; the culture of high salaries has been imported from the United States. Now the brightest Oxbridge graduates go into the City, the law or accountancy and not into education or the civil service. City traders can earn over £1 million a year. Huge pay-offs are often given to top executives, even when their stewardship of companies has failed. The Forbes list of March 2008 revealed that Britain had forty-nine of the world's 1,125 billionaires living within its borders, thirty-five of whom were British. Many of these fortunes will have been drastically reduced by the 2009 world economic crash.

Underclass

Charles Murray (1996) wrote of the 'underclass' in the United States – the 'undeserving poor' living feckless lifestyles, failing to provide role models for young males and indulging in crime, casual welfare fraud and drugs. Some calculate that in the United States during the 1980s, 80% of people suffered a 4% decline in income.

Murray diagnosed a similar tendency in Britain, where he saw an emergent underclass, committing most of the crimes and spreading a negative social message throughout society. Such analyses have been criticised as demonising the poor and neglecting the fact that many people succeed in moving out of the underclass after a period of time.

Social–urban polarisation

Robert Kaplan, in *An Empire Wilderness: Travels into America's Future*, paints a picture of the rich in the United States living in gated suburbs privately guarded while others live in an urban sprawl. Similarly, Murray saw an elite group of high-earning 'New Victorians' in Britain living in protected urban areas with the poor – the 'New Rabble' – living in 'sink' council housing estates.

Crime

The United States saw a huge increase in crime over the period 1960–90, with violent crimes increasing from a total of 288,460 in 1960 to 1.8 million in 1990. Then in the 1990s crime began to decline in the big cities: violent crimes down to 1.4 million in 1999.

Britain witnessed a surge during the 1980s, from 2.5 million serious crimes to over 5 million by the early 1990s. Then figures began to decline too in Britain and Labour boasted a decline of over 40% in the decade after it came to power in 1997. Criminologists think the decline is best explained by economic prosperity. However, perceptions of crime have not declined; the Labour government's drive against loutish behaviour and binge drinking was partly designed to limit the appearance of lawlessness on the streets.

Constitutions

The US constitution was famously written in 1787, after the War of Independence. It carefully laid out the powers of the different elements of government and, subject as it is to reinterpretation by the Supreme Court, has proved flexible and resilient. The constitution is revered and well known in the United States and is the final word in legal disputes.

The British constitution, in contrast, is famously 'unwritten' and has emerged, piecemeal, over a thousand years. Much of it is written, in fact, in the form of statute laws, which describe how, for example, elections should take place; but it is 'uncodified' – not gathered together in one document. After a period of virtually absolute rule, the monarch was forced to seek finance from advisory gatherings of nobles and leading families. These gatherings began to extract a price for the finance they provided, in the coin of permanence and power. In this way Parliament came into existence and slowly power adhered to its two chambers, the Lords and the Commons, especially after the Civil War and the Glorious Revolution (see Chapter 3 for a full treatment). This helps explain the dominance of Parliament in the British system.

Separation of powers

In the United States, the legislature, executive and judiciary are separate and have, in the first two cases, separate democratic legitimacy. The idea was to balance the functions of government so that no single function could win too much power. The spheres of government are distinct and do not overlap as they do in Britain, where, most importantly, the executive is formed out of and is supported by the legislature (Figure 23.1). The US President is elected for four years and even if defeated over legislation remains in power unless impeached, which is a rare occurrence. If British Prime Ministers are defeated on key parts of a programme, for example as happened to Tony Blair over tuition fees in January 2004, then they may have to resign.

This is the single most important difference between the two systems and most other major differences flow from it:

- The President is invulnerable during the official term of office; the Prime Minister is dependent on party support for survival.
- US ministers are free of the requirement of belonging to the legislature; in Britain a minister must be a member of the Commons or Lords.
- The President's relationship with Congress is one of manipulation and bargaining; in Britain the Prime Minister, like the absolute monarchs of old, dominates both legislature and executive.
- The President is able to colour the nature of the Supreme Court long after retirement or electoral defeated; the Prime Minister plays only a peripheral role in appointing top judges.
- The President is more able to bring in a band of advisers and officials; the Prime Minister is more dependent on senior colleagues and the civil service.

Federal state

The United States comprises fifty states, all of which have considerable autonomy, with their own legislatures and governors. The federal government grew exponentially during the twentieth century as centralised programmes and macroeconomic policies grew in importance.

Britain of course is a unitary state, focused on London. Devolved assemblies have taken some power away but Westminster still has the power to remove the assemblies and rule from the centre should it choose.

Amendments

In the United States, it is hard to change the constitution: two-thirds of Congress and then ratification by three-quarters of the states are required. The British constitution, in contrast, is not 'entrenched' by any special procedure and can be amended by a simple majority in both Houses of Parliament plus the royal assent.

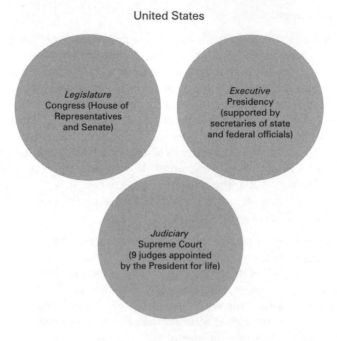

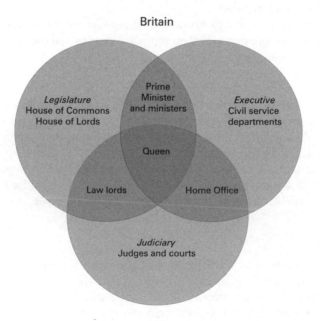

Figure 23.1 *Separation of powers: Britain and the United States compared*

Legislatures

The US Congress comprises the House of Representatives and the Senate. The House of Representatives has 435 members elected by constituencies all over the United States by first past the post for two-year terms. The Senate has 100 members. Two senators are elected for each state for six-year terms, but one-third stand for re-election every two years. With its power over foreign policy and ability to choose whether to ratify presidential appointments, the Senate is much more powerful than Britain's House of Lords.

The British Parliament comprises the House of Lords and the House of Commons. The 732-member House of Lords used to have both life peers and hereditary peers, but most of the latter have now gone, leaving a residual ninety-two. The Lords can only amend legislation and delay it by up to one year. The House of Commons has 646 members elected once every five years from constituencies of some 60,000 voters by simple majority. It is the more powerful chamber, providing the stage on which government is carried out.

Both the President and Congress can initiate legislation but the latter can also 'kill' proposals in committee or defeat them on the floors of either chamber; Congress can aslo apply scrutiny via committees, debates and questions. US committees have access to a wide range of papers and can call on expert opinion. The President controls the executive but not the Congress, and has to use a range of ploys and inducements to get Congress to pass legislation. There is no disciplined party system in Congress as members reserve for themselves the right to vote against the President (even if of the same party); the ethos of individualism encourages non-deferential attitudes and the federal system weakens parties at lower levels.

The British Parliament is in the hands of the biggest party, which forms the government of the day. Given the rigidly disciplined party system, this means government can virtually always pass its legislation and debates are usually merely colourful window-dressing. However, if a Prime Minister cannot win support for a major measure, then resignation usually follows.

With their elected status and powers of scrutiny and effective veto, the two Houses of Congress are more powerful than the two Houses of Parliament.

Executives

The US President is elected for four years on a fixed date via a popular vote, which is, however, mediated via an Electoral College. Each state sends delegates to the College after the general election and the candidate who wins the most votes in a state garners all its delegates. The Florida delegates were crucial in the disputed 2000 presidential election.

Presidents can appoint whoever they like to their Cabinet – subject to Senate ratification (and members of Congress are not eligible) – but can ignore any collective view should they choose. They can initiate legislation but Congress can frustrate their plans and frequently does; the relationship is one of constant and often intense bargaining. The President is head of state and chief of the armed forces. The President can also veto legislation originating in Congress. Wildavsky (1979) discerned 'two Presidents': a domestic and a foreign-policy one. The President is the most powerful person in the world but for much of the time it will not seem like this, as constant lobbying and persuasion are required, just as with anyone else in the political process. Having said that, the office of President has grown enormously in power during the last century.

British Prime Ministers, if they have their party behind them, wield more relative power than the President, but once their party begins to distance itself Prime Ministers are very vulnerable, as discovered by both John Major and his predecessor, Margaret Thatcher. They appoint Cabinet but are limited to those in the legislature – though elevation to the peerage is a useful 'back door' into government by which Prime Ministers can appoint someone to Cabinet and the legislature at the same time.

Both chief executives have substantial staffs but the President has a huge number of aides compared with the Prime Minister. British Cabinet members must all collectively toe the line in terms of policy while their US equivalents do not have the same restrictions. Prime Ministers have tended to become more powerful since Thatcher and many now see Blair's way of bypassing Cabinet, appealing to the country over the heads of Parliament and party and making decisions in small, ad hoc groups, as part of a growing 'presidentialisation' of the office.

President Obama

In November 2008, to the amazement of the world, let alone Americans themselves, the first African American, Barack Obama, was elected President. Arguably it would be more difficult for a black politician to become Prime Minister in Britain as there is no comparable 'black political class' and the parliamentary system allows mostly for incremental advance rather than the sudden success of a presidential campaign.

Political parties

The United States has two big parties, Democrats and Republicans, though 'third' parties do play a role; for example, the Green Party probably denied Al Gore victory in the 2000 presidential election.

Britain has Labour and the Conservatives as its two main parties but the strength of the Liberal Democrats makes this a kind of 'two and a half' party system. In the devolved assemblies nationalists are also powerful players.

After World War II, the difference between the British parties was considerable, from far right to far left, but the political spectrum in the United States was quite narrow, with both major parties supporting capitalism and no socialist party. The United States is not an especially ideological nation but the idea of being 'American' is very important, as it is a key cohering mechanism of the state.

Finance is the big difference between the countries. Elections in the United States are very expensive marketing exercises, utilising advertising and the media, especially television. Congressmen build up their own war chests and reinforce the tendency for incumbents to get re-elected. Presidential candidates must accumulate huge amounts to stand a chance. In Britain, there are much stricter limits on spending and television airtime is controlled stringently. Parties offer manifestos and seek to implement them once in office. However, the discipline shown by British MPs reflects the fact that a political career is virtually impossible outside a party. In the United States, members of the legislature do not need the party so much and voters decide as much on personality grounds as on party affiliation. This means discipline is less and majorities on vital issues are not a foregone conclusion.

Pressure groups

The United States is more open to the influence of pressure groups than Britain. In the former they operate at all levels: local, state and federal. Some 5,000 groups are registered in Washington, DC, and have access to committees and Congress. In Britain, access is not so open and lobbyists use influence and contacts to gain it; moreover, the cohesion and unitary nature of the state encourages pressure groups to concentrate at the centre, with ministers and civil servants. Thatcher and Blair were selective in their attitude to pressure groups and both were cool towards trade unionists.

Pressure groups in both countries try to append themselves to parties via fund-giving and by contact-making. Rules on money-giving are more strict in Britain than in the United States, where lobby groups are clever at evading the rules on funding almost as soon as they are passed. Probably the similarities of operation and importance of pressure groups are about the same in both countries.

Elections

Presidential elections begin with primaries and caucuses to help select candidates at the national conventions. Then the elections follow every four years. As noted above, these are mediated by the Electoral College.

Congress is elected every two years using first past the post.

In Britain, general elections are once every five years at the most but the date is not fixed: it is chosen by the Prime Minister when she or he thinks the contest can be won. There are much fewer stages, too, at the top level, as it is established that the leader of the largest party will be premier after the elections. Candidates are selected via local groups of party officials for the most part. Also, different systems of voting have been introduced in Britain: the devolved assemblies use the amended additional member system (the German system); Northern Ireland use the single transferable vote system; European elections use the regional list system; yet Westminster still uses the first past the post.

Political culture

The election of Barack Obama has shown how different US political culture is from the British. Perhaps the most dramatic difference is religious. In the United States, six out of ten people say religion is very important to them; recall that the original European settlers in the United States left their homelands often because of their strength of faith. In western Europe, the equivalent figure varies from one in Britain and France to two or three out of ten in Germany and Italy. The religious right in the United States has been very effective in fusing politics with religion over issues like abortion, stem cell research and gay marriage. This helps to explain why the outward-facing seaboards tend to be liberal and the interior to be more right wing (or 'Jesus-land' as some have characterised it). The United States is also vigorously patriotic in a way alien to our side of the Atlantic. Bush played up to the US pride in nationhood at a time of war in Iraq and against 'terror' in a way Europeans found distasteful, but which his home audience found heart-warming and even inspiring.

Campaigns

Election campaigns in the United States are very different to those in Britain:

- They last longer, as the primary/caucus/convention procedures take over six months to run their courses. In 2004, campaigning unusually also continued into voting day itself.
- Presidential elections cost huge amounts of money; some estimate the Bush–Kerry contest of 2004 to have cost $2 billion (a small fraction of that would be spent in Britain on an election campaign). Most of the money goes on television advertisements. There are official limits to spending in the United States but they are easy to circumvent: for example, ostensibly 'independent' bodies spring up to sponsor 'attack ads' like the 'Swift Boats Veterans' which undermined John Kerry's record as a Vietnam war hero; Kerry had similar groups working for him and in both cases there were close contacts with their respective party headquarters.

- Televised debates between presidential candidates in US elections play a big role. For example, they enabled Kerry to rise from the dead in the polls and make a credible challenge to Bush from early September 2004 onwards. Kerry won by mastering his subjects and appearing calm and, indeed, presidential. Bush seemed uneasy and alarmed at being rudely contradicted. In Britain, debates have often been suggested but we see our leaders debating frequently in the House and on television, and the Conservatives fear that a debate would place them in a position of being attacked by both Labour and the Liberal Democrats.
- Voting seems to take much longer in the United States, as queues snake their way around voting stations, possibly because voters vote for a raft of policy positions and not just the President.
- Campaigns often focus on the economy and social policy but values are of key importance in the United States, as they help to determine policies on such things as gay marriage, abortion, gun control and stem cell research. In 2004, values-based issues were key in Bush's victory over Kerry: over 20% of voters said they had been decisive factors in determining their votes.

Voting behaviour

In the United States, the Republicans tend to attract the votes of protestant middle- and upper-class rich white voters. Democrats tend to get the votes of minorities – blacks, Jews, people earning less than $30,000 p.a. – and union members, but Catholics tend to split equally. Union membership is low and George Bush Junior won the votes of many Hispanics through assiduous courting and his ability to speak Spanish. The Democrats have historically supported poor people – for example, through the New Deal, Roosevelt's programme to help defeat unemployment in the 1930s – as well as civil rights. Conversely, southerners tend to vote against the Democrats for the same reason.

British voting behaviour has latterly been characterised by a shift from the tendency for working-class voters to support Labour and middle-class voters Conservative to a reduction in class allegiance – 'partisan dealignment'. Now the tendency is still discernible but voters are much more volatile and available to parties which can make a good pitch for their support. The allegiance of the skilled working classes – the C2s – has been crucial in recent decades. In the 1980s, Thatcher won them with policies which they liked – the ability to purchase council houses and reductions in tax – but the decline of public services led them to believe in the programme of New Labour under Tony Blair.

Voter apathy

Both countries have manifested worrying signs of voter disenchantment with the political process. In the United States, citizens have to apply to be on the electoral register. This discourages registration. Bill Clinton's measure to register voters in 1993 at the same time as they applied for a driver's licence added 5 million to the register. In Britain, everyone is automatically included once they are eighteen years of age. Turn-out in mid-term elections in the United States is always under 40% and in presidential elections, despite the huge media coverage, less than 50% have turned out in some recent contests – though it was 54% in 2000. In the closely fought election of November 2004, turn-out was a near record 60% and in 2008, for the first time in forty years, it was over 60% per cent (at 61%). In addition, the United States is a very democratic country, with many elections, and voter fatigue may be a factor.

In Britain, turn-out has been declining since the late 1980s and in the 2001 general election it was only 59.4%. Reasons offered include: the assumption that Labour was going to win; the similarity of the two main parties; disillusionment with politicians.

Political ignorance is widespread in the United States and often undecided 'floating voters' are the least well informed, explaining the emphasis on crude sloganising in such contests.

Some experts explain apathy in terms of a preference for other forms of expressing political opinions, for example via interest groups. Some say the stock of 'social capital' – the tendency of people to join groups and be socially active – is in decline in the United States, while surveys in Britain suggest things are a little better.

Bureaucracies

The US federal civil service compares closely to the British civil service, in that both advise members of the executive. Ministers are usually appointed in the United States on basis of their relationship to the President, while in Britain the service is professional and permanent. British ministers serve usually only a two- or three-year stint before being reshuffled elsewhere. Senior officials change once a new President is elected while in Britain they stay in office, even those in the private offices of ministers. The tendency to appoint 'political' advisers grew under Blair and in this respect US practice is being followed. In both countries bureaucracies have been hived off: through 'Next Step' agencies in Britain and independent regulatory commissions in the United States.

Judiciaries

The US Supeme Court is recognisable as the highest source of authority on the constitution and points of law arising from appeals. In the Britain, a new supreme court was due to be created in 2009 – amid much controversy – but until summer 2003, it was the law lords in the House of Lords who undertook the equivalent role of the US institution.

> ## Box 23.1 How close are British and US attitudes?
>
> 'We have always been kin: kin in blood, kin in religion, kin in representative government, kin in ideals, kin in just and lofty purposes.' Mark Twain on introducing Winston Churchill in 1900.
>
> 'We think the same, we believe in freedom and justice as fundamentals of life.' George Bush with Tony Blair at a Camp David press conference in 2007.
>
> Surveys which merely tell us what we know are often portrayed as a waste of time and money but they can sometimes explode fond myths or adjust established verities. One in the *Economist* on 29 March 2008 did a bit of both, concluding 'Broadly, the differences between the two countries look more striking than the similarities'. Some of the main findings are summarised here.
>
> - The British tend to be more left-wing than Americans on political and social issues, being more tolerant of abortion ('usually acceptable' – Britain 60%, US 30%), homosexuality ('perfectly acceptable' – Britain 45%, US 25%) and premarital sex ('perfectly acceptable' – Britain 75%, US 25%) but (surprisingly) the two nations seem to agree on the death penalty: 'yes always' 20%; 'sometimes' 55%; 'no, it's wrong' 20%.
> - The British also tend to be more to the left on matters such as tax – more in favour of reducing tax for the poor (Britain 40%, US 20%), though both are (surprisingly) heavily opposed to taxing 'the better off' (both 3% in favour), and believing the government should support redundant workers (Britain 40%, US 18%). However, the two more or less agree that 'the profit motive is the best spur to job creation'.
> - The two virtually agreed on Iraq: 'withdraw troops now' around 15%; 'withdraw by end 2008' around 20%; 'set a date for withdrawal by 2009–10' around 25%; and 'stay until country is safe and secure' around 30%.
> - The British tend to think free trade is 'generally a good thing' (55%) while Americans are less keen (30%). The British are less inclined to think globalisation a 'bad thing' (Britain 32%, US 52%). The two seem to agree that 'immigration has helped the domestic economy grow', both at around 25% agree (50% not agree, 20% neither).
> - Alarmingly, large minorities were unconvinced of the dangers of climate change: 'Warming due to humans?' was endorsed by only around 50% in both countries and 'warming but not due to humans?' by around 20%; 'not warming at all' was endorsed by 10% in Britain and by 20% in the United States. Unsurprisingly in the light of this, both countries were, overall, opposed to increased petrol taxes, airline fares and 'clean energy taxes'.

Appointment to the US Supreme Court is by presidential nomination, ratified by Senate. Appointment is for life, so political prejudice is thought to be a
minor problem but in 2001 the crucial vote on Florida election recounts was
made on political lines. Judges are elected in the United States and tend to
be partisan. They may lose their bias with time but they might just as easily
retain them. In Britain, judges are appointed by politicians ultimately but
their bias is thought to relate to their narrow social and educational background, which tends to produce (C)conservative-leaning judges.

Judicial review

In Britain, judges can examine the government's actions and judge them
illegal. The Human Rights Act 1998 made many major issues more political
and in this respect the judiciaries in both countries are converging. However,
the British judiciary has one problem the US judiciary does not have: EU law.
Since 1972, EU law has applied to Britain and when it clashes with domestic
law it is superior. The United States has no comparable situation whereby a
multinational body can challenge the sovereignty of Congress.

References

Kaplan, R. D. (1999) *An Empire Wilderness: Travels into America's Future*, Vintage.
Murray, C. (1996) *The Underclass*, IEA.
Wildavsky, A. (1979) *Speaking Truth to Power*, Little Brown.

Recommended reading

This is not a topic covered in the major textbooks but the following suggestions will
prove useful for further reading. Watts has written by far the best available book,
though the classic de Tocqueville still repays study.

Davies, J. P. (1999) *US Elections Today*, Manchester University Press.
de Tocqueville, A. (1948) *Democracy in America*, Knopf.
Hames, T. and Rae, N. (1998) *Governing America*, Manchester University Press.
Watts, D. (2003) *Understanding US/UK Government and Politics*, Manchester University
    Press.
Welch, S., in Peele, G., *et al.* (eds) (2002) *Developments in American Politics 4*, Palgrave.

Websites

General Social Survey, www.norc.org/GSS+Website.
US Census Bureau, www.census.gov.

24

Britain and the world

Some countries have tended to avoid too much contact with the rest of the world – China for example until very recently – but Britain has long favoured an outward-looking stance and has sought to play a major role both militarily and diplomatically.

Key national interests

Britain's national interests have been conditioned by a lack of plentiful natural resources and an island status that delivers a close relationship with the sea.

Integrity of frontiers

The English Channel was formed over 200,000 years ago and is 350 miles long by a width varying from 21 to 150 miles. Despite successful invasions by the Romans, Nordic longboats and the Normans, in more modern times it has provided a vital defence for the country, especially against Napoleon on the cusp of the eighteenth to nineteenth centuries and against Hitler in 1940. In 1907, the construction of an earlier version of the Channel Tunnel was discontinued for fear a European power might use it to invade; and even in the 1980s, when in construction, similar fears were occasionally voiced.

Primacy of trade

As an island bereft of major natural resources apart from coal, Britain has relied on its close relationship with the sea for its prosperity. From early on, it was a trading nation, exporting overseas metals – mostly tin and later iron – and raw materials like wool and timber (now largely exhausted). Later on, as the home of the Industrial Revolution, Britain manufactured a huge range of goods, especially cotton but also steel and engineered items. This made the country a worldwide economic power but also gave Britain a firm interest in maintaining peace, as the prime condition of successful trading. War was always seen as very much the last resort.

European balance of power

Traditionally, Britain has sought to maintain a stable balance of power on the continent of Europe for fear that a dominant power would threaten its economic interests and ultimately harbour thoughts of invasion. So, it followed that Britain found itself siding against France when it was dominant and then Germany when that country assumed the dominant role.

Empire and decline

Given the familiarity with seafaring, it was natural that British ships should take a lead in exploring the world in the fifteenth and sixteenth centuries. This led to a competitive process with other seafaring nations of discovery and declared interests in far-flung areas – America, Australia and Asia. Over time, the British navy proved itself superior to those of Spain, Holland and France and by the eighteenth century the emergent British Empire had the edge over its rivals. What made Britain the most powerful country in the world by the early twentieth century was the economic pre-eminence which its industrial might had bestowed. By 1920, the British Empire occupied a quarter of the world's landmass – 14 million square miles – and comprised an equal fraction of its peoples – 500 million, of whom 400 million were Indian.

However, Britain's time as a 'superpower' did not last that long. Events in the twentieth century soon reduced its role to something far less exalted.

Economic competition

Having invented industrialism, Britain had no patent upon it and soon the economies of Germany, the United States and Japan began to catch up.

Two World Wars

Britain had to dig deep to help overcome Germany in World War I (1914–18) but World War II effectively left the country bankrupt by 1945, as many of the assets accumulated during the glory days of Empire had been sacrificed in the fight to defeat Hitler. This economic weakness left Britain highly dependent on US economic support in the postwar period. Contrastingly, the United States, relatively unscathed economically by the war, had emerged as the dominant power in the world, both economically and militarily. The Soviet Union, under

Joseph Stalin, sought to match the United States in military terms, as the Cold War ensued, but was never in the same league economically. Britain tried to act as if it was still one of the 'Big Three' but few believed this fiction, except, possibly, certain British politicians on the right.

Relative economic decline

Building on its 2% share of world economic output in 1750, Britain soared to 23% by 1880, when the United States commanded a mere 14.7%. During the middle of the nineteenth century, Britain produced two-fifths of the world's manufactured goods, as well as over half of its iron and coal. From 1870 to 1875, an average of £75 million was invested abroad annually. But already by 1914 Britain's share of world trade had declined to 14.1% as other industrialised nations made up the leeway. The impact of World War I was immense in terms of finance and lost workers, but the weakening effects of World War II were yet greater as assets had to be realised in order to prosecute the conflict and huge loans taken out from the United States in order to sustain it. In his book *Empire*, historian Niall Ferguson controversially argues that the effects of Empire were for the most part beneficent and that Churchill, despite his love of the British Empire, decided to sacrifice it in order to defeat Hitler. However, Britain's relative economic decline for the two to three decades after 1945 was not a topic for debate: it was a fact which any British visitor to European countries, especially Germany, could see with their own eyes. Paul Kennedy's book *The Rise and Fall of Great Powers* argues that it is the resources available to powers which determine their degree of dominance and that relative economic decline almost always heralds a scaling down in the international pecking order. Britain still has one of the largest economies in the world but its share of world trade is now a fraction of what it once was.

End of Empire

As Prime Minister, Clement Attlee very quickly realised that defending Britain's overseas possessions was impossible, given the home country's desperately straightened finances, the far-flung nature of the colonies plus their vulnerability to attack. India and Burma were promptly given independence in 1948, in line with Labour's long-held opposition to imperialism. The Conservatives, however, found it harder to reconcile themselves to the fading away of Empire and were keen to defend its eroding frontiers. Their fatal error occurred in 1956, when Anthony Eden's government collaborated with the French and the Israelis to seize back the Suez Canal after Egypt's Colonel Nasser claimed possession of it. This foolish act brought them face to face with a salutary reality. Eden was forced to back down humiliatingly in the face of US opposition to such 'imperialist' behaviour. It was now clear that Britain had neither the money nor the proxy support of its major ally to maintain its Empire, even if the United States needed British support in the emergent Cold War.

In September 1960, British Prime Minister Harold Macmillan made an address to the South African Parliament in which he stated: 'The wind of change is blowing through this continent. Whether we like it or not, this growth of national consciousness is a political fact.'

The apartheid government received the speech in appalled silence: it would take several more decades before it too came to terms with the new realities. Independence for the African colonies quickly followed until, by the end of the 1960s, there were a mere few stale crumbs of Empire left remaining, scattered around the oceans. The residual diplomatic dividend from the Empire, the Commonwealth, was a free association of former colonies – now independent nations – representing substantial populations but with negligible political clout. Ireland chose to stay out, while India, perhaps surprisingly, opted in. The record of the organisation, which boasts a secretariat in London and regular conferences, is one of difficulty in keeping its own house in order, on matters such as apartheid and various other civil rights violations by members, plus vacuous statements on wider global issues.

The spheres of foreign policy

In his perceptive book *Between Europe and America*, Andrew Gamble (2003, pp. 30–4) recalls Churchill's 1946 invocation of Britain being at the touching point of three spheres: the British Empire; Anglo-America and Europe. Gamble suggests that 'Britain' should now be seen as a 'union' of its devolved

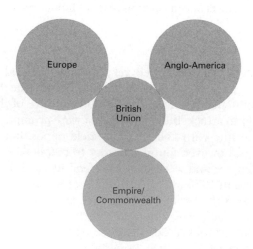

Figure 24.1 *Spheres of British foreign policy*

constituent parts. There were at least three areas in which postwar British foreign policy could invest its emphasis, often represented by three spheres: Europe, America and the Empire/Commonwealth (Figure 24.1). In practical terms, as the above paragraph suggests, the choice is now limited to two, Europe or the United States, though the Empire should not be discounted totally, as it established a tradition for Britain of striding on the world's stage, seeking to influence the direction in which events develop. This has not really changed; doubters are advised to visit the Foreign Office and judge from its still splendid interior whether ministerial incumbents can escape the legacy of Britain's worldwide imperial past.

The European Union as a focus of foreign policy

As Chapter 21 explained, Britain has always been ambivalent about Europe. On the one hand, Churchill, Bevin and others praised the notion of integration but wanted to maintain a distance: this was something which would be good for those European chaps but not necessarily so appropriate for the British. What changed the mind of government was Britain's relative economic decline during the 1950s, while the newly connected signatories of the Treaty of Rome prospered dramatically. It took three applications, a decade and the death of French President Charles de Gaulle for Britain to squeeze its way into the European Community in 1973. But this event was by no means the end of blowing hot and cold over Europe.

A substantial minority of both major parties were opposed to the idea of joining a club of nations that could over-rule its members' domestic law; bending the knee to Community law sounded too much like loss of sovereignty to many in Britain. Socialists suspected the 'capitalist club' of the European Community would erode the achievements of Labour governments. Conservatives feared national identity would be sacrificed to a faceless unelected bureaucracy in Brussels. Only the Liberals agreed that Ted Heath's achievement of winning membership was an unalloyed success. By the 1980s, a 'Euro-sceptic' faction in the ruling Conservative Party had developed, which grew in number as successive treaties strengthened what, with the Maastricht Treaty in 1992, became the European Union (EU). The split over this issue in the Tories made them virtually ungovernable in the 1990s.

The Labour Party, when in government from 1997, also contained doubters, but they were less numerous and caused less trouble. Tony Blair was keen to place Britain 'at the heart of Europe' and he set about reversing the hostility of the Thatcher and Major governments; soon after his election he addressed the French Assembly, with some aplomb, in French. But Gordon Brown was opposed to British entry into the single currency and Blair alienated many of his potential allies in the EU by appearing to be too close to Bill Clinton and then George Bush, especially when he joined the ill fated adventure in Iraq.

The British–US bond: 'special relationship'?

Relations with the United States could scarcely be said to be harmonious in the eighteenth century, when George III was seen as a tyrant and a bitter war of liberation (1775–83) was required to establish the independence of the then thirteen states and the foundation of what was destined to become the world's most powerful nation state. During the next century, economic rivalry between the established great power of Britain and the emerging one of the United States caused more than a few ripples but trade and cultural affinities were accentuated so that someone from America was not really seen as a 'foreigner' when they visited Britain. By the early twentieth century, the United States, with some reluctance, joined in the conflict against the Kaiser but then, repelled by Europe's perennial squabbles, relapsed into isolationism.

It took the subtle political skills of Roosevelt plus the aggression of the Japanese (at Pearl Harbor, on 7 December 1941) to bring American troops flooding back over the Atlantic. World War II cemented a collaboration that united the two countries as never before. American popular culture – notably films and music – were hugely popular and many US soldiers married British girls. But this high point of togetherness masked differences at the top between Churchill and Roosevelt over the conduct of the war and the determination of the United States to receive tangible returns for its loans to Britain of cash and equipment. Despite British receipt of Marshall aid and the warmth between Churchill and Eisenhower, the Suez adventure alienated the United States and brought home to Britain the stern lesson that it had lost the ability to do anything much abroad without US support. Adding some insult to injury a few years later, in 1962, Secretary of State Dean Acheson said in speech at West Point that 'Great Britain has lost an empire yet not yet found a role'. It was difficult to claim at this point that the British–US relationship was as 'special' as was often claimed.

The story since then has been one of Britain seeking to remind the United States of the ties that once bound the two nations, and the White House keeping London, politely, at arm's length. Key points in relations between the two countries have since included:

- the refusal of Harold Wilson to send troops to Vietnam, as Lyndon Johnson would have liked;
- Margaret Thatcher appreciating US help during the Falklands War and bonding with Ronald Reagan – though balking at his 1983 invasion of Grenada;
- John Major helping George Bush Senior in the Gulf War of 1991.

Then came Tony Blair, eager to pursue an 'ethical foreign policy' and to use US power by association and proxy to further some of his own visions for the future of the world.

Labour's ethical foreign policy and the war with Iraq

Tony Blair succeeded in taking Bill Clinton along with him in the Balkans, where the killing in Kosovo was curtailed and Milosevic effectively toppled. Emboldened, perhaps, by such success, he sought to articulate a philosophy of humanitarian intervention, roughly translated as 'where evil exists in the world, it is the duty of moral states to fight it'. In a speech in Chicago in 1999, he spelt out the framework of his ideas on 'international community', which it is worth quoting at some length:

> At the end of this century the US has emerged as by far the strongest state. It has no dreams of world conquest and is not seeking colonies. If anything Americans are too ready to see no need to get involved in affairs of the rest of the world. America's allies are always both relieved and gratified by its continuing readiness to shoulder burdens and responsibilities that come with its sole superpower status. We understand that this is something that we have no right to take for granted, and must match with our own efforts....
>
> [We] may be tempted to think back to the clarity and simplicity of the Cold War. But now we have to establish a new framework. No longer is our existence as states under threat. Now our actions are guided by a more subtle blend of mutual self interest and moral purpose in defending the values we cherish....
>
> The most pressing foreign policy problem we face is to identify the circumstances in which we should get actively involved in other people's conflicts. Non-interference has long been considered an important principle of international order. And it is not one we would want to jettison too readily.... But the principle of non-interference must be qualified in important respects. Acts of genocide can never be a purely internal matter. When oppression produces massive flows of refugees which unsettle neighbouring countries then they can properly be described as 'threats to international peace and security'....
>
> Looking around the world there are many regimes that are undemocratic and engaged in barbarous acts. If we wanted to right every wrong that we see in the modern world then we would do little else than intervene in the affairs of other countries. We would not be able to cope.
>
> So how do we decide when and whether to intervene. I think we need to bear in mind five major considerations[:]
>
> First, are we sure of our case? War is an imperfect instrument for righting humanitarian distress; but armed force is sometimes the only means of dealing with dictators.
>
> Second, have we exhausted all diplomatic options? We should always give peace every chance, as we have in the case of Kosovo.
>
> Third, on the basis of a practical assessment of the situation, are there military operations we can sensibly and prudently undertake?
>
> Fourth, are we prepared for the long term? In the past we talked too much of exit strategies. But having made a commitment we cannot simply walk away

once the fight is over; better to stay with moderate numbers of troops than return for repeat performances with large numbers.

And finally, do we have national interests involved? The mass expulsion of ethnic Albanians from Kosovo demanded the notice of the rest of the world. But it does make a difference that this is taking place in such a combustible part of Europe.

Shortly after this speech, on 11 September 2001, two commercial aircraft were deliberately crashed into the two towers of the World Trade Center in New York, at the instigation of the terrorist organisation Al Qaeda. In the wake of this shocking event, Tony Blair came out unequivocally on the US side; he pledged to stand 'shoulder to shoulder' with Britain's ally and, despite their ideological differences, cemented a strong relationship with George W. Bush (son of the former President). Britain thereupon jointly attacked the assumed 'home base' of the terrorists in Afghanistan, in pursuit of their leader, Osama bin Laden, shielded by the dominant fundamentalist Islamic military group the Taliban. When this victory – albeit limited – was effected, advisers in the White House turned their attention to Saddam Hussein's Iraq, despite his non-involvement in the '9-11' terrorist attacks.

In March 2003, British forces were part of a mainly US attack upon the oil-rich Middle Eastern state. Many in the Pentagon and White House sincerely believed a force of some 70,000 would soon roll over the Iraqi army and that the 'liberated' population would welcome 'coalition forces'. But huge mistakes were made in the planning and execution of the war, which quickly became a nightmare for all concerned, with warring religious militias turning Iraq's cities into infernos of murder and destruction.

At the time of writing, the costs of the war have been huge. Some 4,000 US troops have been killed, with at least 60,000 more wounded, and many thousands returned with severe psychological scars. In March 2008, it was estimated that the occupation consumed some $12 billion a month and could total as much as $3 trillion over the five-year period. A report by the Joint Economic Committee of Congress found that the war had cost an average American family of four $16,900, projected to rise to $37,000 by 2017. Estimates of British troop losses had been under 200, plus a cost of £3.1 billion. But Iraqi civilian losses were among the most horrifying statistics, with estimates running from 200,000 to 800,000. Association with this disaster proved enormously politically damaging for Tony Blair and helped hasten him from office in 2007.

It might be instructive to consider how the Iraq conflict measures up when judged by Blair's five criteria for intervention, quoted above.

- *'Are we sure of our case?'* This has to be a 'no' when it was never endorsed by the United Nations Security Council and the ostensible *casus belli*, the 'weapons of mass destruction', proved to be non-existent.
- *'Have we exhausted all diplomatic options?'* It seemed clear that many wished

to continue seeking an arrangement with Saddam, but strategic and military factors had made a US invasion inevitable anyway.

- *'Are there military operations we can sensibly and prudently undertake?'* In terms of defeating Saddam 'yes', but little or no thought had been applied to winning the peace.
- *'Are we prepared for the long term?'* Most definitely not, as events proved beyond any conceivable doubt.
- *'Do we have national interests involved?'* Britain had scarcely any *direct* economic or military national interests involved but Blair's response was a 'yes' to this question, on the grounds that Saddam was a leader of a 'rogue state', likely to host terrorists and support their efforts to create mayhem, and a democratic Iraq would provide a possible turn of the tide in the Middle East towards a less aggressive and more pro-western stance.

In retrospect, Tony Blair has not expressed any regret at the outcome of the Iraq war, nor has his closest policy adviser, Jonathan Powell. Maybe history will absolve those who made the decision but, from the perspective of six years from invasion day, it seems difficult to imagine how the events of the war can ever be placed into a favourable context, nor made congruent with Blair's own Chicago guidelines. When Obama won election to the White House in 2008 he promised quick withdrawal and this began to be effected in early 2009, with completion scheduled for August 2010.

Having said that, some historians have argued that it would have been more logical for Churchill to have stayed out of World War II and preserved the Empire. Who knows how future events may colour subsequent judgements which currently strike us as ill advised?

A globalised world

Britain now operates in a world in which frontiers have shrunk dramatically. Global commerce has taken off exponentially (Table 24.1) and economies are much more interdependent than they used to be. For example, the practice, for short-term gain, of US banks lending large amounts of money to poor people to buy houses – 'sub-prime' mortgages – created huge repercussions when repayments proved impossible and defaulting took place on a large scale. The availability of credit suddenly dried up and all the major economies were affected to a greater or lesser extent.

Britain must now compete in a world economy where multinational companies can withdraw their activities and move elsewhere, to set up in a more attractive taxation and business environment. This affects every aspect of the economy: Britain needs a vastly more skilled workforce to compete with the millions of graduates being produced by China and India; unions need to recognise that excessive demands may scare off foreign investors to other climes; and government has to adapt regulations to make Britain attractive to investors, even if it means exempting very rich residents from ordinary levels of taxation.

Table 24.1 *The growth of global commerce: some indicators (US $billions)*

Measure (worldwide figures)	Earlier level	1995 level
Foreign direct investment	$66 (1960)	$2,600
Exports	$430 (1950)	$6,000
Official foreign exchange reserves	$100 (1970)	$650
Daily turnover on foreign exchange markets	$100 (1979)	$1,230
Bank deposits by non-residents	$20 (1964)	$7,876
Cross-border loans	$9 (1972)	$372
Cross-border bonds	$1 (1960)	$461
Euro-equity issues	Initiated in 1984	$50
Cross-border share-dealing	$10 (1980)	$120
Daily turnover of derivatives contracts	Small before 1980	$1,162

Source: Baylis, J., and Smith, S. (eds) (1997) *The Globalization of World Politics* (Oxford University Press), table 22.1. By permission of Oxford University Press.

Conclusion: European Union or United States?

Britain has had to come to terms with a huge shrinkage of power worldwide and has had to hand over, with good grace or bad, the vast majority of the Empire, which had been the source of its power and authority. Now shrunk to a medium-sized European power, it has not found the transition an easy one and old mind-sets live on. The connection with the United States has, perhaps, enabled Britain to 'punch above its weight', combined with its seat on the Security Council of the United Nations, its nuclear weapons (delivery systems courtesy of the United States) and with an economy which is the fifth largest in the world. However, apart from access to cutting-edge weapons technology, some intelligence information and assistance during the 1983 Falklands War, critics find it hard to locate any specific benefits which the closeness to the United States currently provides. They suggest Britain wrote the United States a blank cheque over Iraq, for which it has had to pay in the coinage of isolation in Europe and becoming a target for terrorists, who see Britain and the United States as equally evil enemies. Some argue it would be more logical to recognise the facts of economics and geography and invest more political capital in Europe. The EU represents a market of some 500 million people, the biggest in the world, has its own currency and yet has no coherent defence and foreign policy, something which, argue such critics, Britain should be seeking to encourage as part of a move to establish a European centre of world power to match that of the United States, Russia and Asia.

References

Blair, T. (1999) 'Doctrine of the international community', speech by the Prime Minister to the Economic Club, Chicago, available at www.number10.gov.uk/Page1297.

Ferguson, N. (2004) *Empire: How Britain Made the Modern World*, Penguin.

Gamble, A. (2003) *Between Europe and America: The Future of British Politics*, Palgrave Macmillan.

Kennedy, P. M. (1989) *The Rise and Fall of the Great Powers: Economic Change and Military Conflict From 1500 to 2000*, Fontana.

Recommended reading

Jones, B., *et al.* (2007) *Politics UK* (6th edition), Pearson: chapters 2, 28.

Kavanagh, D., *et al.* (2006) *British Politics* (5th edition), Oxford University Press: chapters 6, 31.

Leach, R., *et al.* (2006) *British Politics*, Palgrave: chapter 26.

Moran, M. (2005) *Politics and Governance in the UK*, Palgrave: chapter 4.

Other texts

Byrd, P. (1988) *British Foreign Policy Under Thatcher*, Manchester University Press.

Cooper, R. (2006) 'War and democracy', *Prospect Magazine*, June.

Smith, M., *et al.* (1988) *British Foreign Policy*, Routledge.

Website

Foreign and Commonwealth Office, www.fco.gov.uk.

Index